# MY LIFE: A FRAGMENT

# MY LIFE: A FRAGMENT

An Autobiographical Sketch of
Maulana Mohamed Ali

*Edited and Annotated by*

MUSHIRUL HASAN

MANOHAR
1999

First published 1999



ISBN 81-7304-286-1

*Published by*
Ajay Kumar Jain for
Manohar Publishers & Distributors
2/6 Ansari Road, Daryaganj
New Delhi 110002

*Typeset by*
Wissenschaftskolleg zu Berlin
Institute for Advanced Study Berlin
Fellow Services—Elissa Linke
Wallotstr. 19
D-14193 Berlin
Germany

*Printed at*
Rajkamal Electric Press
B 35/9 G T Karnal Road Indl Area
Delhi 110033

# Contents

# Preface

Since its publication in January 1942, Mohamed Ali's *My Life: A Fragment* has been widely read and used by scholars and generalists alike. In the subcontinent, it is regarded as a major statement by one of the chief protagonists of various Muslim causes. The authenticity of the book, which was originally entitled 'Islam: Kingdom of God', is not in doubt. Its distinct style is consistent with the tone and tenor of its author's letters, articles and speeches.

Afzal Iqbal was the first to edit the manuscript. He had received it in 1939 from Mohammad Mujeeb, the scholar and later vice-chancellor of Delhi's Jamia Millia Islamia. Mujeeb, who had been impressed with Mohamed Ali in the early 1920s when he met him in London as a student, became highly critical of the man and his mission in later years. Having lost interest in editing 'Islam: Kingdom of God', the title Mohamed Ali gave to the book in the making, he would have probably agreed to part with the typescript. 'To this slim and impressive intellectual,' wrote Afzal Iqbal in his introduction to the newly-coined title *My Life*: *A Fragment*, 'I looked for help which he gave me ungrudgingly and in full measure.'

Mohamed Ali was a prolific writer from his student days at Aligarh. Yet he did not consider writing a book until he was interned in 1923, along with Shaukat Ali (1873–1938) and others, after the Karachi trial. On 23 July 1916, he wrote from Chhindwara, then a small and inaccessible town in the Central Provinces (now Madhya Pradesh), to Abdul Majid Daryabadi (1892–1997), one of his numerous admirers at the time:

> You suggest to me that I should write a book during my enforced leisure, and that our people expect one from me. If that is so, I am afraid they don't know me. Firstly, I have neither the patience, perseverance nor the temper of the researchist [*sic*]. Secondly, my emotions are much too strong to permit what intellect I may possess to be exerted in the writing of a book. . . . No, my friend, my brain is far too busy (and so is my heart) to allow of any leisure for such 'pastimes' as authorship. (Abdul Majid Daryabadi Papers, Nehru Memorial Museum and Library, New Delhi)

Soon after being convicted in Karachi, Mohamed Ali set out to write a biography of the Prophet of Islam. But he did not make much progress. He then began writing a multi-volume history of Islam. Having completed the first part in gaol, he was caught up in the political controversies and could not therefore complete the book. 'Curiously enough,' Afzal Iqbal writes, 'Mohamed Ali had never meant to write the present book. He started with the life of the Prophet and ended with his own.' He did, however, write a great deal more than many of his contemporaries. He wrote hundreds of routine letters as editor of the *Comrade* and *Hamdard*, poems to fill a not-so-slim volume, and miscellaneous historical, literary and political pieces to fill another (Rais Ahmad Jafri (ed.), *Selections from Mohamed Ali's Comrade*, Lahore, 1965; and his *Ifadat-i Mohamed Ali*, n.d.; Mohammad Sarwar (ed.), *Mazameen-i Mohamed Ali*, in 2 vols., 1938). During his internment (1911–May 1915; 1921–3) and trips to Europe, he wrote regularly to friends and family members, detailing his routine in gaol, reporting meetings with people who travelled from far and wide to meet him, and dwelling at length on his encounters with various officials in jail (Mushirul Hasan (ed.), *Mohamed Ali in Indian Politics*, in 3 vols.; Shan Muhammad (ed.) *Unpublished Letters of the Ali Brothers*, 1979; and Abu Salman Shahjahanpuri (ed.), *Siyasi Maktubat Rais-al-Ahrar*, 1978). In Europe, where he met scores of public figures and addressed numerous meetings from January to September 1920, he shared his experiences with brother Shaukat and friends (Mohammad Sarwar, *Maulana Mohamed Ali Ka Europe Ka Safar*, 1943).

Mohamed Ali's letters, now mostly published, constitute a major corpus of pan-Islamic literature in the subcontinent and uncover major themes that concerned his generation of educated Muslims. The tone in his correspondence constantly varies from boredom and depression, on the one hand, to exhilaration and conviction on the other, now relaxed and desultory, now indulging in flights of fantasy or burlesque. A flair for the dramatic, coupled with a wry self-awareness, a temperament that allowed the fullest reins to intellectual enthusiasm while never really realising personal ones. This complexity is also revealed in his speeches.

*My Life: A Fragment* is an important personal statement on how some educated Muslims lived through the turbulent decades following the death of Syed Ahmad Khan in 1889. It mirrors their fears and aspirations, as also their commitment to the political and intellectual regeneration of the Muslim communities in the subcontinent. It is, above all, a reflective account of an individual's intellectual and spiritual journey at a time when the anxieties of several Muslim groups were heightened by a number of developments in India and the world of Islam. For this reason, *My Life* is a document of deep religious feeling and serves to illuminate Mohamed Ali's inner self-awareness of Islam. Its author did not claim to be an authority on Islam, but considered his 'first duty' to share his reading and understanding with fellow-Muslims. In his own words: 'Experts often write for experts, but I am so to speak, "the man-in-the-street". The individual experience which I relate will make this clear, and being typical of the history of so many Muslim lives of my generation, it will not, I trust, be altogether lacking in interest.'

Again,

> I have now said all that I need say about my religious antecedents and my present attitude towards Islam and its theology and I fear I have said it at much greater length than I wished, and would have done if I had been able to devote more time that expression and concentration require. But an inherent and almost ineradicable [*sic*] tendency towards diffusion and a fatal attraction for tangents found a good ally in the condition of my prison life when work at a stretch . . . , was impossible and only snippets of time were available for dashing off a few scores of lines at a time. Doubtful as I feel about completing my task I feel almost certain that even if I am enabled to do so within a reasonable time I would not have the leisure for any but the rapidest revision before I hand over the manuscript to the printers. But in the circumstances of which now the reader shares the knowledge with the writer, he thinks he can rely on a generous measure of the reader's indulgence.

The importance of *My Life* is enhanced by the absence of a similar text written by any other leading actor of the period. Shibli Nomani (1857–1914) wrote a great deal, but he died long before the excitement caused by the Khilafat issue. Maulana Abul Kalam Azad (1888–1958) did not write much besides his commentary on the Quran. Jawaharlal Nehru (1889–1964), an admirer of the Maulana's scholarship, noted in his prison diary: 'Free thinker and magnificent writer as he is, he should have turned out a host of splendid books. Yet his record is a very limited one' (Christmas Day, 1942, *Selected Works of Jawaharlal Nehru*, S. Gopal (ed.), vol. 13, p. 39).

At a time when scholars are attempting to delineate the contours of Muslim identity in South Asia, Mohamed Ali's *My Life* enables us to understand how some Muslim constructed their identity in a colonial context. For this reason, this book invites comparison with other texts written around the same time in other countries by Muslim scholars and publicists. At a time when scholars are concerned to unravel the complexity of 'communal' or communitarian identities, it is important to consider how Mohamed Ali reflected on a society that was being gradually transformed by far-reaching political, administrative and bureaucratic changes.

A final editorial point: I have neither modified nor altered the printed text, even though the narrative is often verbose, incoherent, repetitive and full of digressions. I have merely changed some chapter sub-headings (e.g. 'At Mother's Knee' instead of 'At the Mother's Knee; 'Aligarh's *raison d'etre'* instead of 'Aligarh and its *raison d'etre'*), rectified the printing errors, and standardised the spellings, e.g. Kanpur for Cawnpore; Awadh for Oudh; Quran for Qur'an; *madaris* for *madarsahs*; Matthew for Mathew(s); *makatib* for *maktabs*; Medina for Madinah; Umayyad for Omayyad. I have italicised Arabic, Persian and Urdu words and introduced biographical and explanatory notes to make Mohamed Ali's account accessible to the readers.

The introduction, based in part on the arguments and materials presented in my previous publications, has appeared in the volume *Islam, Community and the Nation: Muslim Identities in South Asia and Beyond* (Delhi, 1998). Biographical and explanatory notes are based on: *Shorter Encyclopaedia of Islam*, edited by H.A.R. Gibb and J.H. Kramers (Leiden, 1974); *The Cambridge Encyclopedia*, edited by David Crystal (Cambridge, reprinted with updates and corrections, 1991, 1992); E.J. Brill's *First Encyclopaedia of Islam*, vols. 1–9; *The Oxford Dictionary of the Christian Church*, edited by F.L. Cross and E.A. Livingstone (Oxford, 2nd edition, 1974); *The Encyclopaedia of Islam: Glossary & Index of Technical Terms to Volumes I–VIII*, compiled by J. Van Lent, edited by P.J. Bearman (Leiden, 1997).

I appreciate the help and advice of Alok Bhalla and Aziz al-Azmeh. Their intellectual support spurred me to edit this book. I am grateful to a large number of people, especially Professor Wolf Lepenies, the Rector of the Wissenschaftskolleg zu Berlin (Institute for Advanced Study Berlin). For their courtesy and ungrudging help at the Wissenschaftskolleg, I am much obliged to Barbara Sanders, Corina Pertschi, Christine von Arnim, Mrs Gesine Bottomley, Anja Brockmann and their colleagues in the Fellow Services and the Library. Doris Reichel made life easy with the computer. Elissa Linke scanned, edited and formatted the book for me. I am greatly indebted to her.

*Wissenchaftskolleg zu Berlin* M.H.
*July 1998*

# Introduction

MOHAMED ALI WAS a controversial figure for his contemporaries and for posterity. Government officials associated him with the 'extreme faction of the Muslim community', the 'Advanced Party' and the 'hot-headed Nationalist Party'.[1] He led a clique of noisy and aggressive Muslims of the 'young party', who made the raja's house [Raja of Mahmudabad] their headquarters and lived and agitated at his expense.[2] He left trouble wherever he went, reported the viceroy. He persuaded some students at the Lahore Medical College to raise the tribes against the government in Afghanistan, and caused 'discontent' at Aligarh's M.A.O. College. That is why he and his brother Shaukat Ali were prevented from entering Punjab and the United Provinces (UP).[3]

In recent years some historians have seen in Mohamed Ali a charmer and nothing more; a politician greedy for power, an irresponsible declaimer who drove himself and his followers from one disaster to another. He is charged with inspiring the 'young party' Muslims to manufacture issues and whip up agitations to keep their newspapers going, their organisations active and their coffers full.[4] There are other images as well: the image of an energetic, talented and charismatic figure devoted to Islamic resurgence world over. Writers in India stress Mohamed Ali's commitment to Hindu-Muslim unity, his adherence to the Congress movement, his passion for the country's freedom.[5] Scholars in Pakistan, on the other hand, eulogise his contribution 'to the march of the Muslim nation on the way to its final

[1] Sydenham to Hardinge, 18 March 1913, Hardinge Papers, Cambridge University Library, Cambridge.

[2] Meston to Chelmsford, 20 Aug. 1917, File No. 136 (1), India Office Library and Records (IOLR), London.

[3] Quoted in Afzal Iqbal, *Life and Times of Mohamed Ali* (Delhi, 1978 rpt), p. 113. In May 1915, the Ali brothers were asked to remain in Mehrauli and abstain from political meetings. They were described by Richard Burn (writing for Meston) as 'disseminators of mischief and would-be-traitors', who 'have done any amount of evil at Aligarh. They have tried to stir up trouble in Lucknow and their message is mischievous wherever they go'. Home Poll. D, Proceedings, May 1915, 36, National Archives of India (NAI).

[4] Francis Robinson, *Separatism Among Indian Muslims: The Politics of the United Provinces' Muslims, 1860–1923* (Cambridge, 1974), pp. 178–9; and Judith M. Brown, *Gandhi's Rise to Power: Indian Politics 1915–1922* (Cambridge, 1971), pp. 139–40.

[5] Moin Shakir, *Khilafat to Partition* (Delhi, 1972), pp. 70, 74, 86; S.M. Hadi, *Ali Biradaran aur Unka Zamana* (Delhi, 1978); Shan Muhammad, *Freedom Movement in*

destination'.[6] They romanticise the story of his life and extol his achievements, some real but mostly imaginary. Schools, colleges and streets in Karachi and Lahore are named, as in Delhi, Aligarh and Bombay, after Maulana Mohamed Ali 'Jauhar', the *Rais al-Ahrar* (Leader of the Free Peoples).

What lends credence to such images is the tendency among sections of the Muslim intelligentsia to construct their identity around leaders who had the energy, drive and the skills to articulate the Muslim/Islamic world-view from public platforms.[7] Thus Mohamed Ali is commonly perceived to be more sensitive than others to the predicaments of the Islamic world and more stridently committed to its well-being.[8] He attracts greater notice because he possessed to the full the resources of traditional oratory—its repertoire of tricks. Few orators or political journalists had his combination of qualities: his range of articulate emotions, his capacity for analytical arguments, his pathos, fantasy and wit, and his power to marshal all these towards ends clearly discerned and passionately desired. He also had considerable poetic talent, which combined with his fervour and the desperate situation in which Turkey found herself after the War, to create in him a feeling of impending martyrdom.[9] 'Such sufferings and privations as ours,' he wrote, 'have only too often been the lot of mankind, in all ages and climes.'[10]

---

*India—The Role of Ali Brothers* (Delhi, 1978); Aaj Kal (Delhi, 1978); *Jamia* (Delhi), 'Mohamed Ali Number', April 1979, Jan.–Feb. 1980.

[6] Moinul Haq (ed.), *Mohamed Ali: Life and Work* (Karachi, 1978), p. 41; Nigar, Nov.–Dec. 1976; *Maulana Mohamed Ali Jauhar Sadi Conference* (Karachi, 1978), and for the view that the 'two-nation theory' had been forecasted by Mohamed Ali, see Aziz Ahmad, *Islamic Modernism in India and Pakistan, 1857–1964* (London, 1967), p. 162.

[7] Thus an address presented to Mohamed Ali, following his release from internment, stated: 'It would require a volume to enumerate in detail your services in regard to the M.A.O. College, the Muslim University, the galvanising of the Muslim community through your brilliant newspapers, the *Comrade* and the *Hamdard* . . . the raising of funds for Muslim victims in the Balkan War, the organising of a competent and well-equipped medical mission for the Turkish wounded. Your restoration to liberty is a mark of profound rejoicing to us. . . . Your presence in our midst will stimulate our community into the solidarity seriously imperilled during the last five years of agonising ordeal.' *Leader* (Allahabad), 12 and 15 Jan. 1917.

[8] Mazharul Haq and M.A. Ansari to Hony. Secretary, All India Muslim League, 3 Sept. 1917; and Ansari to A.M. Khwaja, 3 Sept. 1917, in Mushirul Hasan (ed.), *Muslims and the Congress: Select Correspondence of Dr. M.A. Ansari, 1912–1935* (Delhi, 1979), pp. 9–10.

[9] Mohamed Ali, *Kalam-i-Jauhar* (Delhi, 1938); A. Rauf (ed.), *Mohamed Ali aur Unki Shairi* (Karachi, 1963); *Nur-ur Rahman* (ed.), *Divan-i-Jauhar* (Karachi, 1962).

[10] Mohamed Ali to James DuBoulay, 18 Feb. 1919, in Mushirul Hasan (ed.), *Mohamed Ali in Indian Politics: Select Writings* (Karachi, 1985), vol. 2, pp. 192–3.

1

It is you (Syed Ahmad Khan) that had
taught the community its mischiefs;
If we are its culmination;
you are its commencement.[11]

Mohamed Ali was born on 10 December 1878 in Rampur where his grandfather Sheikh Ali Baksh (1813–67) served as a petty official in the court of Nawab Mohammad Yusuf Khan. He aided the British in quelling the disturbances at Bareilly and Moradabad during the 1857 revolt, and received a *khilat* two years later and a *muafi* or a rent-free land with an annual income of 13,000 rupees. The family reaped the rewards of loyalty even after Ali Baksh's death in 1867. Abdul Ali (1848–80), his son, enjoyed the patronage of Rampur's nawab. But he died of cholera in 1880 leaving Abadi Bano Begum (1852–1924), then only 28 years of age, the responsibility of bringing up her five sons and a daughter. The begum's family, which was in direct succession to a number of nobles connected with the Mughals, had suffered during the 1857 upsurge. Her father changed his name and lived for several years as a refugee in the Rampur State territory. Much of the family's property, having been acquired through the generosity of the Mughal rulers, was confiscated by the British government.[12]

Abadi Bano was undeterred by the family's limited resources and the heavy debt incurred by a spend-thrift husband. When approached by Azimuddin Khan, general of Rampur forces, she agreed to send her eldest son to Bareilly.[13] Mohamed Ali recalled:

How she managed to bring up her six little children and how she, an uneducated *purdah* lady, as education is understood in these days, managed to educate us better than our educated and richer uncles educated their own children, is a remarkable story which it is not through egotism that I would like to relate. . . . This miracle was not accomplished without personal privations that would do credit to a hermit living in a cave. It is not, therefore, egotism that has suggested this tribute to a mother's memory, but the sense of a heavy debt that can never be paid off. . . .[14]

[11] Mohamed Ali, in 1923.

[12] The best source for Mohamed Ali's life and career is his own 'autobiography' and his articles published in the Comrade on 21 and 28 Nov. 1924. Much additional information is available in the works of Afzal Iqbal, Rais Ahmad Jafri, Shan Muhammad and Abu Salman Shahjahanpuri. These are listed in my *Mohamed Ali: Ideology and Politics* (Delhi, 1981).

[13] 'People wondered why any mother should be so lacking in love for her children as to send them away from home while they are still so young.' *Comrade*, 5 Dec. 1924.

[14] Ibid., 21 Nov. 1924.

In the graph of Mohamed Ali's life, the steep arc of youth is missing; we see only the flattened curve of maturity. We see him studying a few Persian classics, reading the Quran in Arabic, and observing the religious rituals in a Sunni home. While in Aligarh (1890–98), he is found writing for the college magazine, sharing Shaukat Ali's love for 'the noble and manly game of cricket,' and nursing the ambition of securing 'a nomination for the post of Subordinate Magistrate or Land Revenue Collector.'[15] The 'Big Brother' was impressed with his 'unexpected success' at the B.A. examinations and arranged for his education in England. In Mohamed Ali's own words, 'So before the proverbial nine days of wonder were over, I was on the high seas in the Indian Ocean in the teeth of a raging monsoon, bound for England.'[16]

Within weeks of his arrival in September 1898, Mohamed Ali made his way into English middle class society with the help of the family of T.W. Arnold, who had taught philosophy at the Aligarh College, and its controversial Principal, Theodore Beck. Fazl-i Husain, also in England, found him to be 'a jolly good fellow, very quick in making friends'. They spent 'exceedingly pleasant evenings' discussing literary, philosophical and political issues.[17]

Mohamed Ali reached Oxford on 11 October to study modern history at Lincoln College. He matriculated a year later and secured a second in 1902, missing a first in History by a narrow margin.[18] He impressed his tutors with his vigour, common sense and resourcefulness.[19] James Williams, his guru in Roman and English Law, noticed his 'great capacity for acquiring and remembering information'.[20] His paper on *Macbeth* was written by 'a man of ability, capable of thinking for himself'. Yet these skills did not equip him to qualify the civil service examination, 'thanks to an English spring, and a young man's more or less foolish fancy'.[21] Success eluded him even after returning to India in 1902. Having failed to secure a teaching position at Aligarh owing to sordid manipulations, he opted for the Education Department in Rampur, a position for which

[15] *My Life*, p. 30. The references to this work are based on Afzal Iqbal's text.

[16] Ibid.

[17] Azim Husain, *Fazl-i-Husain: A Political Biography* (Bombay, 1936), p. 20; Iqbal, *Life and Times*, pp. 31–2.

[18] Mohamed Ali to Dewan Tek Chand, n.d., Mohamed Ali Papers (MAP), Jamia Millia Islamia, New Delhi.

[19] Testimonial of Rector, Lincoln College, 19 Oct. 1901, MAP.

[20] Testimonial of James Williams, 14 Oct. 1901, MAP.

[21] *My Life*, p. 32.

his tutors in Oxford had found him suitable. But his brief and inglorious innings ended in November 1902 when he sought refuge in the princely State of Baroda.

Gaekwad Sayaji Rao (1875–1936), the ruler, regarded the new recruit as one on whose shoulders he could place the burden of administrative work, the man who got papers drawn up, orders sent out, correspondence carried on and records kept. But jealous and conservative officials in Baroda, as in Rampur, resented him for his initiative, drive and his proximity to the Gaekwad. Though Mohamed Ali kept himself in the public eye by writing and speaking at conferences, he was set to leave for Bhopal by the end of 1906.[22] Dunlop Smith, private secretary to the viceroy, urged him to stay: 'I quite understand that your surroundings are not always congenial, but after all whose are in every respect.'[23] Around this time Mohamed Ali printed the *Thoughts on the Present Discontent*, based on articles published in the *Times of India* and the *Indian Spectator*. He sent a copy to the viceroy, hoping that it 'would meet with the sympathy and encouragement which India has learnt to associate now with the name of Edward the Peace-Maker'. The viceroy endorsed its contents and wished the book the wide circulation it deserved.[24]

Mohamed Ali stayed in Baroda until 1910, though his heart was not at rest.[25] Activity and companionship were the drugs he craved for. The drab and routine work in the Opium Department offered no solace to his buoyant and exuberant spirit. He yearned for the *mehfils* where he could transmit the flame of his intellectual excitement to others. 'I am fed up with this state . . . [and] tired of this job', he told his Aligarh friend Syed Mahfuz Ali.[26] He was conceited about his Oxford degree and contemptuous of

[22] This is revealed in his exchanges with Syed Mahfuz Ali. It is, however, clear that he took a keen interest in political developments. Although exaggerated claims are made about his influence on the Muslim League deliberations in Dec. 1906, he was regarded as a potentially bright recruit. In Feb. 1907, he lectured in Allahabad. A month later he prepared a text of the Muslim League proceedings which was published as 'Green Book No. 1'. This prompted an explanation from an official. 'I sent in a reply,' wrote Mohamed Ali, 'before the Council. In response, a general confidential circular was issued to government servants. They were told not to contribute articles which were likely to create communal animosity.' Mohamed Ali to Mahfuz Ali, 14 Jan. 1910, M. Sarwar (ed.), *Khutut-i-Mohamed Ali* (Delhi, 1940), pp. 252–4. For Mohamed Ali's speeches, see Home Poll. B, 149, 1913, NAI.

[23] Dunlop Smith to Mohamed Ali, 31 Jan. 1907, MAP.

[24] To Dunlop Smith, 5 Dec. 1907, MAP; and G.K. Gokhale, 8 Feb. 1908, Gokhale Papers (341), NAI.

[25] To Mahfuz Ali, 14 Jan. 1910, *Khutut*, pp. 252–4.

[26] Ibid.

those who sported degrees from Indian universities. He submitted, as he did with monotonous regularity during his internment a few years later, long representations to his superiors commending his own abilities, demanding higher allowances, and criticising those placed above him. 'In spite of being an Indian and having received a very similar education to the rest of the Baroda officials,' he complained to the Gaekwad, 'I found that I differ from them in almost everything, and that it was difficult if not impossible for me to be received by them as one of their own. . . .'[27] Shaukat Ali, himself a civil servant in the Opium Department, felt that his younger brother had crossed the limits of discretion; he admonished him 'to curb yourself a little—you have to work with certain people and you cannot always have your way. If I was your boss, I would strongly object to your correspondence. It borders on insubordination.'[28]

For the time being the prospect of a government job was held out by Dunlop Smith and Harold A. Stuart, the Home Member. But hopes were soon turned into despair, when Mohamed Ali was told that 'the expenses of an Indian private secretary would (not) be justified at present', and that his lack of experience of detective work was a bar for a post in the Home Department.[29] Michael O'Dwyer, later governor of Punjab, recommended him to the nawab of Jaora. But this small princely State could hardly assuage Mohamed Ali's thirst for participation in great events, even in a subordinate capacity.[30]

A career in journalism was the only option, the only avenue through which Mohamed Ali could prove to be of 'any appreciable use to it (Muslim community), while still earning a livelihood'.[31] His journalistic ventures, beginning with the *Comrade* on 14 January 1911, were successful. His own articles, laced with long and tedious quotations, tended to be verbose and repetitive. Yet he created for himself a broad-based readership because he wrote, just as he spoke, with passion and fervour. The *Comrade*, manned by some of his friends and protégés from Aligarh, grew in size; its circulation shot up to 8,500 copies. Its office in Kucha-i Chelan in the old city became a political salon after the paper moved from Calcutta to Delhi, the new capital of British India. 'No paper has so much influence with the students as the *Comrade*, and no individual has the authority over them

[27] To the Gaekwad of Baroda, n.d., MAP.

[28] Shaukat Ali to Mohamed Ali, 4 July 1909, MAP.

[29] G.S. Clark to Mohamed Ali, 2 Nov. 1909; Dunlop Smith to Mohamed Ali, 30 Oct. 1909; H.A. Stuart to Mohamed Ali, 10 Dec. 1909, MAP.

[30] *My Life*, pp. 33–4, and Mohamed Ali to the nawab of Jaora, 23 Nov. 1910, MAP.

[31] Ibid., p. 34.

which is exercised by Mohamed Ali,' reported the UP government in 1914.[32] When he wanted to stop publishing the *Hamdard* at the beginning of his internment, Wilayat Ali, the well-known columnist, begged him not to do so: 'I do not approve of your decision and I do not think many will. . . . You cannot imagine what the loss of *Hamdard* will mean to us—the Musalmans.'[33] Wilayat Ali recognised, as did others, that the *Comrade* and *Hamdard* contributed to a general awakening of educated Muslims who read and financially supported these newspapers.[34]

The *Comrade*, more than the *Hamdard*, served to voice some of Mohamed Ali's main concerns; for example, the promotion of the Aligarh College, his Alma Mater. He wanted the college to serve as a common centre where Muslims from all over the world would congregate and energise a common Islamic consciousness to uphold Muslim interests in India and overseas.[35] Thus, his maiden speech in 1908 on the subject, modelled on the style of Edmund Burke and with quotations from Latin, Arabic, Persian, Urdu and English literature, proved to be the swan song of the first phase of the Muslim University movement.[36] Mohamed Ali supported—some said fomented—a students' strike in 1907. His involvement in college affairs, a story detailed by David Lelyveld, Gail Minault and Francis Robinson, made him the *bete noire* of the board of trustees. The British staff complained to the English novelist E.M. Forster, then visiting India, that they were neither 'trusted to give the help they had hoped nor could they make some way with the students—not much, owing to the influence of the *Comrade*, a forward Islamic newspaper'. The Muslims 'had an air of desperation, which may be habitual, but was impressive'.[37] The college was transformed into a hot-bed of 'sedition';

[32] Home Poll. D, Dec. 1914, 31, NAI.

[33] To Mohamed Ali, 20 Aug. 1915, MAP. See, Abu Salman Shahjahanpuri, *Maulana Mohamed Ali Aur Unki Sahafat* [Maulana Mohamed Ali and his Journalism] (Karachi, 1983).

[34] For the influence of *Comrade*, see K.M. Ashraf, 'Aligarh ki Siyasi Zindagi', in *Aligarh Magazine*, 1953–5, p. 164. 'Throughout the country, only one voice was heard by the people of the north and the south, the east and the west, by the educated and the illiterate, the ulama and the ignorant. . . . ' Abdul Majid Daryabadi, *Maqalat-i Majid* (Bombay, n.d.), pp. 233–4.

[35] *Comrade*, 28 Jan. 1991.

[36] See Gail Minault and David Lelyveld, 'The Campaign for a Muslim University', *Modern Asian Studies*, vol. 8, 1974, p. 145; David Lelyveld, 'Three Aligarh Students: Aftab Ahmad Khan, Ziauddin Ahmad and Mohamed Ali', *Modern Asian Studies*, vol. 9, 1975, pp. 103–16, and his *Aligarh's First Generation: Muslim Solidarity in British India* (Princeton, N.J., 1978), pp. 330–6.

[37] Quoted in P.N. Furbank, *E.M. Forster: A Life: The Growth of the Novelist, 1879–1914* (London, 1978), p. 227.

officials wondered if anything could be done to prevent its students from 'being tampered with' by Mohamed Ali who, for all his professions of loyalty, was 'a dangerous malcontent', 'an element of strife'.[38]

## 2

> Grieve not over imprisonment in the cage, but
> do not forget the actions of the plucker of the rose.
> Oh foolish nightingale! When free in the garden,
> When did you ever find repose?[39]

Historians have traced the break-up of the Anglo-Muslim *entente cordiale*, the growth of political radicalism among some Muslims, and their stridency in areas where colonial policies disturbed the *status quo* most. Some have examined how the anti-Muslim bias of UP's Lieutenant-Governor Anthony Macdonnell, the reunification of Bengal (1911), the rejection of the Muslim University scheme (1912), and the fracas over the Kanpur mosque (1913) convinced a number of educated Muslims that radical self-help was a better solution than mendicancy. Much secondary literature also delineates the role of the men of *Nai Raushni* and the representatives of 'new ideals' and a 'new force', many of whom endorsed the Congress policies and programme. Mohamed Ali emerged as the rallying point for such 'younger men', for he himself held the opinion that the Congress, then dominated by the 'moderates', embodied the 'genuine and vigorous aspirations which move educated India for a well-organised and common national life'.[40] He emphasised, as did Maulana Abul Kalam Azad with greater rigour and consistency, the need for Hindu-Muslim amity and understanding. Without mutual cooperation Hindus and Muslims would 'not only fail but fail ignominiously'. He talked of a 'concordat like that of Canada' and '*a marriage de convenance* [*sic*], honourably contracted and honourably maintained'.[41] In another article—'The Communal Patriot'—he maintained that the two communities, despite their differences, should be mutually tolerant and respectful, and that eventually education and the 'levelling, liberalising tendencies of the

[38] Hardinge to Meston, 14 Nov. 1912; Hardinge to Butler, 29 Oct. 1912; Butler to Hardinge, 3 Nov. 1912, Hardinge Papers. Malcolm Hailey, Chief Commissioner of Delhi, described Mohamed Ali as 'the centre and inspiration of the Pan-Islamic movement'. To H.H. Wheeler, 1 May 1915, Home Poll. D, May 1915, 36, NAI.

[39] Mohamed Ali, translated by Gail Minault, *The Khilafat Movement*, p. 160.

[40] *Comrade*, 30 Dec. 1911.

[41] Ibid.

times' would create political individuality out of diverse creeds and races. He compared the Congress and the Muslim League to two trees growing on either side of a road:

Their trunks stood apart, but their roots were fixed in the same soil, drawing nourishment from the same source. The branches were bound to meet when the stems had reached full stature. . . . The soil was British, the nutriment was common patriotism, the trunks were the two political bodies, and the road was the highway of peaceful progress.[42]

Such views, which were being aired in many quarters, gained wide acceptance. Still, Mohamed Ali's fame spread far and wide only after he and Shaukat Ali were gaoled on 15 May 1915 for an article entitled 'The Choice of the Turks.'[43] On that day thousands congregated to offer their Friday prayers at Delhi's Juma Masjid and 'to bid adieu to the two patriots who had done all they could to promote their cause'.[44] They were first interned at Mehrauli, then transferred to Lansdowne and, finally, to Chhindwara where they arrived on 23 November 1915 wearing 'grey astrakhan cap with large Turkish half moons in the front, also Khuddam-i Kaba badges'. Located 'a considerable distance from their friends' and 'far removed from centres of Muhammadan feeling', Chhindwara was chosen because 'pan-Islamism is faintest' and 'the journey there from the United Provinces as regards visitors is exceedingly tedious'.[45]

The Ali brothers were well on their way towards martyrdom, with various organisations vying with each other to record their 'noble services rendered at the most psychological moment in the history of the community'. Their fame was kept fresh through many protest meetings, and also through the incident, covered by the historians Gail Minault and B.R. Nanda, of the government's conditional offer of their release in 1917. They refused to sign the undertaking suggested by the government; instead

[42] Quoted in Gail Minault, *The Khilafat Movement: Religious Symbolism and Political Mobilization in India* (New York, 1982), p. 19.

[43] The article gave the government 'ample justification for suppressing such writings'. An official note stated on 6 Oct. 1914: 'I do not see how anyone can read the article except as a direct incitement to Turkey to go to war, and practically what it says is that if this does bring them up against Russia and France, they have no cause to love these Powers and it does not matter much. England is practically threatened if she does not evacuate Egypt, and Germany is extolled. If this is not attacking our allies and siding with our enemies it is difficult to know what it is?' Home Poll. A, Oct. 1913, pp. 142–9, NAI. The Ali brothers maintained that they were interned because they freely expressed their allegiance demanded by their Islamic faith. To Viceroy, 24 April 1919, MAP.

[44] *Leader*, 12 and 15 Jan. 1920.

[45] Home Poll. D, Proceedings, Oct. and Dec. 1915, NAI.

they signed another, adding the qualification: 'Without prejudice to our allegiance to Islam'. Leading Congressmen, especially Gandhi, also courted them and pressed for their release. The Mahatma, having met the Ali brothers in Aligarh and Delhi in 1915 and early in 1916, assured Bi Amman—'Mataji'—that he was 'leaving no stone unturned' to secure their immediate and honourable release.[46] Having made Hindu-Muslim unity an essential part of his mission in India since his return from Africa in 1915, Gandhi assumed that Mohamed Ali was an ideal instrument in his hand for creating Hindu-Muslim alliance with the aim of obtaining Swaraj. He was valuable to the Mahatma both as an issue on which to cement a communal concordat, and also because he considered him to be a splendid example of that mingling of Hindu and Muslim cultures which had taken place in the Indo-Gangetic belt.[47] His interest in Mohamed Ali's release was 'quite selfish':[48] 'We have a common goal, and I want to utilise your services to the uttermost in order to reach that goal. In the proper solution of the Mohammedan question lies the realisation of Swaraj.'[49]

Gandhi's initiatives made him popular among north India's Muslims, many of whom participated in the *hartal* organised on 6 April 1919 against the Rowlatt Bills. M.A. Ansari extolled him as the 'intrepid leader of India . . . who has . . . endeared him as much to the Musalman as to the Hindu'. Mohamed Ali's younger colleagues, who regarded the Mahatma as a 'Tolstoy and Buddha combined', endorsed his non-violent programme. Satyagraha, according to Maulana Abdul Bari, the renowned *alim* of Lucknow's Firangi Mahal, was consistent with the Islamic principles.[50] In many parts of the country 'Gandhi', 'Khilafat', 'Swaraj', 'Mohamed Ali' were words that conjured up in the minds of the people a picture of bringing about a better world under the direction of better leaders.[51]

[46] Mahadev Desai (ed.), *Day-to-day with Gandhi* (Varanasi, 1968), vol. 1, pp. 93, 211.

[47] Brown, *Gandhi's Rise to Power*, p. 152.

[48] After arriving in India, Gandhi told a Khilafat meeting that he began to find out 'good Mohammedan leaders'. He was satisfied when he reached Delhi and met the Ali brothers. 'It was a question of love at first sight between us'. Speech at Bombay, 9 May 1919, *The Collected Works of Mahatma Gandhi* (*CWMG*), vol. 15, p. 295.

[49] Gandhi to Mohamed Ali, 18 Nov. 1918, ibid., p. 64.

[50] Hasan (ed.), *Muslims and the Congress*, Appendix 1; Abdur Rahman Siddiqi to Mohamed Ali, 24 March 1919, MAP; WRDCI, March 1919, Home Poll. B, April 1919, pp. 148–52, NAI; also see, A.M. Daryabadi, *Mohamed Ali: Zaati Diary Ke Chand Auraq* (Hyderabad, 1943), p. 20.

[51] W.J. Watson, 'Mohamed Ali and the Khilafat Movement' (unpublished M.A. thesis, McGill University, 1955), p. 14.

Around this time the portrayal of Mohamed Ali as a fiery and relentless anti-colonial crusader was based on the strength of his involvement in nationalist as well as pan-Islamic causes. This image is sustained in much secondary literature published in India and Pakistan. In reality, however, Mohamed Ali's utterances on the Raj and his frequent references to the good that was to accrue from the 'beneficent contact' with Western culture and civilisation explode the myth of his consistent hostility to the colonial government. Notice, for example, how he assured Meston, whose advice he followed in shifting the *Comrade* from Calcutta to Delhi, of his 'anxious desire' to co-operate with him and other well-wishers of his country and community,[52] and pleaded, on another occasion, for 'some pegs' on which to hang his moderate stance on the annulment of Bengal's partition. He insisted that 'well-merited concessions wisely made at a suitable moment' would curb an agitation far more effectively than the strenuous efforts of Muslim leaders.[53] He even suggested that the presence of the British monarch in India should be utilised to bind still more firmly the seventy million Muslims of India to the Empire. No wonder, high-ranking British officers subscribed to the *Comrade* when it began publication in Calcutta.[54] No wonder, the viceroy Hardinge allowed Mohamed Ali to collect and advance a loan to Turkey, patronised the Delhi Crescent Society and supported Ansari's medical mission to Constantinople.[55]

Even when officials rebuffed Mohamed Ali in London during his stay from September to 1 December 1913, he declared his loyalty and appreciated the manifold blessings of British rule in India.[56] When the War with Germany broke out, he was on the side of the British, urging India's Muslims to place their services at the disposal of the government. The article 'The Choice of the Turks' proclaimed the hope that the Khalifa would stay out of the War and save his Muslim countrymen from a conflict of loyalties. Talking to Abdul Majid, the C.I.D. officer, Mohamed Ali defined his position thus:

> His quarrel (Abdul Majid recorded) was not at all with the British Government. He was certainly not so advanced as Messrs. Mazharul Haq, M.A. Jinnah and Lajpat Rai. He believed that is was necessary for Muhammedans that the British Government should and would remain in India much longer than the nationalists

[52] To Meston, 19 Feb. 1913, MAP.

[53] To James DuBoulay, 3 Jan. 1912, MAP.

[54] To F.H. Lucas, 3 Jan. 1912, MAP.

[55] For correspondence with the Viceroy on these issues, see Hardinge Papers (84); Iqbal, *Life and Times*, pp. 77–8.

[56] *Comrade*, 13 Sept. 1913; and Mohamed Ali to James Le Touche, 4 Nov. 1913, MAP.

desired. . . . The Government did not know its real enemies. They will receive in audience Lajpat Rai and other nationalists, . . . but they would consider Mohamed Ali as their enemy.[57]

Mohamed Ali's antipathy towards Pax Brittanica may well have developed during his trip to Europe in 1913, though it was still not explicitly articulated. Meeting writers, journalists and civil servants enabled him to see Turkey from the outside, to observe the strife of the peninsula magnified into the terms of international politics, to watch and appraise the forces remoulding, sometimes deliberately, sometimes almost casually, the destiny of the Ottoman Empire. His exchanges convinced him, perhaps for the first time in his public career, that the British were insensitive to Muslim feelings over the Khilafat, and their ignorance of conditions back home was 'driving them fast to the brink of the precipice'. Hence his indignation at being denied access to senior officials of the Indian House. 'If we are unable to see even His Lordship,' Mohamed Ali told John Morley, 'what could we say to our people on our return except that because some local officials were desirous that we and our co-religionists and many others in our country should be misjudged by our superiors.'[58] Furious at the lack of sensitivity, he was drawn into a kind of *egoisme a deux* in defying their stuffiness. He commented that the government, having taken Muslim loyalty and support for granted, undermined the temporal power of Islam with scant regard for Muslim religious susceptibilities.[59]

Mohamed Ali's internment was the last proverbial straw; Ziauddin Ahmad Barni (d. 1968), a sub-editor of *Hamdard*, traced his mentor's anti-government stance to his confinement in Chhindwara.[60] From here, as also from Lansdowne and Betul, Mohamed Ali expounded on the government's repressive measures, targeting the Indian Civil Service in particular, 'a political party perpetually in office (with) the power to crush its political opponents with all the resources of the State'.[61] He told Delhi's Chief Commissioner, Malcolm Hailey, that he understood 'how hateful must be a man of my character to officials of a certain type'. He recognised the implications of the Defence of India Act, 'which makes even the Archangel Gabriel liable to internment by local governments on the secret

[57] Quoted in B.R. Nanda, *Gandhi, Pan-Islamism, Imperialism and Nationalism* (Bombay, 1989), p. 138.

[58] To John Morley, 2 Nov. 1913, MAP.

[59] To Chelmsford, 24 April 1919, MAP.

[60] 'Maulana Mohamed Ali Jauhar', *Naqqush (Shakhsiat Number)*, Oct. 1956, p. 1161.

[61] To Chelmsford, 24 April 1919, MAP.

testimony of Beelzebub'.[62] In June 1915, he announced that the law under which he was interned was 'tyrannous and unjust'.[63] No government was expected in the twentieth century to claim, even by implication, the right to force a man's conscience. He dwelt on 'the spirit of tyranny', the 'gag of prodigious proportions' prepared 'for silencing more than three hundred million of God's articulate creatures'. The Rowlatt Act 'has ended the reign of law, and substituted a reign of terror in its place'.[64] As a symbol of his protest, Mohamed Ali began to wear half-moons in his grey cap and Khuddam-i Kaaba badge, compared with his European style of dress in previous years.

The enforced leisure made Mohamed Ali more profoundly religious, enabling him to steep himself afresh in his Islamic heritage and to turn to the study of Islam—charting out an unfamiliar subject, getting at its rudiments, and exploring its nuances. In *My Life*, a document of deep religious feelings, he laments not having had access to the traditional Muslim learning. 'It is not without a feeling of deep shame that I have to confess, we boys and girls born and bred in Muslim households were taught far less of our religion than most English boys and girls of our age and position.' He bemoaned that Aligarh 'furnished' students with 'little equipment in the matter of knowledge of faith'. Though he attended Shibli's lectures and referred to the elation of sitting in the Principal's Hall attending his lectures with all the dignity of a quasi-'Undergrad', the Quran practically remained a closed book, and the traditions of the Prophet was no more than a name. In the seclusion of his internment at Mehrauli, however, he studied Maulvi Nazir Ahmad's translation of the Quran and found 'the consolation and contentment that was denied to us outside its pages'.[65] He discovered, after years of ignorance of his Islamic heritage, that the Quran was a 'perennial of truth' and offered a 'complete scheme of life, a perfect code of conduct and a comprehensive social policy.' Thus the main tenets of Islam, which were earlier 'little more than a bundle of doctrines and commandments', acquired 'a new coherence and, as it were, fell suddenly into place, creating an effect of units such as I had never realised before'. *Tauhid* grew upon him as a personal reality, man in the dignity of his 'service' as vicegerent of God, and himself as part of

[62] To Malcolm Hailey, 24 May 1915, ibid.

[63] To Malcolm Hailey, 2 June 1915, ibid.

[64] To Chelmsford, op. cit.

[65] *My Life*, p. 47; S. Abid Husain, *The Destiny of Indian Muslims* (New Delhi, 1965), pp. 24–5; S.M. Ikram, *Modern Muslim India and the Birth of Pakistan* (Lahore, 1970), pp. 42–3.

this great strength. This was Mohamed Ali's 'unique discovery in that small volume revealed some thirteen centuries ago to an Arab of the desert whose name I bore.'[66]

Mohamed Ali read the *Sihah-i Sittah*, a compilation of the Prophet's Traditions (*Hadith*), the works of Imam Ghazzali, T.W. Arnold, Shibli Nomani, the person who made the symbols of Islam a living reality for the Aligarh students, and the poems of Jalaluddin Rumi and Mohammad Iqbal. He experienced 'an exquisite thrill of delight' reading *Asrar-i Khudi* (Secrets of Self), especially because its author Iqbal expressed 'the same basic truth of Islam, which I had in a blundering sort of way discovered for myself'.[67] Studying Islamic history enabled him to see its great men as figures to whom he could talk, and its crises as guides to action in current affairs.[68] Studying Islam was conventional enough for men like Syed Ahmad Khan, Shibli and Azad who did so with greater scholarship, but none with a greater personal need. Mohamed Ali recollected: 'Since I first commenced the study of the Quran I have read a fair amount about Islam from the point of view of Muslims and also of their critics; *but nothing that I have read has altered the significance of Islam for me to which I had stumbled in the first few months of our internment eight years ago* (emphasis added)'.[69] To Gandhi, he wrote:

> Whatever else my internment may or may not have done, it has I believe set the soul free, and that compensates me for so many items on the wrong side of the account. What I could dimly perceive before I now realise with distinctness, and it is this, that the whole aim and end of life is to serve God and obey His commandments. . . . I confess I had never before grasped this truth in all its fullness. . . . *Internment made us seek refuge in the Holy Quran, and for the first time, I have to confess it, I read it through and with new eyes* (emphasis added).[70]

This experience was, in some ways, similar to that of Azad whose three-and-a-half year internment in Ranchi (Bihar) kindled his Islam into warmth and fervour. He began writing the *Tarjuman al-Quran* with his commentary on the opening *Surah Fatihah*, and its themes—Divine Providence, benevolence, justice, unity and guidance, *rabubiyah, rahma, adala, tauhid* and *hidaya.*

[66] *My Life*, p. 96; and Iqbal (ed.), *Selected Writings*, p. 170.

[67] Ibid., p. 127.

[68] A.M. Daryabadi, *Zaati Diary*, p. 14; To A.M. Daryabadi, 22 May and 25 July 1916, in Hasan (ed.), *Mohamed Ali in Indian Politics*, vol. 1, pp. 269–76.

[69] Daryabadi, ibid., p. 14; Mohamed Ali to A.M. Daryabadi, 22 May and 25 July 1916 (Urdu), Daryabadi Papers, New Delhi.

[70] To Gandhi, 20 Feb. 1918, MAP.

Both Azad and Mohamed Ali asserted the transcendental truth of Islam, 'a way of life, a moral code and social polity', a complete set of rules (*qanun-i falah*), as Azad put it. Both believed in the rightness of the Islamic ideals—a complete way of life for an organised community living out Allah's plan under the kind of government which had prevailed in the days of the Prophet. Both held the Islamic principles to be compatible with reason or science. Mohamed Ali underlined this point in 'The Future of Islam', and Azad in the first three issues of *Al-Hilal.*

In Mohamed Ali's view there was just one world of Islam regardless of caste, class, linguistic and regional variations, one vast brotherhood stretching across the continents. This was summed up by the *Comrade* on 18 January 1916.

> It is not only one God, one Prophet and one Kaaba that the Muslims of the world have in common, but in every degree of longitude and latitude they hold the same views of the relations of husband and wife, of parent and child, of master and slave and of neighbour and neighbour. . . . They follow among all races the same laws of marriage, divorce and succession. And they do this in the twentieth century of the Christian era exactly as they did in the sixth and hope to do so to the last syllable of recorded time. . . . There is still the one God to worship and the one Prophet to follow . . . always one unaltered and unalterable Book to soothe and to stimulate, and the one Kaaba to act as the magnetic pole for all true believers from all points of the compass.

In this way Mohamed Ali underlined the primacy of religious loyalty, arguing that Muslims have had a pre-eminent sense of community in their *Weltanschauung*, and especially so in India, where their adherence to Islam made them unique and gave them their 'communal consciousness'. 'I have a culture, a polity, an outlook on life—a complete synthesis which is Islam', he stated in his magisterial style at the London Round Table Conference in 1930. 'Where God commands', he added, 'I am a Muslim first, a Muslim second, a Muslim last, and nothing but a Muslim. If you ask me to enter into your Empire or into your nation by leaving that synthesis, that polity, that culture, that ethics, I will not do it.'[71] He did not believe that by being a Muslim he was any less an Indian. His religious beliefs and nationality never appeared to him to be incompatible. He could—and must—be true to both Islam and India. He explained thus: 'Where India is concerned, where India's freedom is concerned, where the welfare of India is concerned, I am an Indian first, and Indian second,

[71] Afzal Iqbal, *Select Writings and Speeches of Maulana Mohamed Ali* (Lahore, 1944), p. 405.

an Indian last, and nothing but an Indian.' On another occasion he spelt out his position in the following words:

I am a Muslim first and everything else afterwards. As a Muslim, I must be free and subject to no autocrat who demands from me obedience to his orders in defence of those of God. . . . Faith is my motive of conduct in every act . . . and my faith demands freedom. That Swaraj will give me, but it does not demand the subjugation of the Hindu or any one else differing from me in faith. . . . My own freedom and not the enslavement of any other is my creed.[72]

In sum, Mohamed Ali's earlier activities had been directed by 'communal loyalty', but his motivation after his religious experience was Islamic duty. This is not to suggest that he held his community in any lesser esteem or that its mundane welfare was less important to him. On the contrary, his awakening confirmed the rightness of what he had done in the past and made it necessary for him to intensify his endeavours along similar lines.[73]

## 3

Don't think us cheap: the heavens revolve for years
To bring forth man out of the veil of dust.[74]

Mohamed Ali's emotional disposition in religious matters had much to do with the nature and with the promptness of his response to events in Turkey. In this context his concerns cannot be doubted: the opinion that it was all feigned or that he was simply playing the pan-Islamic role cannot be defended. He passionately believed that the basis of Islamic sympathy was not a common domicile or common parentage but a shared outlook on life and culture, and that the Khilafat stood as 'the embodiment of that culture'. He endorsed Azad's description of a 'political centre' (*siyasi markaz*), and designated the Khalifa as the 'personal centre' of Islam and the *Jazirat al-Arab* as its 'local centre'. For these reasons Mohamed Ali warned the government that,

[72] *Mussalman* (Calcutta), 13 May 1921.

[73] According to Watson, Mohamed Ali's loyalty to Islam was expressed in the days before the Turko-Italian War as loyalty to the Indian Muslim community rather than to an abstract way to Allah. His communal consciousness, as he said, was far more secular than religious: his decision to take to journalism was dictated by the 'secular affairs of my country' rather than by a 'religious call'. Then, in the seclusion of his internment, he read through the Quran. Islam possessed him and he discovered the dogmas and ethical codes of his religion. After this experience, argues Watson, his motivation was 'Islamic duty' rather than 'communal loyalty'.

[74] Mir Taqi Mir, translated by Ralph Russell and Khurshidul Islam, in *Three Mughal Poets*, p. 184.

there should be no attempt to remove, whether directly or indirectly, from the independent, indivisible and inalienable sovereignty of the Khalifa, who is the recognised servant of the Holy Places and warden of the Holy Shrines, any portion of the territories in which such Holy Places and shrines are situated. . . . Nor should there be any such attempt to dismember and parcel out even among Muslim Governments, or in any other manner weaken the Khalifa's Empire with the object of weakening the temporal power of Islam, and thereby make it liable to suffer, without adequate power to prevent, the curtailment of its spiritual influence through the temporal power of other creeds.[75]

Again, he stated in London:

Well, so long as there are your Bryces and your 'Big_Sticks', we, too must have some sort of stick for the defence of our faith. . . . If you think you can please the Muslims of India by allowing the Turks to retain Constantinople in such a way that the Khalifa is worst than the Pope . . . for he would in fact be the prisoner of people of an alien race and faith, then, ladies and gentlemen, you know very little of Islam and the Muslims, or of India and the Indians. (*Cheers*) That affront shall never be tolerated, and if you think you can make out that all this 'agitation' is 'fictitious' and 'factitious', then you will be compelling the Indian Muslim soldiery to disprove this lie in a manner that will be far too unambiguous for your tastes or for ours. Beware, beware.[76]

Mohamed Ali envisioned a renascent Islamic world in which all Muslim peoples were united in a strong Islamic world—'the super-natural Sangathan of Muslims in Five Continents'—built around the Khalifa and supporting each other through that institution whenever Muslim security was threatened.[77] The new Khalifa, judged from his views at the Mecca Conference in 1928, was to be based on a democratic, elective rather than a dynastic institution like the *Khilafat-i Rashida.* And the person chosen would be virtuous and faithful to Islam. The Muslims of the world would direct the government and be responsible for its welfare, while their brethren in India—the largest single community—would lead the fight to emancipate Islam.[78]

Mohamed Ali infused vigour into the Central Khilafat Committee and

[75] To Chelmsford, 24 April 1919; Hasan (ed.), *Mohamed Ali in Indian Politics,* vol. 2, p. 236; also, speech in London on 22 April 1920; Iqbal (ed.), Selected Writings, pp. 183–93.

[76] Speech delivered in London on 23 March 1920, in Selected Writings, 2, pp. 20–1.

[77] 'Islam united Muslims by offering a set of common ideals and offered the only rational basis for unity and co-operation among its followers. The sympathies of a Muslim are co-extensive with his religion because they have been bred into him by the inspiring spirit of his creed.' *Comrade*, 12 April 1913.

[78] Watson, op. cit., p. 55.

its provincial and local units to realise the ideal of a renascent Islam. The *Hamdard* was started on 13 June 1913 for the Urdu readers. The Ali brothers travelled widely, delivered lectures, organised mass meetings and galvanised the *ulama* at the Dar al-ulum in Deoband, the Firangi Mahal and the Nadwat al-ulama in Lucknow. In fact, the *ulama* were conscious that they must now be active in addressing themselves to the political, social and religious anxieties of fellow-Muslims, or else see true Islam as they understood it, and their own claims to guide them go by default. This led some of them 'to pocket their pride and in a way even accept the lead of men whom they had but a generation ago finally consigned to perdition'. The orthodox and the anglicised 'were drawn together and as in a flash of lightning, saw that after all they were not so unlike each other as they had imagined'.[79] Once more, Ali remarked:

> Muslim society in India presented a level of uniformity and the bitterest opponents of a generation ago stood shoulder to shoulder. . . . If even a decade previously anyone had ventured to foretell such a result, he would have been laughed at for such a fantastic prophesy. . . .[80]

The annulment of Bengal's partition, the Turko-Italian War, the Kanpur mosque affair and the rejection of the Muslim University scheme added thrust to the converging courses in politics of the modern and the traditionally-educated. The 'temporal misfortunes' of Islam had such a profound impact that 'the wedge that Western education had seemed to insert between the ranks of the religious, and of the men of the "New Light" vanished as if by magic.' A general levelling took place 'without any dependence on the use of force or external authority'.[81]

Mohamed Ali played a pivotal role in strengthening these ties after his release on 28 December 1919. The 'disseminator(s) of mischief and would be traitors' reached Amritsar where, in keeping with the practice that had developed during the War years, the Congress and the Muslim League held simultaneous meetings. He had been imprisoned, Mohamed Ali told the Congress, for denouncing the injustices perpetrated on India and on Islam by the British, and now he must denounce them still, even if it meant returning to prison. At the Muslim League meeting, he expressed his readiness to sacrifice everything he had, including his life, for the sake of Allah and Islam. He made clear that Muslims were subjects of Allah and not of Great Britain. He echoed similar views in London as a member of the Khilafat delegation.

[79] *My Life*, p. 46.
[80] Ibid., p. 47.
[81] Ibid., p. 46.

The delegation, having arrived in England at the end of February 1920 for six months, maintained an exhausting pace, spurred on by Mohamed Ali. He was the debonair gentleman, perfectly dressed, dispensing political wisdom, epigrams, jokes and anecdotes to representative audiences, impressing everyone except the British newspapers and Lloyd George—the man who mattered.[82] He lived well 'in a nice flat with heaps of good food, taxis to go about,'[83] set up meetings with British leaders, spoke at length to various bodies and organised the publication of the *Moslem Outlook* in England and the *Echo de l'Islam* in Paris.

Mohamed Ali returned to Bombay on 4 October 1920, nearly a month after the Calcutta Congress adopted the non-cooperation resolution. His advice was that Muslims must plunge into the campaign with their non-Muslim brethren to achieve the Khilafat aims. Words were soon translated into deeds. He redoubled his efforts, along with Gandhi, Azad and Ansari, to induce the trustees of the Aligarh College to give up the government grant-in-aid. When the demand was rejected, quite a few students set up a break-away national university. This is how the Jamia Millia Islamia was founded.

To begin with, Mohamed Ali devoted some time to giving the Jamia a solid Islamic footing. He revived Shibli's discourses on the Quran and ensured that 'our day began with a full hour devoted to the rapid exegesis of the Quran'. But he was a man on the move and his project in life extended far beyond the confines of a campus. Jamia was too small and too quiet a place for someone accustomed to the humdrum of national politics and one who enjoyed being at the centre of every major event.[84] Predictably enough, he abandoned an institution he had himself founded, and headed for Nagpur to address the Congress, Muslim League and the Khilafat meetings.

Mohamed Ali was among the busiest men in India, speaking before crowds and local committees and galvanising support for the non-cooperation programme. He travelled to eastern and western India from January to February 1921. His presence at the Erode session of the Majlis-

[82] Mohammad Mujeeb, *The Indian Muslims* (London, 1967), p. 537.

[83] Mohamed Ali to Shaukat Ali, 15 May 1920, MAP.

[84] Mushirul Hasan, *A Nationalist Conscience: M.A. Ansari, the Congress and the Raj* (Delhi, 1985), p. 104. Mohamed Ali is reported to have said in Sept. 1923: 'I never conceived of the Jamia's growth and permanence at all. The Jamia's existence today is rather like that of the refugees and the Prophet's helpers at Medina who were lying in wait for the conquest of Mecca. Our real objective is Aligarh which some day we shall conquer.' Quoted in A.G. Noorani, *President, Zakir Husain: A Quest for Excellence* (Bombay, 1967), p. 25. On this point, see Mujeeb, 'Oral History transcript' (407), p. 35, NMML.

ul Ulama in March heightened the Khilafat euphoria, as did his presence in April at Madras where he attracted large crowds of Hindus and Muslims. His fiery speech at Erode nearly got him into trouble again; an apology and an assurance that violence in every form would be eschewed led the government to withdraw the prosecution. From April to August, he spoke in Meerut (9 April), Bulandshahr (12 April), Lucknow (1 May and 7 August), Moradabad (26 July and 6 August), Pilibhit, Sitapur (7 August), and Allahabad (10 August). He was joined by his mother who threw off the veil, appeared before the public and began addressing vast audiences. Her journeys brought hundreds of thousands of rupees to the Khilafat fund. The whole of India was astir. A popular song of the era reflected the spirit:

> So spoke the mother of Mohamed Ali
> Give your life, my son, for the Khilafat.

During this tumultuous period, Mohamed Ali's relationship with Gandhi, with whom he had so little in common, was ambivalent. He was undoubtedly moved by the Mahatma's interest in his release and the Khilafat cause, but he was uncomfortable with his world-view and could not grasp the significance of his political message. His own goals were limited to promoting pan-Islamism. As a result, it was not easy for him to make sense of the Mahatma's vision of a new social and moral order. Gandhi, however, hoped that 'on seeing the success of my experiment in non-violence, (they) will come to realise its excellence and beauty later on'. In May 1920, he referred to a distinct understanding with them that violence would not be allowed to go on side-by-side with non-violence.[85] Mohamed Ali confirmed in December 1923 that he would not use force even if it was required for self-defence.[86]

Mohamed Ali did not press his own viewpoint because he needed Gandhi's support. In fact, he and other Khilafat leaders chose the path of non-violent non-cooperation to 'secure the interests of their country and their faith'. From Paris, he wrote: 'I only wish that I had a Musheer (advisor) here, and if possible Fazlul Haq, though of course the best man to have is Gandhiji himself.'[87] When he was accused of being a Gandhiphile, he replied: 'I cannot find in any community—Jewish, Christian or any other a man who has as noble a character as Mahatma Gandhi. My *pir* and *murshid* is Abdul Bari whom I greatly respect. Yet I

[85] Brown, *Gandhi's Rise to Power*, p. 331, fn. 2; *Day-to-day*, vol. 2, p. 238.

[86] Brown, ibid., pp. 330–1; Robinson, op. cit.

[87] To Shaukat Ali, 15 May 1920, MAP.

can say that I have not found anyone superior to Mahatma Gandhi.'[88] 'After the Prophet, on whom be peace,' he said, 'I consider it my duty to carry out the commands of Gandhiji.'[89]

While Mohamed Ali was reaffirming his loyalty to Gandhi, the Khilafat Conference at Karachi declared that serving in the army or police was *haram* for the Muslims. The expected happened. Mohamed Ali, the Chairman, was arrested two months later. On 26 October 1922 began the trial where he made the famous statement: 'The trial is not "Mohamed Ali and six others *versus* the Crown", but "God *versus* man". The case was therefore between God and man. The whole question was "Shall God dominate over man or shall man dominate over God?".' The jury listened to his rousing speech, but was not impressed. He and five other Muslim leaders were sentenced to two years' rigorous imprisonment on 1 November.

## 4

> Man was first made of clay, and if the song you sing is good
> This world of clay for years to come will listen to your voice.[90]

Mohamed Ali was released on 29 August 1923, and in his first public address spoke of his gloom at finding on his shoulders the burden of freeing Islam and India. He said that he came out 'from a smaller prison to a large one', and that every executive member of the Congress must sign a pledge of readiness to sacrifice life itself for independence. Non-cooperation was still the main plank of his politics: 'If cooperation was *haram* according to the Islamic law two years ago, it cannot become *halal* today.'[91] He criticised the Swaraj Party and its leader, Motilal Nehru, for starting chamber practice in defiance of the Congress decision to boycott British law courts.[92] But three weeks later he himself proposed

[88] To Swami Shraddhanand, 26 March 1924, MAP.

[89] Quoted in Rajmohan Gandhi, *The Good Boatman: A Portrait of Gandhi* (Delhi, 1995), p. 104.

[90] Mir Taqi Mir, translated by Ralph Russell and Khurshidul Islam, *Three Mughal Poets*, p. 184.

[91] Speech at Lahore, in *Bombay Chronicle*, 26 May 1924.

[92] In September 1923 he complained that the Swarajists have 'completely gone back on the entire creed and policy of Gandhi'. 'I have been realising every day that the leaders of the Swaraj Party want to throw Gandhism overboard without some of them having the courage to confess,' he wrote to his Khilafat comrade, Saifuddin Kitchlew. He wanted him to be a peacemaker between him and the 'Gujrati friends', although he advised 'caution and restraint'. Mohamed Ali to Kitchlew, 30 Sept. 1923, Hailey Papers, MSS. EUR. 220 (7-A), IOLR.

the compromise resolution at the Delhi Congress, permitting 'such Congressmen as have no religious or other conscientious objections against entering the legislatures . . . to stand as candidates', and calling for 'united endeavours to achieve Swaraj at the earliest moment'. He was concerned, as he wrote to Jawaharlal Nehru who was induced to accept the Congress secretaryship in Mohamed Ali's year of presidentship,[93] to resolve the differences and unite the Congress factions. Appealing for unity, he stated:

Let the Provincial Congress [UP] assembly send for the sacred soil of Kashi itself the message of the greater and more solid *sangathan*, the *sangathan* of the National Congress. And let us go forth from this Conference truly *shuddh*, purged of all narrowness, bigotry and intolerance in order to free our country from the most cramping slavery—the slavery not only of the body but also of the soul. . . . If there is anything of the old world spirituality in Kashi, let us recommence the work of our great chief, Gandhiji, in the spirit of religious devotion and utter unworldiness.[94]

Whatever the reasons, Mohamed Ali's teaming up with the Swarjists enraged the *ulama*, whose *fatwa* against council entry was repudiated by one of their own spokesman. The 'no-changers', too, accused their idol of betraying the Mahatma's heritage. The front-rank communist leader, M.N. Roy, summed up his resentment:

Much was expected of Mohamed Ali. . . . The hope had been dashed to the ground. The idol showed its clay feet in such a hurry that the admirers were staggered. Mohamed Ali has failed to give the leadership which was expected of him. His pronouncements since he came out of jail are full of mere platitudes and hopeless contradictions. No constructive programme, no positive suggestion as to the future of the movement is to be found in them. He authorises the removal of the ban on the councils, but holds up the edict of the ulemas [*sic*] on the question. He professes to be the standard-bearer of pure Gandhism, but sets his face positively against civil disobedience, without which the political programme of non-cooperation becomes meaningless. He indulges in fearful threats against the government, but finds the demand for the separation from the British empire 'childish and petulant'. He deplores the Hindu-Moslem feuds, but still insists on Khilafat propaganda, which contributed not a little to the success of the enemies of national freedom in

[93] Jawaharlal Nehru, *An Autobiography* (London, 1936), p. 99. 'I have just received your letter, and must 'protest most indignantly' once more against your misplaced modesty. My dear Jawahar! it is just because some members of the Working Committee distrust and dislike your presence as Secretary that I like it.' Mohamed Ali to Nehru, 15 Jan. 1924, MAP.

[94] Mohamed Ali to Nehru, n.d., 1923, in *A Bunch of Old Letters* (Bombay, 1966 edn.), pp. 30–1.

creating communal dissensions. . . . In political questions, he has absolutely no programme to suggest. He harps on the threadbare 'constructive programme' which constructs naught but inaction. Such is the record with which Mohamed Ali goes to Kakinada to furnish the nationalist forces with a new direction.[95]

The main tenor of Mohamed Ali's address at Kakinada was that Hindu-Muslim unity was still necessary if Indians hoped to realise their aims. Similarly, non-cooperation was not outmoded even if one were to grant (only for the sake of argument) that it had failed. He also spoke of his long-standing dream of a 'Federation of Faiths', a 'United Faiths of India'. India's millions were so divided in communities and sects that providence had created for the country the mission to solve a unique problem and work out a new synthesis, which was nothing less than a 'Federation of Faiths'. The synthesis was to be of a federal type, for the lines of cleavage were too deep to allow for any other sort of union. He added:

For more than twenty years I have dreamed the dream of a federation, grander, nobler and infinitely more spiritual than the United States of America, and today when many a political Cassandra prophesies a return to the bad old days of Hindu-Muslim dissensions, I still dream of 'United Faiths of India'. It was in order to translate this dream into reality that I had launched my weekly newspaper, and had significantly called it the *Comrade*—Comrade of all and partisan of none.[96]

The motives for Muslim efforts towards achieving Swaraj were dual. They aimed at freeing India and freeing Islam. The relationship between Indians and the Turks was in the nature of a compact between countries oppressed by the same imperialism. Once India was free and her forces could not be driven to fight against the Turks, the two countries would be safe. Mohamed Ali's contention was that the Turks would have fought for the freedom of their co-religionists, including Indian Muslims, and hence India, if they had not been so weakened. His lack of realism in assessing the Turkish aims did not stop here. He pictured them fighting for an ideal Khalifa, even though the Kemalist revolution was already well on course. He believed that once the Turks were free from their 'distractions', they would revive the glories of the Umayyads or Abbasids and the pristine purity of the *Khilafat-i Rashida*.

Mohamed Ali's elevation to the Congress presidentship helped to legitimise his position in nationalist circles. But within months of his exhortations at Kakinada, he began drifting away from the Congress, or,

[95] G. Adhikari (ed.), *Documents of the History of the Communist Party of India, 1923–1925* (Delhi, 1974), vol. 2, p. 181.

[96] Iqbal (ed.), *Selected Writings*, p. 256.

perhaps, as he would have put it, the Congress drifted away from him. This had a great deal to do with worsening Hindu-Muslim relations and the feeling in some Muslim circles that the Congress was aiding the communal forces in order to establish 'Hindu Raj'. Mohamed Ali developed a point of view from which everything said or done by any Hindu was linked to the Hindu Mahasabha's influence. He saw 'the evil hand of the Hindu Mahasabha everywhere and its tainted mark on every forehead'. Indeed, his 'new mentality' recognised only two divisions in India, Hindu and Muslim, and not nationalist and reactionary or non-cooperating.[97] Commenting on Mohamed Ali's new stance, Nehru could not understand,

how a Hindu or a Moslem can have any political or economic rights as Hindu or Moslem. And I cannot conceive why Moslems or Sikhs or Hindus should lay stress on any such rights. No minority should be unjustly treated. But Maulana Mohamed Ali is well aware that minorities get on well enough as a rule. It is the great majority which requires protection. A handful of foreigners rule India and exploit her millions. A handful of India's rich men exploit her vast peasantry and her workers. It is this great majority of the exploited that demands justice and is likely to have it sooner than many people imagine. I wish Maulana Mohamed Ali would become a champion of this majority and demand political and economic rights for them. But this majority does not consist of Hindus only or Moslems only or Sikhs only. It consists of Hindus and Moslems and Sikhs and others. And if he works for this majority, I am sure he will come to the conclusion that he need attach little importance to the imaginary rights of individuals or groups based on adherence to a religious creed.

Mohamed Ali's main grievance, however, was that Gandhi, whom he had only just described as 'the most Christ-like man of our times', gave a free hand to the 'Lala-Malaviya gang' to pursue the goal of a Hindu Rashtra. The Congress, according to him, was not a national but a Hindu party, unprepared to condemn Hindu fanatics, and unprepared to work towards the creation of a secular society. Gandhi, with whom he worked for ten years through thick and thin, was keen to retain his popularity with the 'Hindus' and, for this reason, reluctant to resolve the Hindu-Muslim deadlock. Mohamed Ali's anxieties were heightened by the growing fissures in the Hindu-Muslim alliance in Bengal and Punjab and the rapid progress of the Arya Samaj, the Hindu Mahasabha, and the *shuddhi* and *sangathan* movements. Commenting on the Delhi riot of

[97] Ansari to Mazharul Haq, 7 Sept. 1929; Hasan (ed.), *Muslims and the Congress*, pp. 86–7.

July 1924 specifically, and on the deteriorating communal situation generally, he wrote: 'And pray Mahatmaji forgive a pang of sorrow, the cry of a well-nigh broken heart, the credit of it all goes, in the first instance, to the misguided spirit of the *sangathan* movement, and the superfluous boasting of the *shuddhi* leaders. . . . I feel sick, positively sick of it all.'[98] At the same time, the 'pseudo-nationalists', he wrote in the *Comrade* on 17 July 1924,

talk and write as nationalists and run down communals [*sic*]; but only in the use of counters and catchwords of nationalism are they nationalists for their hearts are narrow and they can conceive of no future for India except it be one of Hindu dominance and the existence of the Musalmans as a minority living on the sufferance of the Hindu majority, forgetting that such ill-concealed dreams can have but one interpretation, the existence of the Hindu majority itself on the sufferance of the British masters of India. It is my sad conviction that not one of these pseudo-nationalists would have talked so glibly of nationalism, majority rule and mixed electorates, if his own community had not been in the safe position of an overwhelming majority. It is they who are real culprits as narrow communalists, but since the position of their community is safe enough they mouth all the fine phrases of nationalism and parade themselves as nationalists. The Cow question provides the best topic for the exposure of their pseudo-nationalism, for in the name of nationalism they make demands on their fellow-countrymen so absurd that none has ever heard of them in any other country or nation in the world, and it is time that their nationalism was fully exposed.

The publication of the Nehru report in August 1928 set in motion the avalanche of Mohamed Ali's eloquence against Gandhi and the Congress. Soon after returning to India from Europe in October, he stated that the provision of dominion status in the Nehru report was 'inconsistent with the independent spirit of Islam'. Its implication was that the creation was God's, the country was the viceroy's or of the parliament's and the rule was Hindu Mahasabha's.[99] 'Today', he announced on 25 December 1928, 'Mahatma Gandhi and Sir Ali Imam would be sitting under our flag and over them would fly the flag of the Union Jack. The Nehru report in its preamble has admitted the bondage of servitude.' He was outraged that

[98] Mohamed Ali to Gandhi, 21 July 1924, MAP.

[99] 'You make compromises in your constitution everyday with false doctrines, immoral conceptions and wrong ideas, but you make no compromise with our communalists—with separate electorates and reserve seats. Twenty-five per cent is our proportion of the population and yet you will not give us 33 per cent in the Assembly. You are a Jew, a Bania.' See Mushirul Hasan, *Nationalism and Communal Politics in India, 1916–1928* (Delhi, 1979), pp. 287–8.

Muslim representation in the central legislature was fixed at 25 and not 33 per cent, while separate electorates and weightages were done away with.[100] In his view, separate electorates guaranteed that a small minority was not swamped by an overwhelming majority, while weightages ensured that this majority would not establish 'a legalised tyranny of numbers'.[101]

Such views mostly mirrored the fears of government servants and landowners who, having gained political leverage through separate electorates and government nomination, faced the cheerless prospect of being eased out of legislative bodies. Equally, these groups were alarmed by the proposal for adult suffrage. The enfranchisement of over fifteen million voters, mainly tenants, was certain to lead to the ouster of, for example, the landlords from the general constituencies. Not surprisingly, they resisted all forms of provincial advance if their interests were not safeguarded and insisted, moreover, on having separate electorates, weightages, and 'effective' Muslim representation on autonomous institutions created by the legislatures.

Mohamed Ali, now identified with such elements, did his best to turn the tables against his detractors. The first opportunity arose on 21 December. The Ali brothers, in league with some others, disrupted a meeting which was tilted in favour of the Nehru report. When they employed similar tactics elsewhere, several delegates resigned and decided to boycott the forthcoming All India Khilafat Conference that was to be chaired by Mohamed Ali. A few days later Mohamed Ali tried his luck at the All-Parties Muslim Conference in Delhi. He did not need to stifle opposition, for this assembly of loyalists was already converted to the idea that the Nehru report jettisoned their interests.

Mohamed Ali's presence at the Delhi's conference was described as 'a tragedy of Indian public life'. *The Servants of India* commented: 'One's heart sinks at the thought that the Ali brothers should have been among the staunchest supporters of the conference.'[102] Ansari, once his comrade-in-arms, was anguished to find him in the company of the 'Aga Khan and Co.'. He wrote:

> Ever since the Lucknow Convention many of us have been making ceaseless efforts to come to an understanding with the Ali brothers and their friends. . . .

[100] Ibid.

[101] In the very first issue of the Comrade, he had declared separate electorates to be necessary because of 'the distinct and well-defined Hindu and Muslim standpoints in regard to the common, immediate and everyday affairs of Indian life'. *Comrade*, 11 and 28 Jan. 1911, 29 March 1913, 19 Jan. and 6 Feb. 1925.

[102] *Servants of India*, 10 Jan. 1929.

They gradually but surely went on receding from us until at last they found themselves in the company of the Aga Khan and Sir Mohammad Shafi in January last. The willingness with which they associated themselves with people whose only distinction is that they have always been reactionary in regard both to Indian and Muslim affairs was surprising. . . . Indeed the differences that in their origin concerned a few provisions of the Nehru Report have now grown into a conflict of the very outlook. This to my mind explained why the Ali brothers are adopting an irreconcilable attitude although they know very well that they are thereby strengthening the government as well as the communalists, both Hindu and Muslim.[103]

A striking feature of the All-Parties Muslim Conference was that Mohamed Ali sat beside Mohammad Shafi who he had so often derided as a government stooge, and that the Aga Khan was cheered by Azad Sobhani whose vitriolic speeches at Kanpur in 1913 had forced the Khoja leader to quit the Muslim League. Mohamed Ali actually seconded the resolution proposed by Shafi at the Delhi conference. Likewise, leaders like Jinnah, Mohammad Shafi and the Ali brothers, who had not shared a platform before, signed the 'Delhi Manifesto' on 9 March 1929 in order to persuade Muslims to stay away from Congress meetings and processions.

Nehru reacted angrily to Mohamed Ali's signing the 'Delhi Manifesto', declaring it a 'treason' against the Congress by one who had served as its president:

The ex-Presidents of the National Congress are certainly a mixed lot and not always amenable to discipline. Like the king they appear to be above the law. I had ventured to criticise a statement made by one of them forgetful of this truism in Indian politics because of my high regard for this gallant leader in the cause of Indian freedom. He has made history and, if he but will, can do so again. But just when India is stretching her limbs for another and a stiffer struggle, when drooping spirits are reviving, he cries 'halt' and calls back his regiments and battalions. And have not many of those with whom he consorts in this endeavour been the strongest bulwarks of British rule in India and the antagonists of those who strive for freedom?

In his sharp rebuttal on 13 March, Mohamed Ali condemned Congress leaders who defied the party's decisions on non-cooperation, non-violence, Hindu-Muslim unity and untouchability. As a price of his cooperation, Madan Mohan Malaviya, for example, 'wanted to place a revolver in the hands of every Hindu lady, no doubt as a token of non-

[103] Ansari to Mazharul Haq, 7 Sept. 1929, Hasan (ed.), *Muslims and the Congress*, pp. 86–7.

violence, and of course all the Hindu-Muslim riots in which he has never said a word against Hindus are in full conformity with the Congress precepts of Hindu-Muslim unity'. He accused Motilal Nehru for 'killing non-cooperation just as he is killing the Congress today and merging it into the Hindu Mahasabha in spite of his well-known lack of Hindu orthodoxy',[104] and deplored Gandhi's endorsement of the Nehru report. Quoting from his writings of 1924 and 1925 to show that the Mahatma was converted to a different creed and striving for different goals, he pointed out:

> Gandhi has defeated all Muslim attempts for a compromise. He is giving free rein to the communalism of the majority. The Nehru constitution is the legalised tyranny of numbers and is the way to rift and not peace. It recognises the rank communalism of the majority as nationalism. The safeguards proposed to limit the high-handedness of the majority are branded as communal.[105]

Gandhi conceded that the Ali brothers 'had a fairly heavy list of complaints', and that he could not make an impression on them.[106] 'Whatever Maulana Mohamed Ali may think of me, I have nothing but kindly feelings about him. And I feel sure that time will remove misunderstandings. Having no feeling either against Islam or Mussalmans [*sic*], I feel absolutely at ease', he wrote from the Yeravda Central Prison. He hoped in vain that 'if truth is in me, the brothers must capitulate'.[107] Some months earlier, Mohamed Ali had already accused Gandhi of 'fighting for the supremacy of Hinduism (and) the submergence of Muslims'. He refused to join him because his civil disobedience movement was 'for making the seventy millions of Indian Muslims dependent on the Hindu Mahasabha',[108] and doubted whether he would stick to his own programme:

[104] *Nigarishat-i Mohamed Ali, quoted in Abdul Hamid, Muslim Separatism in India, 1858–1947* (Karachi, 1971 edn.), p. 201.

[105] *Times of India*, 5 March 1929.

[106] Gandhi to Motilal Nehru, 12 Aug. 1929, Motilal Nehru Papers (G-1), NMML; see also Gandhi to Shaukat Ali, 17 April 1930, *CWMG*, vol. 43, p. 280.

[107] Gandhi to Horace G. Alexander, 23 Dec. 1930, *CWMG*, vol. 45, p. 26; *Young India*, 3 April 1930, *CWMG*, vol. 43, p. 126.

[108] Quoted in Reginald Coupland, *The Constitutional Problem in India* (Oxford, 1944), pt. 3, p. 111. The position of the 'Nationalist Muslims', on the other hand, was different. This was explained by Ansari to the raja of Mahmudabad: 'Whilst, on the one hand, we consider the policy and programme of the Congress entirely ill-conceived and detrimental to the larger interests of the country today, we do not consider the campaign of civil disobedience conceived in the spirit of antagonism to the Muslims'. To the raja of Mahmudabad, 11 May 1930, Hasan (ed.), *Muslims and the Congress*, p. 121.

Doubtless man who could suddenly call of the non-cooperation campaign at Bardoli in 1922 with the same astonishing about-face can inaugurate a civil disobedience movement in 1930. But what surety is there that he would not again order suspension, just as he did eight years ago, only a few days after serving an ultimatum to the Viceroy?[109]

Moreover, the country was not prepared for civil disobedience: it lacked unity, discipline and self-control. He warned Jawaharlal Nehru: 'Your present colleagues will desert you. They will leave you in the lurch in a crisis. Your own Congressman will send you to the gallows.'[110]

Mohamed Ali's appeal to Muslims to send delegations to London symbolised the collapse of the old alliance on which Gandhi had built the non-cooperation movement. He himself joined a delegation, led by the Aga Khan, with the firm conviction that critical collaboration with the British at the Round Table Conference would bring greater political benefits than 'sedition' in Congress company. But his departure was marked by gloom, for he knew that his mission was condemned as traitorous by those very people with whom he had worked in the past. In fact, the Maulana felt in London that, 'his real place was in the fight in India, not in the futile conference chamber in London'.[111] In Oxford, his Alma Mater, he addressed the students in their tail coats, talked cricket and made them laugh. But he 'made little or no impression and quite failed to put across the case for the Muslims to a youthful but intelligent audience who were to provide a fair number of the nation's political leaders in later years'.[112] His speech at the Round Table Conference, which turned out to be his last sermon, appeared to be the raving of a man isolated, inconsolably bereaved, dying. 'I want to go back to my country,' Mohamed Ali declared, 'with the substance of freedom in my hand. Otherwise I will not go back to a slave country. I would even prefer to die in a foreign country so long as it is a free country, and if you do not give me freedom in India you will have to give me a grave here.' His appeal to the British to give India her freedom or else he would not return alive was no more than a pathetic admission of his failure.[113]

Mohamed Ali, a chronic patient of diabetes, died in London on 3 January 1931 and was buried in Jerusalem. Gandhi, whom he derided with such vehemence during the years 1928-30, had this to say at his

[109] Jafri (ed.), *Nigarishat-i-Mohamed Ali,* pp. 237-72, quoted in Watson, op. cit., p. 92.
[110] Nehru, *An Autobiography,* p. 120.
[111] Ibid.
[112] Benthall Papers (2), Centre for South Asian Studies, Cambridge.
[113] Mujeeb, *Indian Muslims*, p. 539.

death: 'In him I have lost one whom I rejoiced to call brother and friend and the nation has lost a fearless patriot. We had differences of opinion between us, but love that cannot stand the strain of differences is like "a sounding brass and thinking cymbal".' Likewise, reflecting on his role in his *Autobiography*, Nehru observed: 'It was a misfortune for India that he (Mohamed Ali) left the country for Europe in the summer of 1928. A great effort was then made to solve the communal problem. If Mohamed Ali had been here then, it is just conceivable that matters would have shaped differently.' He added:

For whatever the differences on the communal question might have been, there were very few differences on the political issue. He was devoted to the idea of Indian independence. And because of the common political outlook, it was always possible to come to some mutually satisfactory arrangement with him on the communal issue. There was nothing in common between him and the reactionaries who pose as the champions of communal interests.[114]

## 5

Man was first made of clay, and if the song you sing is good
This world of clay for years to come will listen to your voice.[115]

Mohamed Ali had a supreme gift of expression, but he was not one to be identified with any great principle or order, or even a big idea. He relished the trappings of power, the drama of great debates, the high-sounding titles, his name echoing through history. He was too outspoken to be a good manager of people. He excelled at exposing the follies of others but had little to advocate himself; his own thinking was ruthless—he spared nothing and nobody. He had a nimble wit, but sometimes his devastating sarcasm hurt, and he lost many friends.[116] He and his brother Shaukat were 'splendid agitators and very little more'. 'They certainly are not the type of men in whom we would have much faith, were they placed to rule over us', commented Abbas Tyabji, one of Gandhi's lieutenants in Bombay.[117] Edwin Montagu, the secretary of state who had not approved

[114] CWMG, vol. 45, p. 203; Nehru, *An Autobiography*, p. 120.

[115] Mir Taqi Mir, translated by Russell and Islam, *Three Mughal Poets*, p. 270.

[116] Nehru, *An Autobiography*, p. 117.

[117] Quoted in Brown, *Gandhi's Rise to Power*, p. 276. This opinion was shared by others. One of them wrote to Tej Bahadur Sapru: 'Frankly, I am not very much interested in the Ali brothers. I do not believe in them, and to the extent that they are doing right, it is because they are either attracted by Gandhi's glamour, or they feel that they can work more effectively under the kudos of his name.' S.L. Polak to Sapru, 8 July 1981, Sapru Papers, vol. 17,

of Mohamed Ali's internment, found him to be 'a quite typical specimen, full of incurable vanity'.[118]

Mohamed Ali was a passionate man, strong in his resentments as in his affections. He left a strong although not wholly pleasant impression on people who knew him, of a man devoted to his convictions. At the same time he was obstinate, impatient in temper, and choleric in disposition; quick to anger when honour or religion was touched; wild and untameable. He was the man for the people, impetuous, dashing, irrepressible, demanding sympathy by laying his heart open, crying and raising laughter, and believing in God and God's mercy with an intensity that made him at times completely irresponsible.[119] He advocated a strikingly wide range of ideas. Some grossly contradicted one another, some complemented one another, and some appear to have been floated simply to gauge public reaction before being discarded. The Urdu scholar Maulvi Abdul Haq found Mohamed Ali lacking in 'balance and a sense of proportion'. He was no doubt a vocal champion of freedom, but was at the same time ruthless and dictatorial in his public and private conduct. He had an hysterical streak in his personality, lacked consideration for friends, and was, for these reasons, incapable of carrying through his numerous enterprises. Abdul Haq's final judgement was that Mohamed Ali, though a brilliant writer and orator, 'failed' to enhance his stature and reputation in public life.[120]

After all, Mohamed Ali wasted years of his life trying to make a hero out of the Turkish Sultan—as perverse a task as was ever attempted. In his enthusiastic, unrealistic moods, which were frequent enough, he regarded himself as a link not only between Indian Muslims and the Turks,

---

p. 241, National Library, Calcutta. Percival Spear, who met Mohamed Ali at Delhi's St. Stephen's College in 1924, wrote: 'He was a handsome bearded man with striking eyes and clothed in flowing robes. His speech was easy, his manner ingratiating, that of a willing sufferer for a noble cause. To me he seemed to be too suave to be sincere and too insincere to be noble. In fact I took an instant dislike to him.' Percival and Margaret Spear, *India Remembered* (Delhi, 1981), p. 15.

[118] To Chelmsford, 23 June 1920, File No. 6, Chelmsford Papers, IOLR. 'Why we should intern Mohamed Ali for pan-Mohammedanism,' Montagu recorded in his diary on 11 Nov. 1917, 'when we encourage pan-Judaism, I cannot for the life of me understand.' S.D. Waley, *Edwin Montagu: A Memoir and an Account of his Visits to India* (Bombay, 1964), p. 141.

[119] Mujeeb, *Indian Muslims*, p. 536.

[120] Abdul Haq, *Chand Humasr* (Karachi, 1952 edn.), p. 164. Muhammad Sadiq had described this sketch of Mohamed Ali as 'vitriolic'. *Twentieth Century Urdu Literature* (Karachi, 1983), p. 368.

but also between the Turks and the rest of the world.[121] He was insensitive to the implications of the Turkish revolution, which was directed against the tyrannical rule of the Sultan as well as against Western imperialism. Similarly, he was unfamiliar with scholars like Ziya Golp, the intellectual leader of that period, who had dismissed the idea of uniting Muslim nations under one ruler as a messianic hope. That is why when Muslims elsewhere were establishing national states independent of external ties of domination, Mohamed Ali was striving to recreate the Khilafat of the classical theorists.

The invitation to the Amir of Afghanistan to liberate India from British imperialism was an act of indiscretion. On such matters Mohamed Ali seemed to be wanting to forget, as often as he could, the need to be tactful, in order that he might assert with ever greater vehemence the fact that he was a sincere believer in Islam.[122] The idea of Muslim migration (*hijrat*) to Afghanistan, which he endorsed, was both unrealistic and politically inexpedient. His credibility suffered, moreover, on account of the scandal over the 'misuse' of the Khilafat funds and his frequent outbursts that led to growing tensions between the Khilafatists and their Congress allies.[123] The *Comrade* was revived in November 1924, but ceased publication in January 1926. 'Poverty is pestering me', Mohamed wrote. He considered restarting the paper 'and see if I can wipe off the deficit due to those two journals [*Comrade* and *Hamdard*] or I shall retire from public life, and earn 50 rupees from tuitions'.[124] The Ali brothers, having spent more than

[121] Mujeeb, *Indian Muslims*, p. 538.

[122] Azad stated that 'whatever Mohamed Ali said was quite compatible with the teaching of Islam'. Home Poll., 1921, 45, NAI. Later, of course, Mohamed Ali offered a clarification in order to remove the misunderstandings in many quarters. See his presidential address at the Allahabad District Conference in May 1921, Home Poll., 1921, 10, NAI.

[123] For example, the Urdu poet, Brij Narain 'Chakbast' stated that Mohamed Ali's speech at a Khilafat Conference in April 1921 had convinced him that the political turmoil in India was fomented to strengthen Islam and create conditions which would give Afghanistan the excuse to invade the country. He did not think that Muslims could be converted to Indian nationalism because of their extra-territorial loyalties. He was convinced that Mohamed Ali, a pan-Islamist, was not a friend of the Hindus. He argued that Muslim political movements revealed their lack of trust in the Hindus. Gandhi believed that the support of the Ali brothers would enable him to promote his objectives. But, in effect, the Ali brothers used him as their instrument. Chakbast to Sapru, 28 April 1921 (in Urdu), Sapru Papers. In an 'Open letter to the Maulana Sahebs', the editor of *Bharatwasi* took exception to the Khilafatists designating themselves as 'Khadim-i Kaaba' (Servants of Kaaba) and not as 'Khadim-i Hind' (Servants of India). He told the Ali brothers: 'For you swarajya for India is not the first duty. You build the whole edifice on religion, while we build the entire edifice on patriotic considerations.' P. Parasram to the Ali brothers, 8 July 1921, MAP.

[124] *Searchlight*, 17 April 1927.

their means, were in dire financial straits. Delhi's chief commissioner informed the viceroy that Mohamed Ali was 'thoroughly discredited and almost penniless'. He went cap in hand to his former associates and colleagues (the Karachi merchant Haji Abdullah Haroon had already donated 10,000 rupees to revive the *Comrade*), and having failed in almost all quarters he finally secured a grant of 6,000 rupees from the deposed maharaja of Nabha.[125] Some years later, the raja of Alwar bore his travel and treatment expenses in London. Even if these are not illustrations of Mohamed Ali's loss of credibility with his own community, they clearly reveal the gradual reversal of his fortunes.

The Congress politicians, including the 'Nationalist Muslims', gradually deserted Mohamed Ali;[126] yet he clung to the much-maligned Khilafat committees. His defence of Ibn Saud, who had demolished numerous sepulchres held sacred by Muslims, also alienated him from his spiritual mentor, Abdul Bari, and other friends. But he was not impressed. Nor did he learn from his own experiences. During his visit to the Arab lands in June 1926 he discovered the squalor of Mecca and Medina, the barrenness of the surrounding land, the degeneracy of the social conditions, and the mismanagement of the *haj* traffic. Yet he continued to insist that the Khilafat committees were destined to bring about a truly Islamic rule in the Holy Land. He wanted India's Muslims to form a party around the nucleus of the Khilafat group, persuade other Islamic people to their way of thinking, and thus achieve a united Muslim voice. He wanted them to contribute money, time, technical assistance and moral support to the Hijaz, devote themselves wholeheartedly to the reformation of the Centre of Islam, and thus earn the good requital in both worlds. He was confident that it was possible to resist Ibn Saud's arrogation of control of the Holy Land and help re-establish a genuine Islamic rule.[127]

Such romantic visions were nurtured by Mohamed Ali's inflated ego. That is why he paid scant regard to his own comrades who had followed his lead in the past but were no longer prepared to do so in the changed political scenario. His protégés in UP—Khaliquzzaman and Shuaib

[125] David Page, *Prelude to Partition: The Indian Muslims and the Imperial System of Control 1920–32* (Oxford, 1982), pp. 104–5.

[126] For example, one of his former colleagues, Arif Husain Hasvi, resigned from the Hamdard because of Mohamed Ali's communal posture. *Searchlight*, 14 May 1926. Page, op. cit., pp. 100–1.

[127] Watson, op. cit., p. 87; Ahmad, *Islamic Modernism*, p. 139; Rais Ahmad Jafri, *Karawan-i Gumgushta* (Karachi, 1971), pp. 16–18.

Qureshi—opposed his plan of sending three deputations to the Middle East.[128] In neighbouring Delhi, Ansari resigned from the Khilafat committees in July 1926, stating that 'as an Indian owing allegiance first to the motherland' he had to sever his ties with communal and sectional organisations.[129] In Punjab, after their success in the 1924 elections, the Muslim Swarajists took less interest in the Khilafat committee; the main opposition to the Ali brothers came from the Khilafatists under the leadership of Saifuddin Kitchlew. One of Punjab's leading public figures, the poet Iqbal, believed that the Khilafat movement in its dying moments unfolded aspects in which 'no sincere Muslim could join for a single minute'. Turkey, he pointed out, was the first Muslim country to shake off the fetters of medieval mentality and found a way of life of her own.[130]

In sum, Mohamed Ali failed to recognise that 'Muslim identity' in a plural society had to be defined not in relation to the Islamic world but in response to the specific historical and contemporary experiences of the Muslim communities in the subcontinent. This fact had been underlined in Syed Ahmad Khan's rejection of pan-Islamism towards the end of the nineteenth century and was creatively expressed by Azad, Ajmal Khan and Ansari. But Mohamed Ali was swayed by his own religious/Islamic rhetoric. He could not reflect, as did Azad after 1922–3, on the wider implications of the Khilafat movement on inter-community relations. He even refused to accept that Muslims themselves had played the final part in destroying what he was almost single-handedly fighting to maintain. He continued charging at the windmill, hugging an illusion which had become irrelevant to his own community.[131] As he once put it, he had 'an inherent and almost ineradicable tendency towards diffusion and a fatal attraction for tangents'.[132] He could not build the bridges for retreat, because he did not possess the skill to do so. Instead, he aimed 'to destroy all that did not conform to his ideal, even though he could not reconstruct what he had destroyed'.[133] Although he was popular with those who thought it a point of honour to wear Islam on their sleeves, he ultimately undermined his own position and damaged the very causes he aspired to serve.[134]

[128] Page, *Prelude to Partition,* p. 502.

[129] Ansari to Shaukat Ali, 16 July 1926, Hasan (ed.), *Muslims and the Congress,* p. 19.

[130] Page, *Prelude to Partition*, pp. 503–4. For Iqbal, see Annemarie Schimmel, *Gabriel's Wings: A Study into the Religious Ideas of Sir Muhammad Iqbal* (Leiden, 1963), p. 47.

[131] Iqbal, *Life and Times*, p. 413.

[132] Quoted in Nanda, op. cit., p. 201.

[133] Choudhry Khaliquzzaman, *Pathway to Pakistan* (Lahore, 1961), p. 69.

[134] Mujeeb, *Indian Muslims*, p. 538.

I

# Studies at Home and at School

## AN EGOTIST'S APOLOGY

I FEAR I SHALL have to commence my exposition of Islam with a very large slice of egotism. It has, however, been forced upon me not by what I may regard as my merits, but, on the contrary, by my lack of them. This may seem to deprive me of all my title to speak on the subject of Islam; and yet, it is just because I am a very ordinary Muslim with no pretensions whatever to the gradation of schoolmen and still more because I can claim through my ignorance itself a degree of detachment, that I think it would not be altogether unprofitable for the ordinary non-Muslim to give me a fair hearing. Experts often write for experts; but, I am so to speak 'the man-in-the-street', and I write for 'the man-in-the-street'. The individual experience which I relate will make this clear, and being typical of the history of so many Muslim lives of my own generation, it will not, I trust, be altogether lacking in interest.

## ELEMENTARY RELIGIOUS INSTRUCTION

Born in a fairly prosperous and cultured Indian Muslim family in the Rampur State,[1] in the last quarter of the last century, I naturally received some instruction in the faith of Islam. But even though we Muslims—and Orientals generally—sneer at the indifference towards religion displayed in the most progressive countries of Europe today, and so many of us regard the people of Europe as almost Godless, it is not without a feeling of deep shame that I have to confess, we boys and girls born and bred in Muslim households were taught far less of our religion than most English boys and girls of our age and position are taught of theirs. We cannot appreciate too much the vigilance and zealous care of those who keep in mind the undoubted dangers that lurk in a study of Divine Scriptures in translations. But on the other hand we must not overlook the equally indubitable fact that a European child who has his Bible to read

[1] A former Muslim-ruled princely state of Rohilkhand in north India. Its early history is that of the growth of Rohilla power in the region.

in his own mother-tongue knows far more of it than a Muslim child whose mother-tongue is not Arabic knows of the Quran, which he is seldom taught to read in a translation. Like other children of my own age and position, I learnt, when still very young, to read the Quran in Arabic, without, of course, understanding a word of what it meant, and I memorised, without any perceptible effort, a dozen of the shortest *suras* for reciting later on in the daily prayers.[2] I did not need any text-books to learn the simple ritual of the Muslims' prayers, or the method of making the formally prescribed ablutions as a preliminary to the offering of prayers; for the frequent sight of my old teacher, my elder brothers and cousins, and others in the mosque in our street, and, in fact, of my mother and other ladies of the family and members of our household, was sufficient for a general guidance. These and the few simple rules for observing other forms of prescribed cleanliness are best learnt in the course of daily practice, and though elementary text-books abound, they are referred to only in case of doubt even by the young, or just to memorise a few Arabic texts that form part of the daily prayers, but are not taken from the Quran itself.

## AN *ALIM'S* RELIGIOUS STUDIES

Had I belonged to one of the families that specialise in religious learning, I would, no doubt, have spent half a life-time in the study of the Quran and its *Tafseer* or exegesis, of *Hadith* or the Traditions of the Prophet, of *Fiqh* or Muslim Jurisprudence, (including not only Law, as understood in European countries, but also ordinances regarding prayers, fasts, alms-giving and pilgrimage, and in fact, every religious duty prescribed for a Muslim) and of *Aqaid* and *Kalam*[3] or Dogmatics and Dialectics, which form the scholastic philosophy of the Musalmans regarding their creed, in other words 'Theology' in the narrower sense, together with logic which forms the substratum of this branch of religious studies.

As a necessary preliminary to these religious studies, I would have had to receive instruction for a number of years in Arabic grammar, and along with it in some secular Arabic literature, and after having finished at any age from twenty to thirty, the entire syllabus of studies followed in the Arabic schools dotted all over northern and eastern India, I would

[2] As Quranic term, *sura* refers to a unit of revelation.

[3] Or, *ilm al-kalam,* the term for theology, one of the religious sciences of Islam and the discipline which brings to the service of religious beliefs discursive arguments.

have set up as an *Alim* and teacher, giving instruction, in my turn, in the same text-books to younger men similarly inclined or situated.

## AN AVERAGE MUSLIM'S STUDIES

But, as I did not belong to such a family, all that I had to do was to read with my old red-bearded pedagogue, who was innocent of all knowledge of Mathematics, History and Geography, not to mention Natural Science, half a dozen or more text-books in Persian, like the *Gulistan* and *Bostan* of Sadi;[4] the letters of Aurangzeb,[5] Nizami's *Sikandarnama* or Epic about Alexander's conquest of Persia;[6] Firdausi's more famous *Shahnama*,[7] and some prose works composed in less intelligible and more ornate though not more graceful Persian than Sadi's, such as Zahuri's *Sih-nasr* or that delightful but malicious lampoon of Nimat Khan-i-Ali[8] on Aurangzeb and his conquest of the Shia[9] kingdoms of the Deccan.[10] But these were purely cultural and literary, not religious studies. It is true one learnt a

[4] Shaikh Sadi (1213/19–1292) of Shiraz is one of the most renowned authors of Persia. His fame rests on the *Bustan*, the *Gulistan* and his *ghazals*. The *Bustan* and *Gulistan* are collections of moralising anecdotes.

[5] (1618-1707); the last of the great Mughal Emperors (1658–1707). He died at Ahmednagar.

[6] Nizami Ganjawi (d. 1217) is one of the great Persian poets and thinkers. His five masterpieces are known collectively as the *Khamsa*, the Five Treasures. Firdausi was his source of inspiration in composing the *Sikandarnama* or *Iskandar-nama*. The *Sharif-nama*, the first portion of the *Sikandarnama*, is devoted to Alexander's conquest of the world. The second part portrays Alexander as a great sage and prophet. Alexander achieved his military success over Persia in a series of battles: Granicus (334 B.C.), Issus (333 B.C.), and Gaugmela (331 B.C.).

[7] Abul Qasim Firdausi (940–1020), the poet of *Shahnama*, an epic of about 60,000 lines. Its composition lasted 35 years (completed in February 1010) and was dedicated to Sultan Mahmud of Ghazna.

[8] (d. 1710); he entered the service of Shah Jahan and attained his highest honours under Aurangzeb.

[9] After the death of the Prophet, the followers of Ali staked his claim to be the Khalifa. They became known as 'partisans of Ali' or *Shia Ali*, usually anglicised as Shiites. They believe that Ali and his followers were both temporal rulers and *Imams*. The most important group is the 'twelver' Shias, who believe that there were twelve *imams*—Ali and his descendants—after the Prophet Mohammad, and that the twelfth did not die, but disappeared, and one day will return to bring justice to the world.

[10] The region bounded by the Eastern Ghats and the Western Ghats; includes most of Karnataka, south Andhra Pradesh, south-east Maharashtra and north-west Tamil Nadu States. The Carnatic plain areas was the arena for the British struggle against the French for control of India during the eighteenth century.

great deal of the ideals of Muslim life and even of Muslim religion in the text-books in Persian in use in these *makatib* [private schools] and *madaris* [public schools] and particularly from books on *Akhlaq* or good morals and manners. But they did not directly aim at religious instruction, and in fact, one or two of the books so often taught as good literature in those days, were, on account of their unusually erotic nature, by no means fit for the instruction of youth.

## THIRD 'INFIDEL' IN A FAMILY

As it was, hardly before I had finished a couple of these Persian text-books, I was sent to a school recently founded at Rampur and subsequently to another at Bareilly, some forty miles from my home, to learn English, and of course, along with it, the usual school subjects of Arithmetic, History and Geography. For unlike most of our cousins whose parents were averse to endangering their salvation by subjecting them to 'the Godless influence of English education', two of my brothers had already been sent to the school at Bareilly by our mother. She had become a widow at the age of 27, when cholera had suddenly cut short of our young father's life after a few hours' illness. She refused to remarry, and hiding the anguish of her heart under a light bantering tone, told those who advised her to do so, that she had had a husband to look after her long enough and now she had herself five husbands and a wife to look after, referring, of course to her five boys and one girl, the eldest of whom was only thirteen and an invalid, and the youngest of whom, the present writer, was not yet two. Women are generally more religious, or at least more superstitious than men; but our mother, who brought us up without any other assistance, although intensely religious, was remarkably free from prejudice and superstition. When the younger of these two brothers of mine, Shaukat,[11] was selected by her for a course of English education, the uncle who was managing our property refused to sanction an allowance for his school expenses, remarking, in all sincerity, but also with all the bitterness characteristic of the times and more specially of the place, that one 'infidel' was bad enough in a family! But our mother was determined and secretly pawned some personal jewellery of her own with the help of

[11] Shaukat Ali (1873–1938); educated at the Aligarh college in 1888; sub-deputy agent till 1912; founded the Anjuman-i-Khuddam-i Kaaba with Maulana Abul Bari in Lucknow in 1913; interned with Mohamed Ali from May 1915 to December 1919, and again in 1923; president of the Khilafat Conference at Kakinada in 1923; Mohamed Ali chaired the Congress session in the same city.

the maid-servant of a Hindu neighbour, who was a banker, and packed off the second would-be 'infidel' of the family also to Bareilly, with the assurance that she had enough money in her own hands now to pay for Shaukat's schooling at least for sometime to come. When our uncle had been thus outwitted by a resolute woman whose self-reliance throughout a long life of hardships and difficulties had only been equalled by her implicit trust in the bountiful providence of God, he got her trinkets released from pawn and paid for the schooling of both his nephews from the proceeds of our property. And so, when yet another 'infidel' sought perdition, he accepted the inevitable, and I proceeded to Bareilly without any clandestine negotiations of my mother with a pawn-broker's maid. As in so many other things in my life, Shaukat had thus paved the way for me and made it smooth.

## PREJUDICE AGAINST ENGLISH CULTURE AND EDUCATION

Here I may remark that the prejudice against English education was still very strong in Upper India. It had been the centre of Muslim political life for eight centuries and even when the rule of India passed away from Muslim hands by slow and hardly perceptible degrees in the century between the Battle of Plassey[12] and the Indian Mutiny, the Musalmans of Upper India did not cease to regard the new rulers of India as something very inferior to themselves in civilisation and culture. This storm of ill-will and disdain had been gathering for a whole century and was precipitated among other things by the aggressive activity of Christian missionaries. The Mutiny began as an affair of the sepoys of the Indian Army; but in the storm-centre of my province where it had to be fought out if English rule was to continue in India, it soon attracted to itself many forms of discontent which had been gathering force and volume for more than a generation, and religion was inextricably mixed up with politics. Although so many Musalmans had at enormous risks assisted the English at a time when hardly any could have predicted their eventual success with any degree of assurance, it was the Muslim aristocracy in that province that suffered most in the terrible aftermath of the Mutiny. In fact, in its permanent results even more than in some of its terrors it could, without any considerable exaggeration be compared to the social upheaval

[12] The battles of Plassey in 1757 and Buxar in 1764 put an end to the independence of Bengal and the establishment of East India Company's rule.

that the French Revolution meant to the old nobility of France. The remnants of Muslim aristocracy, deprived of all influence and many of their possessions, certainly did not expect the return of the Muslim rule. Nevertheless, a whole generation kept sullenly aloof from all contact with the culture of the new rulers of India, which in their heart of hearts they still despised, and Musalmans of these regions were in no mood to take advantage of the education provided by the Universities of Calcutta, Bombay and Madras founded in the very year in which the Mutiny convulsed these provinces. The Punjab had to be without a University for another quarter of a century, and even then it had to interlard English education with a great display of the encouragement of Oriental lore. My own province had to wait for some years longer, and then, too, it was not the University established by Government that induced the bulk of Musalmans to throw off their old prejudices against English education but one projected by a Musalman of Delhi who strenuously protested against the complete divorce of religious from secular learning.[13] Few indeed can realise today the feelings of those Upper India Muslims who sulked in their tents for so long, or the difficulties of the pioneers of English education among them like Syed Ahmad Khan, who founded within two decades of the Mutiny the Aligarh College which is now the first chartered Muslim University in India.[14] One of his aunts, it is said, maintained throughout the rest of her life her refusal to see him only on account of his taking too kindly to the culture of the foreigner and the infidel, though her nephew, despite the heterodoxy of his somewhat aggressive rationalism in interpreting the Quran and his militant opposition to superstitions and shackling customs unauthorised by Islam, was a zealous and even stern Muslim in his polemics in defence of his creed against European and Christian critics and an unbending conservative Indian in social matters such as the seclusion of women.

## THE 'OASIS' IN 'BRITISH' INDIA

This attitude of the Indian Musalmans towards English culture and education took an even more hostile form in our own state of Rampur. It was the only tract in the province still under Indian and a Muslim ruler,

[13] The Allahabad University was established in 1887, followed by the Banaras Hindu University in 1916.

[14] Syed Ahmad Khan (1817–1898); born in Delhi in a family connected with the Mughal court; joined the service of the East India Company as *Sadr-Amin* in 1838; stationed in Bijnor when the rebellion in Meerut broke out on 10 May 1857; wrote an account of the

and was on that account a veritable oasis in the surrounding 'British' India. The principal inhabitants of Rampur were, like those of the rest of the British division of Rohilkhand,[15] descendants of Rohillas[16] that had come from Afghanistan. Warren Hastings[17] had fought against the Rohillas one of the most unpopular wars for a purely mercenary reason, when British forces were, so to speak, hired by the ruler of Awadh; and the state of Rampur was the remnant of their independent territory which had extended *az sang ta Gang* (i.e. from the Himalayas to the Ganges). They could not bear much love for the English whose services had been obtained against them in exchange for hard cash. When the Mutiny broke out and raged in all its fury at Meerut and Delhi, both within a hundred miles of Rampur, it soon spread to the surrounding Rohilla country. Nevertheless, the ruler of Rampur actually rendered invaluable assistance to the hard-pressed British from that isolated centre in spite of the unpopularity of the British cause among the Rohillas. This unpopularity before long involved the ruler himself who had otherwise been very popular and deserved to be loved by his subjects for his great generosity. In fact it is related that his own soldiers when changing guard outside his sleeping apartment, and pointing out the various articles of value in their charge to the relieving soldiers would mention his gold bed and conclude the list with the bitter aside: 'And the infidel that sleeps in that gold bed!'

After the Mutiny, when neither the court of Delhi, nor even that of Lucknow was left to attract the remnant of Muslim learning, Rampur could still offer it a refuge and an asylum. The next ruler, who has left to his successors as legacy many of the most valuable Arabic and Persian manuscripts which they greatly cherish, and which make, with the many additions made by them, the finest collection in all India, was himself no mean scholar. This emphasised the cultural conservatism of Rampur all

causes of the Indian Revolt; visited England in 1869 and, on his return, founded a college at Ghazipur; also established the Scientific Society in 1864; chief protagonist of Western education among the Muslims; founded the M.A.O. College at Aligarh in May 1875. Of his many writings of a later period should be named his *Essays on the Life of Mohammad* (1870), and a Quran commentary in Urdu called *Tafsir al-Quran* which goes as far as Sura xvii.

[15] 'The Land of the Rohillas' is the historical appellation of an area of about 12,800 square miles between the Himalayas and the Ganga, including Katahr and the districts of Sambhal and Budaun.

[16] Name given to Afghans of various tribes who came from Roh and settled in the seventeenth and eighteenth centuries in the western part of modern Uttar Pradesh.

[17] (1732–1818) became the Governor-General of Bengal in 1774. He was charged with corruption but was acquitted after a seven-year trial.

the more, and marked it off from the rest of the province, even though, as we have seen, it bore little love for the new learning. Its antagonism to English education may well be judged from an amusing incident that occurred towards the end of the last century. In course of time even that little bit of old unadulterated *Indian* India came to be connected with the rest of the world by telegraph wires, and one day a Rampur Pathan had the surprise of his life in getting a telegram. It was, of course, in English and when he and his friends had recovered from the first shock of surprise, they found that they had now to face the inevitable problem, who was to decipher this strange message from a heathen world? At last, somebody happened to remember that some of the boys of our family had been sent away to learn English, and mentioned this to the perplexed recipient of the telegraphic message. The moment he offered this solution of his difficulty the rest of the company expressed their pious disbelief in the information, and one of them burst out: '*Astaghfirullah'* (God forgive!). What do you say? My dear man, they are gentlemen!'

## EDUCATION WITHOUT A TEACHER AND TEXT-BOOK

Well, 'gentlemen' though we believed ourselves to be, we had nevertheless been impious enough to study English even though we had to leave Rampur for the sake of our education. As for myself, in one of their vacations, my brothers Zulfiqar and Shaukat had constituted themselves my pedagogues in English and before long the progressive administrator on whose advice mother had sent my brothers to the Bareilly school had founded a similar school in Rampur itself. I had studied there for some months, and when I was about to enter my twelfth year, I was permitted to accompany my elder brothers to Bareilly. This departure from the code of Rampur gentility, even if not an approach to 'infidelity' as our uncle had put it, had no doubt an adverse effect on us so far as religious education was concerned. I have already explained in some detail what poor chance there was for a youth who did not belong to a family that specialised in religious learning of receiving any but the most elementary religious education; and had the curriculum of our *makatib* provided *all* the knowledge of his religion that such a Muslim youth could acquire, his religious equipment would have indeed been scandalously small, particularly for the inhabitant of a place that prided itself on being the latter-day centre of Muslim learning. But not all education is to be had in schools and out of text-books even in the West; and those who have such notions of education will certainly find the East a puzzle to them. Some of the wisest and greatest men of the East have been, like our Prophet himself (on whom be Allah's benedictions and peace), wholly illiterate, owing nothing to teacher or text-book.

## MOSQUE AS A CLUB; HOME AS A SCHOOL

But apart from such exceptional cases, there is this general consideration to be kept in mind, that so much depends on the general condition and atmosphere of society. Take the case of a large University town like Oxford even today. How much can a man not learn, say, from the shop-windows of its booksellers? But so far as religion and the East are concerned, for all but a small minority, far the larger portion of the people's stock of religious knowledge comes from breathing in the air of the place in which they live, and the circle in which they move. To take a parallel case, whence does the average man in Europe get his knowledge of politics? Not certainly from books and political philosophers, and not always from newspapers either. To many men their club, their favourite cafe and their public-house supply most of their political wisdom—or unwisdom. And what politics is to the West today, religion is still to the East. Where a few men gather together, and they are not preternaturally lacking in gravity, the conversation is sure, before long, to take a religious or spiritual turn, even though their theology may not be sufficiently edifying for schoolmen. An English writer[18] intimately acquainted with Indian Muslim society remarks of Musalmans that 'they are ready to speak in season and out of season' of their faith and quotes in support Doughty's observation about the Arabs that 'their talk is continually (without hypocrisy) of religion which is of genial devout remembrance to them' [C.M. Doughty, *Travels in Arabian Deserts*, vol. 2, p. 39.]. And what could serve as better meeting-place than a mosque? Unlike a Church a mosque is not a silent place with a dim religious light, deserted for the greater part of the week; but on the contrary, a very airy and well-lit place, a fairly busy haunt of men. It is a humming hive of the Muslims, the more devout of whom at least gather there oftener and with greater regularity than do the habitués of clubs and cafes in their customary haunts. And then, of course, there is the home.

[18] This refers to T.W. Arnold (1864–1930) who came to Aligarh as philosophy professor in 1888 and was intellectually close to Shibli Numani (see fn. 23); author of many books, including *Preaching of Islam.* When during the summer recess of 1892 Arnold decided to travel to England, Shibli proposed to join him, at least up to Port Said, from where Arnold would proceed to England and Shibli to Istanbul, Beirut and Cairo (before returning to India by the very beginning of November of the same year).

When the conversation of the secluded half of humanity in the East is not about children and the cares and duties of the household, at least in three cases out of four it is about religion. But it must be admitted that it is not dogmatic theology and the little differences of form and ritual which obsess the schoolman and which the better educated menfolk discuss only too often, that forms the chief topic of our women's conversation when it turns on religion. It is rather about the spirit and the substance of faith, the Ethics of Islam, that has been transmitted down the ages, very often in the form of legends and folklore which would not stand the severe test of the Traditionalists.

## HOME CIRCLE

If my father had been alive, or if my brothers had been older or had all remained at home, I would have had the advantage of getting better acquainted even with Muslim dogmatics, dialectics and of course that portion at least of Muslim jurisprudence which deals with the ritual of worship. A Muslim home has two distinct divisions, the *mardana* and the *zenana,* or as the Turks call it the *selamlik* and the *haremlik,* that is to say, apartments where the male members of the family usually pass the day and receive their male visitors, and those where ladies live and where only those male members of the family can come before whom these ladies can appear without a veil. When our father died, our mother shut up the adjoining new house that father had recently built to receive his friends, for none of us was old enough to need a separate *mardana* and some years later she herself moved into it lending the old *zenana* house to her brother and his family. And although a house with us five brothers and two cousins living in the adjoining old *zenana* house which they had so long shared with us was bound to be a noisy place, and our boisterousness no doubt made us a tremendous nuisance, still mother preferred that we should be for the greater part of the day under her own eyes. So, instead of allowing us to play with our numerous cousins in their houses, all close to our own, and of course in the street which was practically monopolised by us, though legally still a public thoroughfare of the less frequented sort, she should let us invite a whole heap of these cousins to our house and romp all over the place, even though we ruined the terraces and cost mother no end of money in repairing the leaky roofs in the heavy monsoon rains. Nevertheless, there was one place where we could elude her vigilance and yet still be within the bounds. That was the *mardana* house of our eldest uncle and the fear that he inspired in all of us was enough to procure us freedom to cross the street and go there whenever we cared. Here there was an endless succession of visitors belonging to all strata of Rampur society. Ours was one of the principal families engaged in administration, and apart from visitors of equal status who came to pay a social call, many others also came in who had any petition to make to the ruler of the state and sought our uncle's intercession or perhaps a favour to ask directly from himself. Everyone had an easy access and I cannot think of any place where such a variety of people congregated daily as at my uncle's, specially on Friday mornings, it became all the more 'democratic'—and, I fear, not a little less noisy—on account of my uncle's hobby of quail-fighting which attracted quail-trainers of the whole state. Here could be seen in the freest intercourse men in the very humblest rank of society, as well as the haughtiest members of the Rampur nobility and court. But not being Rohillas, whose tastes were as a rule more martial than literary, our uncles used to receive for Rampuris quite an unusual number of visitors from among the scholars and literary men that had found the Nawab's court their last harbour of refuge when the political storms had destroyed the courts of Delhi and Lucknow. It is true that much of their erudite conversation was above the understanding of boys of our age; but it could not fail to rouse a literary curiosity which was stimulated, and to some extent satisfied, in the company of our grown up cousins. As I was the youngest son of the youngest son of my grandfather, some of these cousins were only a few years younger than my own parents. They had their own separate apartments, on the ground floor of their father's *mardana,* where there used to be a similar endless succession of visitors everyday. Youth's code of decorum was not so rigorous and the conversation here was more lively than on the upper storey, even if it was not so erudite. When free from our *maktab* and its red-bearded pedagogue, and fatigued with fairly long intervals of play, we used to drop in and listen with great interest to the animated discussions of our cousins and their friends and visitors, and I must confess this experience of my childhood was a liberal education in itself.

## OUR MOTHER

And then there was the religious schooling we unconsciously received from our mother. I must rigorously restrain myself, otherwise there is no knowing to what lengths I may not digress when I am on that ever congenial topic—our mother. Suffice it to say that although she was practically illiterate, as I shall presently explain, I have, in all my experience of men of all sorts of types, come across none that I could call wiser and certainly none that was more truly godly and spiritual than our mother.

Muslim society in India in the days of its decadence had sinned against the light in nothing so much as in condemning womanhood to all but universal ignorance. What used to be the general rule in the best days of Islam had, about this time, been whittled down to a few rare exceptions—women who could have intelligently followed the learned conversation of the most erudite scholars and who could partake, after their daily round of domestic duties, joys of literature not unoften in more than one language. They were still taught to read the Quran in the original Arabic which they could, of course, understand no more than the majority of men themselves. Some could read Urdu, which was their vernacular, and were thus enabled to read a few religious 'tracts'—for the most part metrical compositions, more legend than literature, supposed to impart good moral instruction. This additional accomplishment, however, was not a part of my mother's literary equipment. But she possessed enough intellectual curiosity not to be satisfied with what little she knew and she possessed a memory that is nothing short of a marvel. My father would often bring into the *zenana* the book he might be reading and one of these books evidently proved so attractive that he would read it in bed far into the night. It so happened that occasionally he forgot to take it along with him when he went to the *mardana* next day and that is how mother was enabled to have *her* innings. A cousin of ours, who was the favourite of both of my parents, and who subsequently became my father-in-law [Azmat Ali Khan], used to be very often with my father and was very frequently coming to my mother with messages from him in the course of the day, when father was himself too busy to come, besides paying visits to my mother on his own account. The attractions of the book that so often formed my father's nocturnal literature impelled my mother to ask this nephew what it was and since it turned out to be a remarkably good romance, mother eagerly asked him to read it to her whenever she could get an opportunity to taste this 'forbidden fruit'. And so astonishingly good was her memory that although she had heard these portions of the book read out to her only once, and that too fairly rapidly, she could gradually make out the words when she began to glance at the book herself, on account of the similarity of the *Nastaliq* script, in which Urdu and Persian are written, with the *Naskh* script in which Arabic and of course the Quran, which she could read, are written.[19] And it was in this manner that our mother learnt to read Urdu, though she cannot *write* it to this day. She tells us how the attractions of

[19] A script which is said in the works on calligraphy to have been formed by joining NASKH and TALLIQ, which compound gradually came to be pronounced as nastaliq. The invention of this script goes back as far as the thirteenth century.

the book and her own memory very nearly betrayed her secret to father, for once she repeated whole passages out of the book in her sleep to his great astonishment. And well he may have felt astonished, for we cannot help wondering even now how she can repeat to the eager circle of her grandchildren, in love with Bi Amma's stories, whole volumes of romances, including translations of English works of fiction which she had read only once. All that we could ourselves repeat even of our favourite novel would be scarcely better than the proverbial silent man's retailing of the story of Jacob and Joseph: 'Was a Prophet; had lost a son; and found him again!'

## AT MOTHER'S KNEE

However, it was not merely for reading fiction that our mother utilised her ability to read Urdu acquired in this novel manner. Musalmans have always had a horror of translations of their Holy Writ, for fear of people forming the habit of relying upon man's words rather than on those of God; and I believe the Turks, who are perhaps the most rigidly orthodox nation among the Musalmans, have to this day no translation of the Quran in Turkish. In India the first translation into Urdu was smuggled into general acceptance and favour under the garb of the briefest of brief *Tafseers* or Commentaries, and not long afterwards the Quran was printed together with a Persian translation and this Urdu 'Commentary', which was really a very *literal,* though somewhat expanded translation, both being the work of members of the same great family of divines of Delhi whose piety and learning were universally acknowledged in the country.[20] These two translations were printed along with the Quran in the interlinear style which has grown customary, and allusions to historical events were explained, and other useful information supplied in fairly frequent marginal notes. In these days such copies of the Quran are to be found in many households and yet I have only too often come across men who could read the Urdu translation with far greater ease than the Arabic original, which of course, they did not understand and who would yet be content with their unintelligent reading of the Arabic original without any desire to comprehend its meaning by reading the interlinear translation in their own vernacular. But this has never been the case with our mother. On her busiest day she would not neglect to read her Urdu translation along with

[20] This refers to the family of Shah Waliullah (1703–62) of Delhi and Shah Abdul Aziz (1746–1824). Shah Rafiuddin and Shah Abdul Qadir translated the Quran into Urdu.

the word of God in Arabic, though her sight is now very weak, and even her glasses cannot magnify the smaller Urdu print in her old copy of the Quran to make them half as legible to her as the larger Arabic print. She has all her life been in great demand on account of the capital way she has of retailing stories, and it is not only children that gather round her; for few 'grown-ups' can resist the temptation of spending an evening in this fashion in her company. She has a large repertoire to choose from; and it includes many a story of ancient Prophets partly culled from the Quran and partly from the legends and folklore of Jews and Arabs which, for all their apocryphal character, serve admirably to point a moral. When as children we used to sit round her forming an eager circle of listeners taking in every word of these old-world tales so faithfully and charmingly repeated, she would amplify them with comments of her own in short moral discourses that have lingered in our memories more than the vast majority of lectures of *savants* and sermons of preachers. But far the more important lesson for her children was contained in the rigorously ascetic character of life which she maintained ever since her widowhood at that early age, but which at the same time never robbed her of the least iota of her geniality and the joy of living so that except for her very simple fare and her still simpler dress and her occupying herself needlessly with the drudgeries less than with the superintendence of her large household, one would have thought that she was the merriest of merry widows. These lessons were of inestimable value to us later on in the battle of life, which the circumstances of our family had made more than ordinarily hard to wage. For not only had our father died so young, but he had left his inexperienced widow to maintain and educate half a dozen children out of the proceeds of an estate that his generous, not to say lavish, way of life had left sadly encumbered with debts. Nevertheless, it must be confessed that all this moral and spiritual training that we received from our mother, however high its practical value, left us still very ignorant about the details of Islamic faith and its history. And then on top of all this came the migration to a school where we were to receive the new godless education of the West without so much as a mention of Allah and His Prophet, and His Holy Book.

## GODLESS EDUCATION IN SCHOOL

The British Government professed a complete religious neutrality, and carried it into practice by a rigorous exclusion of all religious, and even moral teaching, except such as the boys were left to find for themselves in the literature provided in the 'Readers' in English and Oriental languages. On the other hand the entire outlook of the education which the Government did provide for the youth of India was 'Modern' in its destructiveness. It tended to breed in the student an arrogant omniscience, and to destroy along with age-old blind beliefs in superstition all respect for tradition and authority. No doubt in course of time it led to the awakening of a genuine spirit of inquiry and a search for Truth. But in its first onset it was mainly destructive, and what little it substituted in the place of the superstitions it destroyed, was itself based on blind beliefs and superstitions, albeit 'modern'. However, since it was so clearly revolutionary, there was no lack of liveliness in our schools and colleges. If at home our cousins had held animated discussions about religion and dogma which we could no longer attend, we had here in the 'Boarding House' of our school still more animated discussions that centred round natural science and philosophy, even if our pretentious scientists and philosophers had only the most elementary and superficial ideas on the subjects in debate. In this particular school, however, the Musalmans were in a minority; but it was an assertive, not to say aggressive minority, with the result that in spite of all the destruction wrought in old-world ideas by this onset of our western education, we were unconsciously impelled to maintain the old pride of faith for all our pleasant relations with the majority of our school-fellows who were Hindus.

## ALIGARH'S *RAISON D'ETRE*

I was not long at this school, for as soon as Shaukat had matriculated we both joined our brother Zulfiqar who had left the Bareilly school a couple of years earlier and had subsequently gone to Aligarh after matriculating. This was the well-known, and in a way notorious, institution founded on the models of English public schools and residential colleges some ten or twelve years previously by the 'Naturee' Musalman, Sir Syed Ahmad Khan. By his staunch loyalty to the cause of the English during the Mutiny, when he was employed as a subordinate judge in one of the affected districts in the land of the Rohillas, he had acquired considerable influence in official circles, and a distinguished position in the country generally which his great talents and beneficent activities in any case amply deserved. I have already alluded to his unorthodox rationalism in religion and his militant zeal in social reform which had given great offence to his people and had estranged from him some of his nearest relations and had made him altogether the best hated man among his orthodox and conservative co-religionists. And yet it was this ultra loyalist and arch-heretic who had raised the standard of revolt against the government in education, and based his dissent on no other ground than a Muslim's passionate attachment to his faith. Christian missionary colleges and schools which received from the state grants-in-aid out of funds so largely contributed by non-Christian tax-payers, but in which non-Christian students were compelled to attend Bible classes, were, of course, *anathema maranatha* to the Muslims. But Syed Ahmad Khan had no less aversion to the schools and colleges of a religiously neutral government and he attributed the backwardness of his co-religionists in Western education to their sound instinct and the cherished traditions of their past which would not tolerate such a thing as a complete divorce between secular and religious education. It was this policy that the government had felt itself compelled to pursue; and it was precisely this policy which made the Musalmans keep aloof from its educational institutions; and Syed Ahmad Khan not only correctly explained but vigorously justified this attitude of his co-religionists. But he was too practical a reformer to be content with railing at the evil; while he railed at the evil he also worked for the good. Long before he retired from the service of the government, he had prepared a complete scheme for the foundation of a Muslim University, open to all religions, communities and denominations and absolutely free from the taint of religious or racial tastes, yet mainly and primarily intended for his own community for the youth of which it was to provide religious as well as secular instruction. Above all, it was to create for young Musalmans a centre with the true Islamic atmosphere, so that its alumni would not merely be educated and cultured men, but educated and cultured Musalmans. The old world had crumbled down before his own eyes, after a slow and, at one time, almost imperceptible decay and although he had not himself seen Europe—except just once very late in life, when he went to England to arrange for the education of his sons at an English University—he had come into contact with the new Western world in the persons of the English officials; and in spite of his very elementary acquaintance with the English language, he had resolutely set himself to acquire as intimate an acquaintance as he could with Western ways of thought and modes of life. England, in fact the whole of Europe, had received a new secular evangelic in Darwin's *Origin of Species* and the revolutionising theory of Evolution,[21] and Syed Ahmad Khan, who had

[21] The form of the theory of evolution put forward by Charles Darwin (1809–82), especially in the works *The Origin of Species* (1859) and *The Descent of Man* (1871).

already been impressed so greatly by the progressiveness of Europe, came under the spell of Western science. No wonder that in his newly awakened enthusiasm he attributed to it an omniscience that even in the light of its marvellous developments must now be confessed to have been somewhat exaggerated. With a Tacitus[22]-like antithesis he credited Europe with every good quality in which he found his own people deficient; but for all this he never wavered for a moment in his belief in the eternal truth of Islam and the capacity of the Muslims to rise to the highest pinnacle of human greatness. All he wanted was to build a bridge that would connect his ancient faith with this new science, and the ideal that he placed before himself, when framing his scheme of the Muslim University of the future, is best expressed in his own words. 'Science,' he said, 'shall be in our right hand and philosophy in our left; and on our head shall be the crown of "There is no God but Allah and Mohammad is His Apostle."' His University was to secure the best graduates of Oxford and Cambridge for its professors and for the guides, philosophers and friends of his 'young barbarians all at play'. But its policy would be determined finally by Muslims, who alone would be represented on its supreme governing body.

## RELIGIOUS INSTRUCTION AT ALIGARH

It is outside my present purpose to follow the fortunes of the great institution which he eventually founded as soon as he was freed from the shackles of government service, or to examine, except in one particular, how far the actual came to correspond with the ideal. The one exception that I must permit myself, however, relates to religious education. Aligarh did produce a fine amalgam of the East and the West in many things, and in spite of its progress in Western science and literature, it maintained a communal pride that often acted as an effective motive to right conduct on the part of its alumni. But it must be confessed that it furnished them with precious little equipment in the matter of knowledge of their faith. They were progressive enough, and they were proud enough of being Musalmans, but they were, alas, far too ignorant of their religion. No doubt the ancillary position in which Aligarh stood as a college affiliated to a purely examining University rigorously neutral in religion and wholly colourless in its learning—unless one may call it Western and English—did not permit it any efflorescence and orientation in the direction of more

[22] (*c*. 55–120); Roman historian and orator. His concise and vivid prose style was a major influence on later writers.

specialised Muslim culture and Eastern lore, such as one would expect from an educational institution mainly and primarily intended for Indian Musalmans. But this was not all, nor, in fact, the main difficulty with regard to the scanty religious equipment of the students. No doubt some time was devoted to the religious instruction of the Muslim students, and additional text-books were fixed by a committee of the governing body from which questions were set at every examination, and no one could expect promotion to a higher class or form without satisfying the examiners regarding his proficiency in 'Theology'. But the fact was that while Sir Syed Ahmad lived himself, he was in actual practice the only supreme governing body of the institution and in order to avoid repelling Muslim parents whose orthodoxy was shocked by the aggressive rationalism of the Founder, and to attract their boys to Aligarh, he had passed a sort of self-denying ordinance that not only his own religious books would not be taught at Aligarh, but that he would not even be a member of the committee that regulated religious instruction. In this way a very colourless and really moribund committee which never did any work, prescribed, perhaps once for all, some very elementary text-books in what was euphemistically called 'Theology'. These text-books for the most part only prescribed rules for ceremonial cleanliness, and contained the ritual of prayers, or provided for the 'advanced' student some of the principal laws of Islam regulating marriage, dower and divorce. The Quran practically remained a closed book to us, and the Traditions [*Hadith*] of the Prophet were no more than a name, while only for a time some of the college classes read what should be called a 'Primer' dealing with the life of the Prophet, for it did not extend beyond a score of pages in size. Of 'Theology' in the sense of Dogmatics and Dialectics, there was no trace in any text-book. Oriental languages have always languished in Indian Universities and the scant importance that is attached to them is unconsciously suggested by their official description under the head of 'Second Language'. English, of course, is understood to be the 'First Language' and not only is the greatest attention paid for its own sake but, ridiculously enough, all subjects are taught in it, to the almost entire exclusion of the Indian student's own vernacular, as a medium of instruction, except in the very lowest forms. It was, therefore, customary for a long time to employ ill-paid and neglected drones for teaching such languages as Arabic, Persian and Sanskrit, and unless a student had received an unusually lengthened previous education in his 'Second Language' at home, or possessed an exceptional literary taste which nothing could crush or kill, his knowledge of this 'Second Language' remained scandalously defective, and his acquaintance, at the end of his educational career, with its rich and abundant literature was generally of the most distant and meagre character. And it was such dull drones that were pitchforked at Aligarh into the 'Faculty of Theology' to teach his religion to the Muslim youth *once a week,* in the hour consecrated on other days to the 'Second Language'. The result was that the 'Theology Hour' was even more enjoyable than the 'Recreation Hour' because truancy in that hour, and, failing that, engagement in the diverting pastime of writing humorous verse or drawing rude and rough caricatures of all who were the pet aversion of boys, not excluding the venerable pedagogue himself, had the added poignancy of the forbidden fruit. What little information the text-books furnished us could be 'mugged up' overnight and squirted out on the 'Answer Books' in the examination hall next morning. At Aligarh, too, there were frequent animated discussions among the students; but when they did not relate to Western literature, philosophy or science, they centred round Indian politics, which in my school and college days was far more concerned with the claims of the various contending communities of India than with claims of the Indian people against the British Government. Our communal consciousness was, therefore, far more secular than religions, and although we considered Islam to be the final message for mankind and the only true faith, and could strenuously and even intelligently enough argue about the superiority of its chief tenets, we were shamefully ignorant of the details of its teaching and of its world-wide and centuries-old history. When this was the case in the most notable and admittedly premier educational institution of Musalmans in India, I shudder to contemplate the condition of our co-religionists studying in missionary and government schools and colleges where year in and year out the name of Islam was never so much as mentioned.

## ACQUAINTANCE WITH THE QURAN

Nevertheless we used to have a long vacation of two months or more once a year, when we used to go home and have perfect leisure to listen to the lively discussions in the circle of our cousins. In fact we could now take a modest share in them occasionally, for the higher status that English education had given us made up for the disparity in our ages.

But Aligarh itself presented one bright spot in all this cimmerian darkness and I must not omit to mention it. This was no other than a College Professor of rare charms and an entirely new literary outlook whom Sir Syed Ahmad Khan had been able to attract to Aligarh. He was Shibli Numani, Professor of Arabic and Persian, an ardent lover of poetry and of Islamic History.[23] Besides some exquisite verses in Persian, he has left several biographical and historical works as monuments of research and scholarship. The last of these, which promises also to be the greatest, is the life of the Prophet in several volumes. Of these, so far only two have been published by his literary executors; but he had managed to complete it just before his greatly mourned and wholly unexpected death. His ordinary daily lectures at Aligarh on Persian and Arabic were most attractive, but, unfortunately for me, he had retired from the College before I matriculated from the school attached to it, and so I could not attend them. Nevertheless, I was fortunate enough, although still a school boy, to attend his all too brief lectures to the undergraduates on the Quran. For half an hour every morning, just before the College students commenced their secular studies, he used to give in the Principal's Hall, a rapid exegesis of the Quran, explaining and amplifying the holy text, and although, being only in the school I could not ordinarily have had the privilege of listening to these charming little discourses of Shibli, a lucky chance enabled me to be one of his pupils. The school building was a separate one, though in the same ground as the College buildings and the 'Boarding Houses' or students' residential quarters, but through lack of accommodation in the school building, for sometime the class which I had joined as a small boy not yet in his teens, was crowded out of it and was consequently accommodated in a lecture room in the College building adjoining the hall where Shibli gave his exegesis of the Quran. Happening to be standing just outside the Hall one morning, when Shibli commenced his discourse, I stayed on intently listening and thereafter no 'grown-up' Collegian was ever so punctual in his attendance outside the regular college hours as one little schoolboy who nevertheless dearly loved to play the truant in his own class. I used to accompany my two elder brothers from the Dining Hall after breakfast and when they noticed my eagerness to listen to Shibli, they mentioned it to him since he had already had occasion to know of my existence. When I had first come to Aligarh from the school at Bareilly I knew no Arabic at all; but one day I startled my brother Shaukat by translating to him with astonishing accuracy some Arabic verses that he was reciting. He asked me how I knew these verses and even their meaning, when I explained that I had happened to read them in Shibli's life of the

[23] Shibli Numani (1857–1914); historian, biographer, literary critic and Urdu poet; appointed as Assistant Professor in Arabic and later as Professor of Persian at the M.A.O. College on 1 February 1883; one of the founders of Lucknow's Nadwat al-ulama.

Abbasid Khalifa Al-Mamun,[24] which was among my brother's books and that I had found the translation also there. As he learnt, that I had made no effort to memorise them, but that they had remained impressed in my memory on account of their affecting pathos and simplicity, he was sufficiently interested in this explanation to mention it to Shibli himself. But the Professor was incredulous and had his curiosity still further aroused by learning that at the immature age of 11 I dabbled in Urdu verse as well. So he arranged to take me by surprise and one day I found myself in his College room being examined in the contents of his book Al-Mamun. I had hurriedly read that book only once just to pass the time when my brothers were attending their lectures and I had not yet been admitted into the collegiate school; but I think the result of this test of memory proved satisfactory. Then I was given an Urdu verse for composing a *ghazal* [a love lyric] in that metre with that rhyme. I fear I could not claim burial in the 'Poet's Corner' on the strength of those verses, nor were they such that today I 'would not willingly let die'. But what I composed certainly passed the test of Prosody, and I was amply rewarded for my success in Shibli's searching examination by being invited to dine with him one evening along with my two brothers. I must confess that I paid a poor compliment to Shibli's charm of conversation for when the dinner came to be served, somewhat late in the evening, he found a diminutive poet curled up comfortably in the largest easy chair in the room, and when roused from his poetic reveries to such prosaic realities as pilaff and puddings, rubbing his eyes as hard as he could to avoid the suspicion of sleep. Evidently finding now that I was more complimentary to his erudition and eloquence than I had been to his pre-praudial conversation earlier and I had been listening to his lectures from behind a door, he graciously invited me to come inside and thereafter I had the exquisite elation of sitting in the Principal's Hall attending Shibli's lectures on the Quran with all the dignity of a quasi-'Undergrad'.

## SUBSEQUENT RESULTS

This was how I first made the acquaintance of the meaning of the Quran. And yet, alas, it was doomed to bc of short duration, for only a few months later my class was also accommodated in the school building and the

[24] Son of Harun Rashid and a patron of learning. His rationalistic tendencies made him join the Mutazalites. In his reign poetry and learning reached their golden age. It was then that lived men like al-Waqidi, al-Bukhari and the jurist Ahmad b. Hanbal.

distance between that and the college building where Shibli lectured made it impossible for me to reach the former in proper time for my school work if I attended Shibli's lectures as well. And, if I am not mistaken, Shibli himself did not continue these discourses of his very long, though I cannot imagine that anything but some dire necessity, such as a later breakfast hour fixed by the caterers in the Dining Hall, would have induced him to discontinue lectures that were, I thought, remarkably well-attended. These all two brief half-hours have, however, lingered in my memory all these years. When the Government honoured me with a nomination on a committee that was to frame a scheme for a new type of a local and residential University at Dacca and in particular to prescribe a degree course of 'Islamic Studies' in consideration of the very large Muslim population in Eastern Bengal, I requested the committee to beg the learned Shibli that he might assist us with his views. To this he readily consented, and when he came to Dacca, I recalled those half-hour lectures of his on the Quran. He was pleased to note that I still remembered them and one result of those lectures of his, I had listened to so many years ago, was that the very disappointing 'scratch-crew' of Maulanas, old style as well as new, that formed the 'Islamic Studies' Sub-Committee, decided to include in the syllabus of these studies *Tarjumat-ul-Quran*. This translation of the Quran was to be distinct from the *Tafseer* or Exegesis, which in the ordinary Arabic *madaris*, is too full of Grammar and Dogmatics and other dry-as-dust details and never seems to proceed beyond a third of the entire Quran even in a career of ten or fifteen years. In the Jamia Millia Islamia or the National Muslim University that rose out of what I must still regard as the ashes of the 'Proposed Muslim University' at Aligarh and of which I was the first Rector, *Shaikhul Jamia*, I saw to it from the first day that these discourses of Shibli were revived, and our day began with a full hour devoted to the rapid exegesis of the Quran, though alas, there was no Shibli any longer to discourse on the Holy Text.[25]

## I ATTRACT MY 'BIG BROTHER'S' NOTICE

After eight years at Aligarh, four in the school and the remaining four in the College, I obtained my B.A. degree from the Government University of Allahabad, which examined the alumni of all colleges and schools in my own Province, and in some adjoining provinces and territories of Indian

[25] The Jamia Millia Islamia was founded in October 1920 in response to Gandhi's call to boycott government-aided educational institutions during the Non-Cooperation movement. Mohamed Ali was one of its founders, though he did not keep up his links with the institution.

rulers. As my success in the examination proved far better than my deserts, it induced my brother Shaukat to try his hand at a miracle and somehow procure sufficient funds to send me to Oxford. Being senior to me by the somewhat large margin of six years and having been the captain of the famous Cricket XI of the Aligarh College, besides being the Secretary of the College Union and many other things which made him a very big 'boss' indeed, he had not condescended to take much notice of an inconsequential schoolboy like me. This was in spite of the fact that I earned regularly every year a small scholarship as one of the best boys in my class, and thereby helped him to dress as a smart cricket captain at Aligarh should, for which even our joint pocket money, which of course he pocketed for both of us, did not apparently suffice. And on the few occasions on which he did take notice of his little brother, it must be confessed that the little brother ardently prayed for perfectly uninterrupted obscurity, for these were the occasions when some of my schoolmates complained to him of my militancy and I became in my turn the object of even more militant attentions from my 'big brother'. Colonel Wedgwood, MP, has conveyed a very correct impression of his bulk by describing him in an *English Review* as 'Seven feet by five', and although he did not in those days break the scales as he did in the gaol on our imprisonment, he turned them at a heavy enough weight as my tingling ears, when he had soundly boxed them, could honestly testify.[26] He was indeed my 'big brother' in every sense of the word, and I agreed with Sadi, that wise man of the East who said, 'Be a dog but do not be a younger brother'. My unexpected success in the examination for my degree, however, arrested his attention and being then in a superior grade of the service of government he set about to make ample amends to me for his past neglect. Ordinarily, I would have, in all likelihood, secured a nomination from my college for the post of subordinate magistrate or land-revenue collector in some district in my province at the ripe age of about 20 and would have begun to earn a modest salary not much less than my brother's, reaching after some fifteen years according to the scale of promotion then current, a figure

[26] The Turkish visitor Halide Edib described Shaukat Ali as 'a very big man in every sense. . . . He has a flowing beard, a shock of picturesque grey hair, and eyes which twinkle like those of a mischievous boy. His dress is suggestive of the vagueness of his politics. He wears a long shirt over tight Indian trousers and leggings; and a loose Arab Mashlak (mantle) with a Turkish Kalpak (fur cap) in the fashion of about sixteen years ago. His attire is reminiscent of a combination of Indian, Muslim, Arab and Turk; in a word, it is reflection of Pan-Islamism. . . . In caricatures he is represented as a big baby to whom the King gives a pretty doll so as to keep him quiet.'

which used to form the initial salary of an Indian civilian. But my brother had now far higher aspirations for me, and I have not yet met his equal in planning greatly and, what is more, also executing greatly. As I said, the raising of funds sufficient to cover the cost of my education in England was nothing short of a miracle, and unlike most miracles in this unbelieving age, his certainly managed to come off. So, before the proverbial nine days of wonder were over, I was on the high seas in the Indian Ocean in the teeth of a raging monsoon, bound for England—all the way by the sea, if you please, just because it gave my wonder-working brother a week more than the overland route would have done to gather in the promised shekels and remit the proceeds of the loan by cable to 'Coupon, London'.

## AT OXFORD

And what chance was there for me to learn anything more about my religion while at Oxford? In addition to studying for my 'Schools', I had to commence like a schoolboy once more, the study of Latin, to be able to translate in a few months 'unseen' passages from Tacitus[27] and Cicero[28] in my preliminary examination—which was an almost hopeless task. And then there were half a dozen additional subjects of the most miscellaneous character that one had to take up for the Indian Civil Service Competition, if one happened to be neither a classical nor a mathematical scholar. To cut the story short, I had at Oxford, where I took an Honours degree in Modern History, an excellent opportunity of acquainting myself with a portion of the history of my co-religionists as the period of general history that I selected for my 'School', covered the rise and growth of the Muslim power and included most of the earlier Crusades. But of the religion that had proved the sword and buckler of these Muslims of an older day, I could learn nothing further at Oxford. While awaiting the result of my Indian degree examination I had been greatly attracted by a new translation of the Quran into good easily intelligible Urdu, that my brother had procured for his wife and himself; and I had had a copy of it sent on to me at Oxford. Fired by my own religious zeal and financed by the affections of a generous brother, I had the Quran bound most sumptuously in calf by the book binder of the Bodleian, and it looked superb on the otherwise meagrely furnished book-shelf in my college room. But alas, for the

[27] Connelius Tacitus (*c.* 55–120), Roman historian.

[28] Marcus Tullius Cicero (106–43 B.C.); Roman orator, statesman, and man of letters.

inconsistency of human nature, the best bound books are not those that are oftenest read, and the Quran which I had so eagerly sent for from home, remained far too often a mere ornament of my book-shelf. Of course I occasionally read it and its fascination was such that once I took it up, I could not be induced to close it for some hours. But I must confess with shame that the one book I should have studied above all others was not taken up as often as it should have been, and though I was now supposed to have 'completed' my education, I realised later that, in fact, I had not even begun it.

II

# The Awakening

## IN PUBLIC SERVICE

After four years I returned to India after taking my degree, though not as a member of the much coveted Indian Civil Service, thanks to an English spring, and a young man's more or less foolish fancy. I had now a specious enough excuse for not pursuing any religious studies in the strenuous life that one must lead who aspires to distinction in the Public Service under a watchful and critical administrator like the Gaekwar of Baroda. I joined His Highness' service, sometime after resigning my appointment as the Chief Educational Officer in my own State of Rampur, where too love of my house and of its loveable people had given to my desire of distinction an added impetus and kept me fully engaged in the work of my department. While at Rampur, I had been greatly concerned to find that even in a Muslim state no religious instruction had been provided in the English school, and when I, who had been one of its first pupils, was at its head, I arranged that at least the afternoon prayer should not be neglected. I found the boys keen enough to devote even their recreation hour to it; and the Hindu boys attended Hindu theology with the school Pundits, while the Musalmans offered their prayers. This much I could do without reference to my superior authority; but I left the service of my chief at Rampur soon after my first year, and was unable on that account to push matters any further.

## I BECOME A JOURNALIST

A time was, however, to come when I could say I paid more homage to my faith than dipping occasionally into the Quran and arranging for the prayers of some Muslim boys in my charge. For towards the end of 1910, I left Baroda also and set up as a journalist at Calcutta with a weekly newspaper of my own. This was a rather serious departure to make, specially for one who had given, in Bacon's[1] expressive phrase, so many

[1] Francis Bacon (1561–1626), English philosopher and statesman.

hostages to fortune in the shape of wife and children. I had achieved, if I may say so, a fair degree of success in my work as a Baroda official, and could only relinquish it by disguising my departure as two years' 'leave without pay'. When no further disguise was possible, and I placed my resignation in the hands of the Gaekwar, I found him most unwilling to accept it, and in the last resort prepared to extend my leave. All this was no doubt flattering enough to my vanity, and an ample recompense for some strenuous work which had cost me my unusually robust health, but felt that thenceforward my work lay in another direction. While still in the Baroda service I had to decline offers of administrative posts of greater responsibility than my Baroda office in two other states and my final refusal of yet a third similar offer still more tempting was sent as soon as the first issue of the *Comrade* was out. In fact, in a half-serious imitation of Nelson's famous incident of applying the telescope to his blind eye, I had kept a bulky telegram pressing me to accept the minister's post in this last State [Jaora, a state in Central India] unopened, until the *Comrade* was on sale in the streets of Calcutta.[2] For I had suspected that the unopened telegram must be from the young Prince whose pressing offer was being forcibly backed by no less a person than Sir Michael O'Dwyer [then governor of Punjab], and I wished to avoid all temptation at the last moment.[3] By this change I had to give up an assured if modest income, and the prospects of all future advance, and like a plunger stake all the money I could gather from any quarter practically on one throw of the die as an Editor-Proprietor and subsequently as that unholy but costly trinity—an Editor-Proprietor cum Printer.

## THE *COMRADE* AND ITS DREAMS

And yet I did all this not so much because journalism had ever attracted me. What is more, I had not even for a brief space, served my apprenticeship in a profession that is as exacting as any other, beyond writing occasionally for the *Times of India*, of Bombay, to which Mr. Lovat Fraser had first invited me to contribute.[4] The reason which so irresistibly impelled me to take up journalism was that the affairs of my community just at that juncture made it the only avenue through which I could hope to reach a place in which I could prove of any appreciable use

[2] The Jaora State was in the Malwa Agency of Central India with a population of 84,202 in 1910. Its ruler Iftikhar Ali Khan had succeeded his father in 1895.

[3] For details, see my Introduction.

[4] These were later published as the 'Thoughts on the Present Discontent'.

to it, while still earning a livelihood. But even now it was not a *religious* call that dictated this sudden, and as it proved, momentous change from the career in which I had comfortably settled down. It was more the secular affairs of my community that seemed to require this alteration in my plans. A great controversy which had gone on throughout the Morley-Minto *Regime* with regard to the claims of the Indian Musalmans to be represented as a *community* in the legislatures and the local bodies of the country had just then culminated in the reforms which recognised and to a great extent satisfied this claim.[5] In this controversy I had taken my full share, and I felt that I should now assist my community in taking its proper share in the political life of the country. I was particularly anxious to help it to understand that, while endeavouring to satisfy the pressing needs of the present which may inevitably bring it now and then into conflict with other elements in the body politic, it should never lose sight of the prospects of the future when ultimately all communal interests had to be adjusted in order to harmonise with the paramount interests of India. I had long been convinced that here in this country of hundreds of millions of human beings, intensely attached to religion, and yet infinitely split up into communities, sects and denominations, Providence had created for us the mission of solving a unique problem and working out a new synthesis. It was nothing less than a Federation of Faiths. The lines of cleavage were too deeply marked to permit a unity other than federal and yet the cleavage was not territorial or racial in character but religious, and I had been dreaming for some time dreams of a 'United Faiths of India'. The *Comrade*—'comrade of all and partisan of none'—was to be the organ that was to voice these views, and prepare the Musalmans to make their proper contribution to territorial patriotism without abating a jot of the fervour of their extra-territorial sympathies which is the quintessence of Islam.

## OUTLOOK IN 1911

When I first thought of making this change in my career I did not expect that any but a small fraction of my attention and energies would be attracted by Muslim politics outside the confines of my own country. It is true that affairs in Egypt did not present a very reassuring appearance; nor did the New Constitutions in Turkey and Persia receive, after an initial outburst of welcome, their full measure of sympathy which we in India felt to be due to such heroic and hazardous enterprises from the one European Power

[5] The Act of 1909 granted separate electorates to the Muslims.

with which we had all along been almost exclusively concerned. The only other European power on our political horizon had been Russia, and so long as after the overthrow of France a hundred years previously, she was the most considerable of the Continental Powers and had aggravated that situation by aiming at being a yet greater power on the Continent of Asia; everyone in India had been taught by the masters of Indian destinies to regard her as an enemy of mankind whom it was the peculiar mission of England to thwart and to defeat. But the rapid rise of Japan,[6] and its signal success in defeating Russia in the Far East, while it encouraged other Oriental nations to hold up their heads in hope, so radically altered the position of Russia that from being an inveterate enemy she became a friend and in all but name an ally of England though it was her victorious adversary, Japan, that had been the latter's ally. This speedily reacted on Eastern politics not only in Persia where Russia openly stood out as a high-handed dictator and where it was soon to rain and hail ultimatums, but also in Turkey, where the rivalries of the Slavs[7] and the Teutons[8] now asserted themselves with an added vehemence in the form of a struggle between *Entente* and Alliance made the Near-East once more the storm-centre of politics. All this was no doubt disquieting enough to an Indian Musalman who had been brought up from his childhood to regard England as the friend and Russia as the enemy of Muslim states like Turkey, and who was now about to launch his frail bark on the turbulent sea of journalism. But the political controversies of Hindus and Musalmans appeared none the less to be our immediate concern in India, and the passions that these inter-communal differences had unfortunately roused just a little previously, had lent to them the semblance of an acute international conflict. Turkey and Persia seemed comparatively remote.

## BEGINNING OF TROUBLES

But things did not proceed quite as I had so optimistically planned. 1911, when I made my first bow in front of the journalistic footlights, proved a fateful year for Muslim countries. The new Governments of Turkey, Persia

[6] Japan waged successful wars with China, 1894–5, and Russia, 1904–5. It annexed Korea in 1910.

[7] The largest group of European peoples sharing a common ethnic and linguistic origin, consisting of Russians, Ukrainians, Byelorussians, Poles, Czechs, Slovaks, Bulgarians, Serbs, Croats, Montenegrins, and Macedonians.

[8] The reference is to the order of German knights which grew out of a hospital community in 1190.

and Morocco,[9] all began to meet with squalls in their initial voyage of reform and progress and these squalls soon developed into regular storms. In India too the year did not end before the eventful announcement by the King in person at his Coronation Durbar at Delhi of a radical modification of the Partition of Bengal,[10] which had no doubt improved the depressed condition of the large Muslim majority in Eastern Bengal whose support the officials had enlisted on their side and which two successive Governments in England and India had declared to be a 'settled fact'.[11] Thus it was that the Musalmans felt themselves to be betrayed both in India and abroad and in being their spokesman I soon lost grace with the official world. For me, as for other Musalmans who took any appreciable part in the affairs of their community, the year 1912 opened with far different prospects from those of 1911. Up to the last I entertained the hope that things would ultimately right themselves. But this did not, and the year ended even worse than it began. The sad disillusionment with regard to international morality for which the shameless brigandage of Italy in Tripoli[12] was responsible had greatly affected me in the autumn of 1911. It was destined to be followed by a still sadder experience in the autumn of 1912, when I had migrated to Delhi with the Government of India.

## SAD THOUGHTS AND THEIR SEQUEL

My feelings during the disastrous war in the Balkans,[13] were at one time so over-powering that I must confess I even contemplated suicide. Paradoxical as it no doubt appears, even that act of moral cowardice needs

[9] The Treaty of Fez (1912) established Spanish Morocco (capital Tetouan) and French Morocco (capital: Rabat).

[10] In three articles, published in Comrade on 23 December 1911 and thereafter, the time, place and procedure for transferring the capital and for the annulment of Bengal's partition were sharply criticised. See also Mohamed Ali to F.H. Lucas, 3 January 1912, in Hasan (ed.), *Mohamed Ali in Indian Politics*, vol. 1, pp. 38–41.

[11] The partition of Bengal was annulled in 1911 by the Viceroy, Hardinge. 'Agitate and you will get your heads chopped. This is the moral we are given,' wrote a correspondent in the *Mussalman*, a Calcutta newspaper.

[12] The Italian troops landed in Tripoli (Libya) on 5 October 1911.

[13] In 1912, Bulgaria, Serbia, Greece, and Montenegro attacked Turkey, securing swift victories. A preliminary peace was drawn up by the Great Powers in May 1913, in which Turkey surrendered most of her European territories on condition that a new state of Albania was created. Disputes between the Balkan allies over the spoils of war led to a second war, in which Bulgaria attacked her former allies, and was defeated.

some courage and I very often wonder whether I could have mustered enough of it to take the final plunge on that fateful night. The latest message of Reuters that had reached me was that the Bulgarians were only 25 miles from the walls of Constantinople—from Constantinople, a name that had for five centuries been sacred to every Muslim as the centre of his highest hopes.[14] This is the first time that I have made this confession of what I must call my weakness, except for a hasty outburst in the course of animated but friendly discussion when I blurted out something about the mental torture of that night to the Editor of an English newspaper in India. A month or two later what was my shock when I discovered a reference to it in the columns, of the London *Times*, pointing a moral and adorning the tale of one of its Indian correspondents. But fortunately my identity was sufficiently covered by my Alma Mater, for I think I appeared only as 'a graduate of an English University'. To return to that autumn night in 1912, I was saved a trial of my courage as well as cowardice by the unexpected appearance of a Muslim friend who had graduated from Oxford not long before and was on this occasion accompanied by an English fellow-graduate of that University who was his guest and had expressed a desire to see an Indian *nautch*.[15] Arrangements had been made *Sub rosa* and the place selected was the house of a barrister who was my next door neighbour. My friend insisted on my company, and hard as I pleaded the excuse of a busy Editor and still harder the state of my feelings after that last message of Reuters, my friend would not take any denial and almost bodily lifted me from the Editorial Sanctum and carried me by main force to the private *nautch* party next door. Thus it was that instead of being a horror of broken bones and bleeding body supposed to have accidentally fallen down from a third storey, there I was 'assisting' at the 'orgy' that had been arranged by my young friend to gratify the curiosity of a brother Oxonian.

## REACTION TO BRITISH FOREIGN POLICY

The attitude of England towards the enemies of Turkey, Persia and Morocco had begun to alienate the sympathies of Indian Musalmans ever since 1911; and this estrangement could not but react on their relations with the British officials in India, who in spite of their detestation of the

[14] Once the capital of Constantine. From 1453 it was the Turkish capital until this was transferred to Ankara in 1923.

[15] Syed Ross Masood (1889–1937), the grandson of Syed Ahmad Khan, was educated in New College, Oxford, where he obtained a bad second class in History which, he said,

radical politicians in power at home could not help looking askance at Indians daring to criticise an English Government with a candour and a courage unusual for a subject race. In 1913 I was precipitated into open conflict with the official world when they declared the forfeiture of a pamphlet I had received along with several other Indian Musalmans from Turkey, appealing to England for Christian succour against the Balkan Allies whose Macedonian atrocities were therein depicted. I could not tamely submit to this and tried conclusions with government by carrying up for the first time, to the High Court of Calcutta the Indian journalists' grievances against that hateful and hasty piece of legislation, the Indian Press Act of 1910 which I only learnt in prison has now at long last been repealed. While this litigation was going on, the fatal developments following on the demolition of part of a small mosque at Kanpur[16] embittered Indian Muslim feelings still more, and I had to proceed to England to appeal to the Home Government and persuade it to alter a policy, Indian as well as foreign, that seemed to bear no good to anybody, and was sure to alienate still further the Musalman subjects of His

---

was more than he deserved; returned to India in February 1912 and elected trustee of Aligarh college on 26 January 1913; was an influential personage in Hyderabad as Director of Public Instruction and played a large part in the planning of Hyderabad's now Osmania University; appointed vice-chancellor of Aligarh Muslim University in 1929 but was outvoted in the University Court over the matter of a staff appointment in 1936; served as Minister of Education in Bhopal; died of kidney disease on 30 July 1937. His 'princely manners and good looks, the vividness and demonstrativeness, charmed and excited' E.M. Forster; 'and gradually . . . he fell in love with Masood'. 'There never was anyone like him,' wrote Forster in his tribute, 'and there never will be anyone like him.'

The reference is to E.M. Forster and his friend Syed Ross Masood, grandson of Syed Ahmad Khan. The nautch was organised by Dr Ansari, according to Forster, in Delhi at a time when emotions were high over the plight of Turkey in the Balkan war. Mohamed Ali was, however, persuaded by Ross Masood to go to the nautch. He told the story to a journalist, and not long afterwards, there appeared in the London Times a report of how a leading Muslim agitator, on the very eve of Turkey's defeat, had spent his evening at an 'orgy'.

[16] As part of the Improvement Scheme, the Kanpur Municipality obtained the UP government's permission to construct the A.B. Road in April 1909. The Improvement Trust Committee passed a resolution to the effect that the eastern portion of the Macchli Bazar mosque should be acquired and a plot to the north of the mosque be given in compensation. The Muslims of Kanpur submitted a memorial to the Lieutenant-Governor on 12 April 1913 and public meetings were held in different parts of the city.

Contrary to intelligence reports, Mohamed Ali was striving for a peaceful solution and was in constant touch with the Viceroy and the Lieutenant-Governor. The Comrade, however, continued to publish articles on the 'Cownpore Sacrilege' in which a crowd of over 20,000 Muslims was fired at by Tyler, the District Magistrate, leaving 17 dead and many wounded. This incident, which inflamed Muslim passions everywhere, occurred on 3 August.

Majesty.[17] In this I partly succeeded; but within a year of it events of far greater magnitude occurred in which the entire world was involved. The War and events leading to the participation of Turkey not on the same side as England undid all the good that we had expected to follow the friendly deputation of the Indian Musalmans which we had taken to wait on Lord Hardinge earlier in the year and which had been received by that viceroy with every show of goodwill.[18]

## REACTION TO TURKISH POLITICS

From November 1914, to the time of my conviction and sentence of imprisonment at Karachi, seven years later, almost to a day, Government and I have not been able to see things eye to eye. The result was that once more through the instrumentality of the Press Act, my press was forced to suspend its activities on the very day that War was declared by England against Turkey, and when at Russia's obvious pressure the plans to partition Turkey among the Allies were complete and it was settled that Constantinople, the seat of the Khilafat, was at long last, to become Tsargrad, in fulfilment of the ambitions of Peter the Great, and when early in the summer of 1915 the forces of General Sir Ian Hamilton were ready to land on the Gallipoli[19] peninsula preparatory to the forcing of the Dardanelles,[20] and the occupation of Constantinople was expected at an early date, I was ordered to be interned under the Defence of India Act. My brother Shaukat who had up to that time never taken any part in politics and had in fact just retired with an extraordinary pension after 17 years spent in the public service was also interned. During all this time his activities outside his official duties had been confined to education, and

[17] The reference is to the Macchli Bazar mosque. The Raja of Mahmudabad (1879–1931) and Mazharul Haq (1866–1930) of Bihar negotiated with James Meston, the Lieutenant-Governor of the United Provinces, in resolving the crisis. Mohamed Ali's own claim is a bit exaggerated.

[18] Hardinge (1858–1944) was Viceroy of India from 1900 to 1916. The annulment of Bengal's partition, the rejection of the Muslim University Scheme and the Kanpur mosque affair happened during his viceroyalty. To begin with, he was on the best of term with Mohamed Ali, but relations turned sour around 1913. The Viceroy then urged the Secretary of State not to encourage the 'self-imposed' mission of Mohamed Ali and Wazir Hasan to London. He described the former as a 'mischievous agitator'.

[19] A narrow peninsula extending south-west from the coast of Istanbul province, north-west Turkey; between the Dardanelles and the Aegean Sea. It was the site of a major campaign during World War I (1915–16).

[20] Scene of an unsuccessful campaign in World War I.

particularly to the educational reform of our old College at Aligarh for which he had successfully organised the 'Old Boys' Association'. When the King announced his intention of coming to Delhi to hold his Coronation Durbar, my brother took furlough for two years in order to assist in the evolution of that College into a Muslim University which he so keenly wanted to be opened by His Majesty himself.[21] His incessant touring throughout the country had resulted in contributions to the University Fund that well exceeded two out of a total of three million rupees collected for that purpose. But finding that even such a purely non-political activity was not immune from being regarded by some officials as questionable, he decided to retire from public service and to devote himself entirely to communal work.

## THE 'DEENDARS' AND 'NAI RAUSHANI'

The international developments which had resulted in the disintegration of the already enfeebled temporal power of Islam were bound to exercise a great influence on the Musalmans. But few could have prophesied the precise form this reaction was to take. Western education had thrust, so to speak, a wedge into the ranks of Indian Muslim society. The old type of Indian Muslim, who was either a theologian or still under the theologian's influence, finding that he was unable to stop the progress of an avalanche of *bedeeni* or 'irreligiousness', had taken with all the greater zeal to a sterile ritualism and shook off from the skirt of his orthodox gown the dust of 'worldliness'. Few of this class were any longer wholly 'unworldly'; but all prided themselves on their 'other-worldliness', which consisted chiefly in leaving a world which no longer heeded their fulminations and *fatawa* to manage its own affairs, and go to the perdition that they predicted for it. The younger men—the men of the *Nai Raushani* or 'New Light'—had the pretensions not only to be men of light, but also men of leading, dominated the public life of their community. For a long time educational propaganda was the crying need of Musalmans and educational conferences and touring deputations and lectures were organised by the men of 'New Light'. Latterly they had been encouraged by the Government itself to take a more assertive part in politics and had organised political propaganda with the same zeal and energy for securing their proper share of the communal representation. As I have already

[21]In 1898, the idea of a university was revived by the colleagues and contemporaries of Syed Ahmad Khan. The Sir Syed Memorial Fund Committee was constituted in 1899; it was replaced by the Muslim University Foundation Committee in 1911 with the Aga Khan as President and Nawab Viqarul Mulk as Secretary.

indicated, their zeal was more communal than religious; they knew so little of their religion and their orthodoxy was more than suspect. They did not sneer at religion but they certainly sneered at the 'religious', and their social 'reform' had begun with a very outspoken criticism of the ancient time-worn customs of the east and had ended in their almost complete adoption of western ways. From the so-called 'England-Returned' who was a barrister or an Indian civilian, a doctor or an engineer,[22] was full of Huxley[23] and Herbert Spencer,[24] often took wine, was in just a few cases not without a partiality even for pork, and occasionally had married an English wife, to the clerk in a Government office or a ticket collector on a railway whose acquaintance with English began and ended in the lowest form of a 'Zillah School', but who could not speak his own language without introducing some English equivalents for some of the commonest words in the vernacular regardless of their absurd incongruity and who would wear a coat or waistcoat more or less of European cut even when the rest of the costume was purely Eastern, there were many shades of the 'Anglicised' and 'Europeanised' Indian Muslim whose chief concern was this world and not the next, but who bore the name of Muslim with as much pride and glory as the most orthodox 'other-worldly' divine.

## VIEWS OF THE 'REFORMED'

The less intellectual seldom worried about the theological dogmas, even when the tide of a superficial and for that reason all the more aggressive rationalism make it easy for them to believe precisely as their fathers had believed, particularly on the subject of the supernatural with which later-day Islam had been lavishly supplied by the more numerous but less learned class of Muslim *Waiz* or preacher; the line of least resistance which readily lent itself for such purposes was cheerfully followed and in a hazy, undefined way to separate religion from life just as most people separate this world from the next and do not believe that they are required to argue or think about such things too nicely. The more intellectual or the more venturesome satisfied their mental cravings by ridiculing the mildewed conservatism and literal interpretation of sacred texts, and contented themselves with the gratifying belief that they at least were among the

[22] This refers to the writings of Wilayat Ali 'Bambooque' (1887–1918), an Aligarh graduate, a contemporary of Raja Ghulam Husain and Choudhry Khaliquzzaman, and a regular contributor to Mohamed Ali s *Comrade*. He wrote humorous and satirical sketches.

[23] The reference is to Aldous (Leonard) Huxley (1894–1963), well-known novelist.

[24] Herbert Spencer (1820–1903), philosopher, sociologist and writer on education.

'reformed' though they never took the trouble to define what their 'reformed' beliefs were and how they fitted in with the sacred texts to which, if required, they would have acknowledged their completest [*sic*] allegiance as unhesitatingly as the most orthodox.

## EUROPE'S TEMPORAL AGGRESSION

It was to a society thus constituted that European temporal aggression presented an ultimatum. We in India who had already lost our own Empire several generations if not a whole century ago, were not probably expected to feel as acutely as we did the loss of our co-religionists in Persia, in Egypt and in Tripoli, and in far-off Morocco. But the temporal losses of Turkey which we were advised by Europe to 'cut' touched a peculiar chord in our sub-consciousness, the chord of religion; for the Ruler of Turkey was the Khalifa or Successor of the Prophet and *Amir al-Muminin* or Chief of the Faithful, and the Khilafat was as essentially our religious concern as the Quran or the *Sunna* of the Prophet. It needed no alarmist cry of 'Religion in danger' to rouse the Musalmans in India, if religion had still any real hold on them. That indeed was the great test. Was Islam only a label for the Indian Muslim or had it a real living concern with worldly life? It is idle to speculate now what would have happened if in such a crisis Indian Musalmans had also reached the stage of indifferentism if not practical unbelief, that is lamented by the religious among the most civilised and progressive sections of Western Christendom. But no doubt many a progressive European believed that even if Muslim orthodoxy in India could not be brought by such a remarkable succession of the 'failures of Islam' to view its conservatism and narrowness differently, at least those who had received a Western education, those who had learnt to sneer at the religiosity of an earlier day and for many of whom Europe's materialism had such fatal fascination, would now be weaned off from such remnants of spirituality as still lingered as a result of their Eastern heredity in some remote corner of their being. These, at least, they thought, would now solidly vote for a complete renunciation of such useless remnants and for dropping off all such hampering impedimenta in their march towards the secularism of Europe which had given it such a complete victory over the unprogressive and superstitious East.

## RELIGION WITH A BRIEF CREED AND NO CLERGY

Perhaps I am anticipating my reposition of the essential characteristics of Islam; but it is my firm belief that what prevented such a consummation was the fact that in reality Islam had so little of dogma with which to overburden a Muslim. Christianity has been in recent times so skilfully idealised by the new school of its writers of Apologetics that none of the Church Councils that were held from time to time to regulate Christian belief and anathematise successive heresies and schisms could recognise it. In fact, even to the most latitudinarian student of religion it is so featureless that it is not easily possible to be identified with any religion. And yet, except for that large class which from abhorring theology has come to abhor religion itself, even this so-called religion without 'theology' has a theology which presents great difficulties to the least critical of believers unless of course he permits his beliefs to benumb and paralyse his intellect. The Church can fill tomes with its theology but even the briefest catechism would require the proverbial half-sheet of note-paper to contain the truncated dogma of reformed and modernised Christianity. But when you compare this with Islam you will find that even the half-sheet is superfluous, for a postage stamp would be ample to cover its creed. And I do believe the postage stamps of Muslim States contain the *Kalima* or 'Creed' for Muslims. 'There is no God but Allah and Mohammad is His Messenger' is all his dogma and it makes no great call on his powers of thinking or on his credulity. When this great storm overtook the Muslim he had no unessential freight to throw overboard and lighten the ship. He could have of course thrown Islam itself overboard, but that he hugged as his life-belt and the world is waiting to see if he can that way weather the storm. Moreover, 'the absence of a priestly ideal, of any theory of the separateness of the religious teacher from the common body of the believers or of the necessity of a special consecration and authorisation for the performance of religious functions', which has resulted in Islam in an added feeling of responsibility resting on the individual believer and in a general level of uniformity in Muslim society unknown in communities that maintain a priesthood, has also tended to keep religion undivorced from life among the Musalmans, and to make it the concern of all alike. These two essential characteristics of Islam, as we shall presently see, helped the Indian Muslim to answer Europe's ultimatum.[25]

[25] The alliance between the ulama and the Western-educated Muslims is analysed in several works. See, for example, Francis Robinson, *Separatism Among Indian Muslims: The Politics of United Provinces' Muslims, 1860–1923* (Cambridge, 1975); Gail Minault, *The Khilafat Movement: Religious Symbolism and Political Mobilisation in India* (Columbia University Press, 1982); Mushirul Hasan, *Nationalism and Communal Politics in India, 1885–1930* (Delhi, 1930).

## IMPACT OF INTERNATIONAL POLITICS ON INDIAN MUSLIMS

The temporal misfortunes of Islam, therefore, drew the Muslims to their religion as if inevitably and the wedge that Western education had seemed to insert between the ranks of the religious, and of the men of the 'New Light' vanished as if by magic. The orthodox and the anglicised were drawn together and, as in a flash of lightning, saw that after all they were not so unlike each other as they had imagined. The men of the 'New Light' were, as I have said, in a sense, the men of leading as well, and they at any rate had not shrunk from the affairs of this world like their *deendar* co-religionists, who had, almost as if making a virtue of necessity, retired from public life and became recluses, when they had gradually lost most of their former hold on the people. Moreover, they alone could understand and explain what precisely Europe was doing and threatened to do directly to the temporal power of Islam and indirectly to its spiritual influence in the world. Their outspoken championship of Islamic states in the Indian press and on the public platform, no greatly impressed these semi-recluses, and informal and tentative overtures from both sides soon followed. Be it said to the credit of the *ulama* that they did not hesitate at this juncture to pocket their pride and in a way even accept the lead of men whom they had but a generation ago finally consigned to perdition. But, if revenge is a word that may be used in this connection, they had their fill of it in the transformation that these temporal misfortunes of Islam wrought in the spiritual temper and tone of 'the men of light and leading': Only those of the *ulama* whose concern seemed to be the retention of their own quasi-priestly authority more than the maintenance of orthodoxy still kept aloof, and these for the most part exhibited a deplorable pusillanimity when faced with some unpleasant consequences of religious zeal. Among the anglicised also, there was a section that sought the limelight for its own interest rather than of the community, and in the hour of danger it quietly slank away into dark corners. Just as the selfish among the *ulama* had sought to cover their self-seeking cowardice under an extreme narrowness and fanaticism of bigotry and had anathematised all others as involved in different degrees of heresy, so too these political leaders who forsook their erstwhile associates in the press and on the platform pretended to sneer at the latter's return to the obscurantism and bigotry of the *Mullahs*. Thus we and the *ulama* who now began to associate with us in our communal work were attacked by two sections of Indian Musalmans who were brothers under their skins, for the opposite faults of being too religious and not sufficiently religious at one and the same time. But neither section was sufficiently considerable to affect the situation vitally. Once more Muslim society in India presented a level of uniformity and the bitterest opponents of a generation ago stood shoulder to shoulder, working together with great zeal and with a mutual appreciation of the good points which each lacked himself, but which the other possessed. If even a decade previously anyone had ventured to foretell such a result, he would have been laughed at for such a fantastic prophesy; for it was little short of a miracle in an age which had assured itself that miracles were things that did not occur.

## 'THE BOOK OUR MOTHER READ'

Like other men of my own class, particularly the 'Old Boys of Aligarh', I was now impelled to make a close study of my religion, and although most of us found even then little time for such a study, for there was much other work to do in order to stave off the disaster—as far as poor helpless India could be expected to do that—we could no longer let things drift in the old complacent way. Both my brother and I now turned more and more to the Quran and found in it the consolation and contentment that was denied to us outside its pages. As Whittier[26] has so truly said:

> We search the world for truth we cull
> The good, the pure, the beautiful,
> From grave-stone and written scroll,
> From the old flower fields of the soul;
> And weary seekers of the best,
> We come back laden from our guest,
> To find that all the sages said
> Is in the book our mothers read.

## THE PARABLE
## 'LIKENING A GOOD WORD TO A GOOD TREE'

Biologists tell us that the plasma from which seeds originate possesses a 'natural and physiological immortality', and I recently read in an *English Review* a series of stories which go to prove that certain seeds actually possess a kind of perennial life, persisting in some cases through different geological eras. A Scotsman had discovered six grains of oats in an Egyptian Sarcophagus unopened for 2600 years. He planted two, one of

[26] John Greenleaf Whittier (1807–92); US Quaker poet and author of a collection of poems and stories.

which germinated and produced a fairly long stalk with twelve grains of oats. In another case a gentleman discovered a little pre-glacial plant which came up constantly out of the fibre he used to prepare from Yorkshire moss in his hot-house. This plant can live now only in countries like the West Indies and Tropical America, and he infers that its seeds must have survived since the date when lions and tigers roamed in British tropical forests and when there were cacti and palms on all British river sides. The manner in which the seed of Islam has today suddenly germinated in some of the most completely Europeanised and 'materialised' Muslims in India, and no doubt elsewhere also, goes to prove that the spiritual plasma possesses in no smaller degree a 'natural immortality'. In fact the Quran should have prepared us for this phenomenon if we had assimilated the truth it conveys in the familiar verses:

> Seest thou not how Allah putteth forth a parable likening a good word to a good tree; its root is firmly fixed and its branches are in the sky; it yieldeth its fruit in all seasons by the will of its Lord, and Allah setteth forth these similitudes to men that haply they may mind. And the likeness of an evil word is as an evil tree uprooted from the surface of the soil: it hath no stability. Allah will establish them that believe with the steadfast word in this world's life and in the hereafter, and the unjust shall He lead astray; and Allah doeth what He pleaseth.

The Muslim's 'creed' is called the *Kalima-i Tayyiba* or the 'good word' and as each child comes forth into the world this 'good word' is uttered into its ear. And every Muslim prays that this 'good word' may be the last on his tongue as he departs from this world. He that is cognisant of 'a grain in the darkness of the Earth', 'He that cleaveth the seed and the stone', must have willed that even after a whole 'geological era' of gross materialism, the seed of Islam which He had caused to be planted in some obscure corner of our being, should germinate in our souls and we can only live in the sustaining belief that like the 'good tree' of the parable, the 'good word' of our 'creed' now 'firmly fixed in the soil, would one day reach the skies with its branches, and yield fruit in all seasons by the will of its Lord', that since it has pre-ordained 'stability' none shall succeed in 'uprooting it from the surface of the soil', but that 'Allah will' establish us with 'the steadfast word both in this world's life and in the Hereafter'.

## EXPANDED HORIZON

There is no doubt that there has been an almost complete transformation in the mental outlook and mode of life of so many of the younger Musalmans of India during the last decade. The reaction has extended very far and has taken such unexpected forms that regular 'cnuts' who used to dream of nothing but what would be the 'mode' in the *next* century A.C. have begun to haunt in the *Sunna* or Tradition of the Prophet for the fashion plates of Year 1 A.H.! Young dandies who were on the look-out for the latest toilet preparations like European women of the smartest of smart sets, and were 'fondly proud of a well-trimmed moustache as a European girl of her curls, are now to be seen in some cases with the most ungainly beards turning grey with the dust of an Indian summer'. But it must not be imagined that there has been any fanatical and irrational revulsion against everything Western. On the contrary no one values what the West has taught them in the way of *real* progress than these men. They feel more eager than ever to multiply the facilities for imparting to their co-religionists and fellow-countrymen an instruction in the best that Europe has yet to teach them, and particularly for the rapid diffusion of its scientific knowledge throughout the East. Their newly-awakened spirituality has not driven them into an unthinking hostility towards the material progress of Europe. Only they want its material progress without the gross materialism that would one day spell its ruin. They have for their guide the sane and sound philosophy of their broad-minded Prophet who had taught them to 'leave the foul, and take the clean', to 'seek knowledge even if it be in China', and to regard wisdom wherever they found it, as their own 'lost patrimony' to which they were entitled even more than those with whom they found it. It would, therefore, be perhaps more accurate to say that instead of a transformation of their outlook, there was rather an enlargement of the field of their vision. Their mental and spiritual horizon has suddenly expanded and they have been brought into the closest touch, on the one side, with the old world conservatism and orthodoxy, and on the other, with the masses whose troubles they now began to share as comrades in arms, and no longer as commanders who only deigned to issue instructions to them—'for their good'. A general levelling up has taken place in the Muslim community which has made it a power in the land such as it had never been before, and that without any dependence on the use of force or external authority.

## THE PILGRIM'S BROKER—NEW STYLE

Nothing could better illustrate this development than the story of my brother Shaukat. In conjunction with Maulana Abdul Bari Sahib,[27] the

[27] Maulana Abdul Bari (1876–1926) was the spiritual mentor of the Ali brothers; one of the founders of the Anjuman-i Khuddam-i Kaaba; took a leading part in the Khilafat and Non-Cooperation movements and acted in unison with Gandhi on a number of issues; president of the Jamiyat al-ulama-i-Hind in 1923.

head of the famous house of Firangi Mahal (Lucknow) which has given to India a most unique combination of saintly Sufis and doctors of Muslim learning during an unbroken succession of four centuries, my brother took the leading part in founding in the summer of 1913 the Society of 'Servants of the Kaaba'. This was to unite the Musalmans of every sect in maintaining inviolate the sanctity of the three *Harams* of Islam at Mecca, Medina and Jerusalem. Every 'Servant of Kaaba' solemnly repeats the religious pledge to maintain this sanctity at whatever cost to himself whenever its violation is threatened, as Italy once did during the Tripoli War, and towards the expenses of the organisation every Servant, rich or poor, contributes the humble mite of one rupee on the day of the Holy Pilgrimage. As an immediate necessity the troubles of the Indian pilgrims in securing passages for the voyage to the Holy Places drew my brother to Bombay. There he found that the only way in which he could assist these long-suffering thousands who were 'Allah's guests' in that thriving port, was to take the humiliating license of a 'Pilgrims' Broker' for the sale of passages and to enlist the services of equally ardent and competent Muslims as 'Brokers' Servants' in order to obtain the necessary *locus standi.* He was determined to do that; but the new 'Pilgrims' Broker' became an altogether new man also. This occupation entirely changed his mode of life. From a smart, half-Europeanised, fashionably dressed officer of Government who used to be in great request at European gym-khanas and clubs on account of his sporting exploits as a famous captain of Aligarh cricketers, and who prided himself on his pretty taste in silk shirts, which only his enormous build could rescue from being regarded as the height of foppery, he became a poorly, not to say shabbily, dressed Bombaywalla in a loose long green coat of queer cut. On the erstwhile smooth cheeks and chin was now to be seen a shaggy beard which, as he himself used to say, was his fiercest protest against Europe and Christendom. In Bhindi Bazaar and its noisome purlieus he soon became a familiar sight, trudging stoutly along the busy thoroughfares that led to overcrowded 'Pilgrim Shelters'. Here lay the most helpless mass of humanity huddled together, awaiting a favourable turn in the passage-market and in the meantime compelled to eat away in this macabre-like suspense the meagre savings of half a life-time, thus reducing the very means with which it could avail itself of the long-waited for opportunity of securing a cheap passage to the Holy Land of Islam. To the Shipping Company that had gradually acquired a monopoly of this traffic, and relying on that used to commence its pilgrimage season with cheap passages and after thus luring these helpless creatures to the only port of embarkation, used to raise them when they arrived there from the remotest corners of India, and from neighbouring countries. as well, my 'Broker' brother's and his 'Broker's Servants' some of whom were graduates and well-to-do members of some of the best families, must have been as great a nuisance as he on his side found the company to be. After a prolonged controversy he came to the conclusion that the best solution of this terrible problem would be a Shipping Company for the pilgrim traffic established by the charitable Muslims themselves, beginning with Indian Muslim Princes who should contribute one or more boats according to the rank and revenue of their states; but which should be run on sound enough business lines, so that losses could be avoided. Such small profits as resulted could be utilised to increase the comforts and conveniences of 'Allah's guests' and to repatriate those whom some sudden misfortune during the pilgrimage had thrown upon the charity of their co-religionists. This was all the 'Politics' that attracted my brother even on retirement from service under the Government. He was in the thick of the Pilgrimage season when the War broke out and practically put a stop to the pilgrimage and consequently to the activities of my brother at Bombay. Long before the next pilgrimage season arrived, this quaint 'Pilgrims' Broker' was sharing internment and exile with myself.

III

# My Troubles and the Remedy

## THE PRESS ACT

UNDER THE PRESS ACT, publishers of newspapers and periodicals and keepers of printing presses had to deposit with Government security for good behaviour. But Indian Musalmans, whose politics had long been preponderatingly favourable to Government and in fact but too often savoured of sycophancy according to the more forward sister communities in India, were believed to be fairly innocuous when I commenced my journalistic career in 1911, and my British printers were accordingly exempted from the deposit of a security. When I migrated to Delhi about two years later, and had to become the keeper of a press myself in the new-old capital of India that lacked the printing facilities of Calcutta, I was already something of a suspect and I had to see several-high officials before I was exempted from this deposit. The ground officially assigned for this great favour was that I had been similarly treated in Calcutta two years ago and had in the meantime served a period of apprenticeship in 'respectability'! But alas, I could not long rely on that 'respectability' for I had been the recipient, as I have already mentioned, of a pamphlet from Turkey regarding the atrocities of the Balkan Allies in Macedonia. It was an appeal to Christians and in particular to Englishmen, the old Allies of Crimea and friends of the Congress at Berlin.[1] It bore the title 'Come over into Macedonia and help us',[2] which the Christian reader will readily recognise as a quotation from the Acts of the Apostles, and reminiscent of the entry of Christianity into Europe through the energy and ardour of St. Paul, the 'apostle of the gentiles'. Like me, Lord Lamington, who had but lately been the Governor of Bombay, had received that morning an appeal

[1]An International Congress (1878) following the Russian defeat of Turkey in 1877–8. The chief results were: Serbia, Rumania and Bulgaria achieved independence from Turkey; Austria-Hungary occupied Bosnia-Herzegovina; Russia made some gains but conceded a reduction in the size of Bulgaria.

[2]This pamphlet was proscribed by the government of Bengal on 18 July 1913. Though Mohamed Ali questioned the validity of the order, his application was dismissed by Sir Lawrence Jenkins. The issues of Comrade (17, 24, 31 May and 17 June 1913, and Hamdard (7–8, 14, 17, 19, 21, 24–8 June 1913) were forfeited.

to which Sir Adam Block, an Englishman and President of the Commission of Ottoman Debt, had contributed a foreword in support, and the ex-Governor of Bombay had been so greatly affected by its perusal that he had based on this pamphlet a smaller tract intended for broadcast distribution, and this tract bore on it the sign of the cross in red. When even such a publication was declared forfeited under the Press Act by one Local Government in India after another, following the lead of the Government of India itself which was the local Government for the Imperial Enclave at Delhi, I had, as I have stated, petitioned the High Court of Calcutta to set aside the order of the Bengal Government.[3] The object in selecting that tribunal being to appeal to a judicial body as independent of the executive as one could expect to find in this country. As Sir Lawrence Jenkins, the Chief Justice, said in his masterly judgement, I lost my book, but I retained my reputation, and what I valued still more, I gained a judgement which tore up the Press Act, the authors and sponsors of which had thus been pilloried for the first time in a court of law in India. An English barrister of great eminence, the brilliant and generous-hearted Eardley Norton had accepted my brief without accepting any fee, while an Indian politician whose 'sweet reasonableness' before long made him a counsellor and adviser of the highest British officials in India and England, Mr. Bhupendra Nath Basu, had been my 'Honorary' Solicitor. The Government of Bengal had almost succeeded in briefing against me Lord Sinha, the unwilling author of the Act, but just as I was stepping into the Court of the Chief Justice and his two senior most 'brothers' who formed the 'Bench' for my case, Lord Sinha whispered into my ear that he would not appear in the case. In fact, a fortnight later we sailed together in the 'Judge's boat' to England, and when I was arranging with English friends to induce Lord Crewe,[4] then Secretary of State for India, to receive a deputation which would press the repeal of this obnoxious legislation,[5] we almost induced Lord Sinha to lead it. Perhaps his eleventh hour refusal in both cases was due to the fact that it was during his term of office as the Law Member of the Government of India that the Press Bill had been hurriedly hammered into shape, and finally turned into the India Press

[3]At the Calcutta High Court, a special bench listened to an application made by Norton on behalf of Mohamed Ali. For the proceedings and judgement, see *Comrade*, 6 and 20 September 1913.

[4]He was secretary of state for the colonies (1908–10) before assuming charge as Secretary of State for India (1910–15).

[5]He refused to meet Mohamed Ali during his visit to London. See Hasan (ed.), *Mohamed Ali in Indian Politics: Select Writings*, vol. 1, pp. 38–40.

Act of 1910 on the anvil of the Imperial Council and if as an unwilling parent he was reluctant to praise the baby thrust into his arms as his own pet child, he now felt some delicacy, in being the foremost to attempt to kill it and give it a Christian burial. That consummation has at long last been achieved; but, as ever in Politics, the man who had to figure as the petitioner in the 'leading case' under the Act had to suffer a good deal in his own person before that final achievement.

## THE PRESS ACT AGAIN

The sequel of this case was that the Magistrate of Delhi demanded an immediate deposit of the maximum amount of security from the keeper of my press, and the fact that I was then absent in Calcutta made no difference to him. My lawyers at Delhi not desiring to close the printing press and stop all my journalistic activities deposited the amount entirely on their own responsibility, and a year later, on the very day that England declared war on Turkey, that security was declared forfeited, and another five times as heavy was demanded, together with the entire plant of the printing press, worth about half a lakh of rupees, which would be declared forfeited, for the second offence along with the additional monetary security. This was because of an article provoked by a 'Leader' of the London *Times* on 'The Choice of the Turks',[6] which had appeared more than a month previously, and I may add that once more my generous friend Mr. Norton had agreed to appear for me in the Calcutta High Court, though as it turned out, he was unavoidably detained that day in a murder case in which he had already been appearing, which went beyond the week in which it was expected to be decided. Sir Lawrence Jenkins and his brother judges threw out the case, as Lord Sinha had predicted, on the ground that they had no jurisdiction, for this time the Government of Bengal had taken care *not* to declare the forfeiture of the offending issue of the *Comrade*. In fact the Police Commissioner of Calcutta had returned to me the copy that I had surrendered for confiscation, even though the Government of India had declared its forfeiture 'wherever found'. Lord Sinha had, however, advised me to take the case to the Chief Court at

[6]According to a British official, the article 'gives us ample justification for suppressing such writings on the part of Mohamed Ali'. In a note submitted on 6 October 1914, it was stated: 'I do not see how anyone can read the article except as a direct incitement to Turkey to go to war. . . . England is practically threatened if she does not evacuate Egypt, and Germany is extolled. If this is not attacking our Allies and siding with our enemies it is difficult to know what it is?'

Lahore which exercised jurisdiction over the Imperial Capital, although it was itself dependent on the local Government of the Punjab. He naively declared that I was certain to lose it at Lahore, but equally certain to win the appeal to the Privy Council. Whatever the offending article may have done to offend the Government or the successive Governments in England, it had not the least reference or relevance to 'the Government by law established in British India' which it was declared to have had 'a tendency to bring into hatred or contempt' even though it openly preached loyalty to it with earnestness and sustained vigour. Several papers in England, including the *Morning Post* and the *Daily Telegraph*, in fact published very favourable reviews of that article about the very time that my press was forced to close down for publishing it and the *New Statesman* vigorously took up my cause when the astounding news reached it that it was precisely for publishing this article which it had favourably noticed some weeks earlier that I had been made to suffer such a heavy loss.

To return to my story, two parts of Lord Sinha's prophecy were fulfilled to the letter inasmuch as the Calcutta High Court did not entertain my application and the Lahore Chief Court decided against me in a judgement characteristic of that hand-maiden of the executive. But, alas, before I could reach the portals of the Privy Council and test the last and more hopeful part of Lord Sinha's prophecy, another door was closed on me, the door of internment under the Defence of India Act.

## EXIT 'THE COMRADE'

The *Comrade* could not, therefore, reappear unless I chose to risk the loss of ten thousand rupees and a fifty thousand rupees worth of printing press, which I would have been most foolish to do. It would have been only throwing good money after bad, and in fact there was no longer much work for a journal conducted in the language of India's rulers and designed to act as an intermediary between them and the people of India. It was an expensive publication because it had to worm its way into official circles when a less pleasing appearance would have given it an immediate *darwaza band* (literally, 'door closed') that far-franker Anglo-Indian expression which does service in India for the conventional 'lie' of 'Not at home'. Care had also to be taken to interlard matters of the most vital interest to the India of the Indians with lighter reading in the form of verse, short stories and humour, not that Indians did not in course of time come to appreciate these features which were unusual in Indian journalism. But if the *Comrade* had been meant only for them many of these could have been dispensed with and the paper and printing would have been less expensive. Thus the cost would have been greatly reduced, enabling me to make possible a corresponding reduction in the subscription which was unusually high for an Indian weekly review. For a poor community the educated Indians who were in the main Musalmans had made an unexpectedly generous response and the circulation had increased five-fold in less than four years. Fresh subscribers were still enlisting; but, alas, the old ones were falling into hopeless arrears, a habit with which Indian journalists are not unfamiliar. And as the *Comrade* had practically no 'adds' it had from the first been a drain on my resources and on the resources of those who had generously come to my assistance soon after my journalistic *debut.* However reluctant I was to say 'Good-bye' or at least 'Au revoir' to my 'Comrade' for four of the most strenuous years of my life, the cessation of its publication meant financial relief.

## A PRINTER AND PUBLISHER'S TROUBLES

But I was far from having said farewell to journalism itself. The *Comrade* was only a part of my scheme as a journalist and would-be publisher and when I had followed the Government of India to Delhi and in the absence of printing facilities in the new capital had been forced to become my own printer, I had found that to be the proper moment for enlarging the sphere of my work by publishing a daily newspaper in Urdu, the vernacular of so large a part of the Indian population and specially of the Musalmans. The script used for Urdu is the *Nastaliq* or Persianised form of the Arabic *Naskh*; but although it was a most artistic script in which all the angularities of the latter had been gracefully rounded and was the delight of the calligraphist, it was the absolute despair of the typographist. Christian missionaries had made an indescribably ugly compromise between the two, mainly, I believe because even the *Naskh* needed an extraordinarily large variety of types for printing in a script which was a sort of 'shorthand'. Sir Syed Ahmad Khan, who had been a pioneer in so many other directions, had made use of this type; but his journalism was hardly of the 'popular' variety and few indeed were thereby familiarised with this type. As the printing machines needed for the *Comrade* would have remained idle for four days or more in the week, and as I was anxious to be rid of dependence upon the vagaries of the calligraphists employed for lithography in Indian printing presses, I had decided to use type, but having long ago sickened of this ugly 'compromise' and finally despairing of *Nastaliq* type, I had ordered pure *Naskh* type from Beirut. For up-to-date journalism lithography could never do, but it was no easy matter to wean off the people from the *Nastaliq* script and to familiarise them with the *Naskh*. However, the commotion caused by the sudden outbreak of the Balkan War in the autumn of 1912 when I transferred myself to Delhi and intended to issue my Urdu daily paper, provided the best possible chance for the success of this new departure, for I had gathered together a very competent staff of sub-editors for the *Hamdard* and was frequently receiving direct messages from Turkey through the assistance of my friend Dr. Ansari, who had organised in conjunction with myself and taken over to the famous Tehatalja lines and to Chanak in the Dardannelles an All-India Medical Mission.[7] But the Beirut firm inordinately delayed the despatch of the type, and when it arrived it was insufficient and badly assorted for the purposes of 'copy' in the Urdu language. A second supply was ordered and was again delayed so that the first issue of the *Hamdard* could not appear for some eight months after the scheduled time. With a large staff of journalists whom I had already engaged living in enforced idleness for such a long period and expecting to commence work any day, and a printing press which had no work to do during the better part of the week, what I must have suffered in pocket can easily be understood to have been considerable. But what I suffered in mental worry and chagrin was felt as a far severer strain.

## MORE TROUBLE

When at long last the *Hamdard* was issued, the Balkan War was all but over, and a newspaper printed from movable types in an unfamiliar script could not ride, as it were, on the crest of a wave. Its circulation did not increase as rapidly as one would have expected, even after making all allowances for the fact that sensationalism was strictly a taboo, and the leader-writers who were inclined to follow the prevailing fashion of sprinkling red pepper with a rather lavish hand were never allowed to forget that the new publication had its own traditions to establish. All this was disheartening enough and if the book-keepers could have influenced

[7]Mukhtar Ahmad Ansari (1880–1936) led the Indian Medical Mission to Constantinople, 1912–13, for which he received a special award from the Ottoman Consul-General; founded the Home Rule League in Delhi and was elected its president; played a leading part in the Khilafat movement. According to Meston, 'in Moslem circles he [Ansari] commands considerable respect. . . . His work in the Medical Mission during the last Turkish War is a matter of pride to them.' Ansari worked closely with the Ali brothers, though they became estranged from him over the Nehru Committee Report of August 1928.

the policy of the paper, there would have been little to distinguish it from some of its more thriving contemporaries. But I lost my faith neither in my own ideals nor in my people's ultimate appreciation of them, even though I was far from making the two ends meet financially. On top of all this came yet another trouble with the new type. Even with a circulation much smaller than I had expected, it began to show very early traces that it would not wear well. Within a year it required to be replaced and I was certainly not prepared to depend once more on our Beirut suppliers who had caused me so much loss and worry. I had already made an attempt to prepare matrices for a type-foundry of our own; but now my friends advised me to 'cut my losses' on printing from movable type and to have my paper lithographed in the familiar *Nastaliq* script. I had refused to listen to them in the autumn of 1912 when they advised me not to wait for the Beirut type, but to issue the *Hamdard* immediately on the outbreak of the Balkan War as an ordinary lithographed paper and while saving myself the losses I was incurring with an idle editorial staff, give to the people a newspaper that they badly wanted. Now they pressed the point once more and urged me to profit from a year's experience of a paper appearing in an unpopular script. I could not of course make the printing press pay if it printed only the *Comrade* and was compelled to add to my other worries those of a job printer, and even then, through inexperience and in fact want of interest in the business failed to prevent heavy financial loss. But three machines were purchased for lithographing the *Hamdard* and so true was the forecast of these advisers of mine that the circulation of the *Hamdard* in its new script began to go up by leaps and bounds. Two months later the European War broke out, and for once luck seemed to favour me, though I would far rather have had my bad luck as before than make money out of such excitement as a war breeds. But that I was not destined to do for long after all. For, as I have said, immediately on the outbreak of War between the Allies and Turkey, the security deposited for my printing press was declared forfeited on account of an article that had appeared in the *Comrade*.

## 'THE CHOICE OF THE TURKS'

That article had been written under the stress of a great crisis, while I was still bed-ridden owing to diabetic trouble which had necessitated some six weeks previously a surgeon's attention to an abscess under a toe nail. I had sat up for forty hours to write twenty fateful columns, foregoing sleep and rest and almost all food, except some very strong coffee, which

I seldom used to take, and I had corrected the proofs in a moving train, while on my way to Rampur to bury a dearly beloved cousin, the husband of my only sister, who had died suddenly. Another leading article had already been set in type for that issue of the *Comrade,* but the issue was delayed so that this article could be substituted and reach England and Turkey in time to prevent, if it possibly could, the outbreak of hostilities to which the *Times'* leading article seemed to be driving the old Allies of Crimea. I had surveyed the whole situation and had rapidly sketched the history of Turkey's relations with various European Powers, and particularly with England with a view to contrast the old friendly attitude, and its undoubted advantages to the two Powers one of whom had at its head a ruler who was the Chief of the Faithful, and the Successor of their Prophet, while the other numbered far the largest Muslim population as members of its far-flung Empire. It was not unoften that the leader writers of the *Hamdard* 'lifted' a leading article of mine or my dearly lamented friend and sub-editor, the late Ghulam Husain,[8] and made it serve the purpose of a leader or two in the Urdu stable-companion of the *Comrade,* and here was material enough to last them a whole week or more. But just as one of my most brilliant sub-editors was dressing up a portion of the 'Choice of the Turks' in its oriental garb for the *Hamdard* came the peremptory order that it was wholly taboo.

## THE *HAMDARD* SUFFERS

The *Hamdard* was intended to educate the people whereas the *Comrade* had to be their spokesman as well, and to act as a medium between them and their rulers, and I was anxious to exclude from the former all exciting topics such as could not be avoided from the latter in the heat of advocacy. More than one protest and appeal reached me from the sub-editors of the *Hamdard,* but I was adamant and the readers of the *Hamdard* were not permitted to overhear what passed between the *Comrade* and the Government in power in England. And yet when the security of the press was declared forfeited, the unoffending *Hamdard* had to close its doors as well. It was pointed out to the magistrate that the machines which had

[8]Raja Ghulam Husain (1882-1917); commenced his public career as Mohamed Ali's associate in the *Comrade*. He joined the *Indian Daily Telegraph* after the *Comrade* ceased publication; launched the *New Era* on 7 April 1917. As sub-editor of the *Comrade*, his was 'a sobering influence on the brave enthusiast of the Muslim cause, Mohamed Ali, whose generous impulses proved more profitable when allied with the "sweetness and light" of his admirable colleague'.

printed the offending article of the *Comrade* did not and in fact could not lithograph the *Hamdard* for which other machines had been purchased months ago and used ever since. But he was inexorable and the letter of the law was thrown in my face by his pointing out that the *Hamdard* machines too were covered by the same security, and could not be set up as a separate press even with the deposit of an initial security, but that for these too I must deposit the enhanced security, as part of an offending press, and no doubt see them forfeited along with that enhanced security for the 'next offence'! Immediately on the declaration of forfeiture those who sympathised with me began to pour subscriptions on me to enable me to deposit the maximum enhanced security of ten thousand rupees and in fact the amount was oversubscribed. But everybody advised me against paying in the first security on account of the liability of the plant itself to forfeiture on the next occasion, and since I had decided not to issue the *Comrade* again as long as the War lasted, and Government was not in a mood to listen patiently to the advocacy of such causes as I had espoused, it was decided to set up another printing press for lithographing the *Hamdard* and pay the maximum initial security of 2,000 rupees for it. All this took time and what with the purchasing of new plant and the payment of a large staff of editors, translators, calligraphists and lithographers, while the new press was being set up I exhausted all the subscription that had poured in so generously and was in addition considerably out of pocket.

## ILL-HEALTH AND INTERNMENT

The worry and the additional work and constant travelling involved in the Press Act litigation at Calcutta and then at Lahore had played havoc with my health and my doctors cheerfully guaranteed my death within an easily measurable distance of time if I did not take the 'long leave' which had long been overdue, so that some three months after the revival of the *Hamdard* I handed over charge of the paper to my sub-editors and of the management to my brother Shaukat and left for Rampur. Soon after my arrival the Inspector General of Police of the United Provinces, which was ruled over by Lord Meston,[9] once on the friendliest terms with me, but who had been since the Kanpur Mosque trouble about two years ago openly hostile, followed me to my haven of refugee and arranged with H.H. the Nawab of Rampur for my 'internment' there.[10] However, as the

[9]James Scorgie Meston (1865–1943); Lieutenant-Governor of the United Provinces.

[10]Nawab Hamid Ali Khan (1875–1930) was ruler of the surviving remnants of Rohilla power in Rampur. He interned Mohamed Ali at the suggestion of Meston.

excessive heat injured my health still further His Highness permitted me to go to the hills, and just when on our way there I arrived at Delhi in company with my medical adviser and friend Dr. Ansari who was going to share a house with me at Mussoorie, came the Delhi Government's order of internment. It was extended even to my brother Shaukat, whose only offence apart from his strenuous work for the pilgrims, had so far been his management of my financial affairs during the previous month in my absence from Delhi and his successful advocacy which procured the cancellation of the order of internment wrung out of His Highness the Nawab of Rampur.

## 'QUTUB SAHIB'

The Imperial enclave did not extend outside the city of Delhi beyond the limits of the police station of Mehrauli.[11] This was the earliest capital of Muslim India, and there a small earthen mound has covered for seven centuries the last remains of the saint Qutubuddin,[12] the disciple of Muinuddin Chishti of Ajmer and in his turn the preceptor of Nizamuddin Aulia.[13] This unpretentious little grave round about which cluster the tombs of many a pious Muslim and form with the usual mosque the *Dargah* of the Saint has given Mehrauli its unofficial title of the Qutub Sahib, though the ordinary visitor out sight-seeing would naturally think that this distinction was due to that wonderfully imposing monument of early Muslim piety and art in India, the Qutub Minar. It was to this place that we were ordered to proceed and to remain 'interned' within the 'notified area' which is the rather clumsy name for the smaller variety of municipality. The place has still the remains of a large palace built by the Slave and Khilji dynasties and an uncompleted mosque the *Quwwat-ul-Islam* or 'Power of Islam' of which the unique Qutub Minar was to be only one of the several minarets. Near it and adjoining the *Dargah* are the ruins of the stucco and plaster palaces built by the last of the Mughals, the

[11]The village next to Qutub Minar. The Ali brothers were interned in May 1915 and were asked by Malcolm Hailey, Chief Commissioner of Delhi, to abstain from political and public meetings.

[12]Khwaja Qutubuddin Bakhtiyar Kaki (d. 1235–6) buried near the Qutub Minar in Delhi. His Khalifa was Babi Farid Ganjshakar (d. 1268–9), whose shrine is at Pak Pattan in Montgomery (Punjab).

[13]Khwaja Muinuddin Chishti (1142–1236); founder of the Chishti order. His shrine at Ajmer is the most popular place of pilgrimage in the subcontinent. The Mughal Emperor, Akbar, made a pilgrimage to it on foot. One of his most distinguished disciples was Nizamuddin Auliya (1238–1324), whose shrine is at Nizamuddin (west) in New Delhi.

pensioner of the East India Company illustrating unmistakable contrast between the first things and the last things in Muslim rule in India. There is a small bazaar large enough for the needs of those who come over from Delhi and of course other parts of India as well, to visit the shrine, and at every hundred yards or so there is a mosque, more or less in ruins, at one time no doubt filled five times a day by the residents, but now wholly untenanted except for wild pigeons and bats and scarcely ever receiving even a sight-seeing visitor. The only exception is the unique little mosque known as 'Aulia Masjid', which is still a place of pilgrimage and is in perfect state of preservation because there was so little indeed to preserve. Under a spreading *Pipal* tree are still marked on the ground two little rectangular spaces close to each other to show where the great saint and Sufi of Chisht—Muinuddin—used to offer his prayers when visiting his disciple Qutubuddin, who used to join him in his devotions. Pious disciples afterwards erected in front of this place a little wall some four feet high, pierced in the centre by a *mehrab* or the usual niche for the Imam who leads the service in a mosque and by its side is the tiniest little *mimbar* or three-stepped pulpit of the Indian mosques. Few feet below the level of the floor is the magnificent tank of Shamsuddin Iltutmish,[14] the contemporary of the Saint of Muslim India's oldest capital built on a site where in a dream he had seen simultaneously with the Saint the Vision of Prophet on horse back. There is neither a dome nor a minaret in this mosque and the only roof is the bluest of blue skies which on a moonlit night pours down through the leaves of the *Pipal* overhead a light far more suggestive of heaven than 'the dim religious light' of cathedrals and mausoleum. There are still some houses in Mehrauli, but hardly one is habitable for they are the relics of the last days of Muslim rule when brick had replaced stone even for royal palaces and pleasure resorts and the aftermath of the Mutiny, even where it left any heirs to reclaim the property of their ancestors, left them in no condition to maintain the luxury of a suburban retreat. Practically the only house kept in any kind of repair was secured for us from the scion of a well-known Mughal family as a loan for a month after which we hoped to secure something else. But if there was a scarcity of habitation for the living there was none of it for the dead. Mehrauli is one vast graveyard, and for miles around the eye sees nothing but graves, graves, graves. It was in this extensive 'God's Acre' that we were left to study at leisure God's Book that we had so long neglected, and to rediscover the ever-living truth in this grave of Empires.

[14] He succeeded Qutubuddin Aibak in 1210 and consolidated Turkish rule in India.

## PICNICKING PILGRIMS

But even though private motor cars were still scarce and taxis had not invaded the revived capital of India, Mehrauli was at none too great a distance for *tongas*, and other forms of hackney carriages which brought every day cart loads of visitors from Delhi to see us and to offer us their sympathies and an endless supply of fruits which made our place look like a fruiterer's stall. Our kitchen though maintained on a very modest scale began to find itself overworked for we could not think of sending away our visitors without a meal, and it was not unusual after a few days to have three or four meals cooked one after another without any interruption to provide a long succession of breakfasts beginning at ten and ending at two or even later. Evidently our visitors soon realised this, for soon afterwards we began to get by the morning's post a short note intimating that a party of friends would be visiting us in the forenoon or the afternoon and that we should not order any meals at all! For on top of the four wheelers that used to bring the pilgrims would be huge *degs* or vats containing curries and pilaff and sweet rice and the local bakeries had already been asked to supply 'hot from the oven' the *Sheermals* or milk-bread for which Qutub Sahib had still a great reputation. Thus it turned out that our hermitage was even more crowded than our houses at Delhi where at all times of the day, and almost of the night as well, we used to have a succession of visitors. The study of the Holy Book had certainly commenced and for the first two hours or so of the morning when the 'pilgrims' would be starting or be still on the road we had leisure enough; but there was none after that, even though our mother had insisted on sharing our exile in order, as she tried to justify her unbending resolve to save us from 'unwelcome intruders'. The Government had perhaps also had time to realise that we might just as well have been left at Delhi, for just when we were looking out for another house to which to shift after our first month of internment, came an order warning us to be ready within a few hours to proceed to an unknown destination with an escort of Delhi Police.

## EXILE

We had hardly done packing a few things for the mysterious journey when a European Police officer motored up with his men with a view to escort us to the confines of the small Imperial Enclave. Curiously enough, the officer was no other than the one who had received, as the captain of his Police Team, the Winner's Cup in the Hockey Tournament which those who had presented it had requested my brother Shaukat as the doyen of sportsmen to hand over to the winners. Of course, he had made the customary little speech, closing with the usual homily to 'play the game' in life as well as in sport, and I recall that on this occasion the Police officer was as sporting as he could well be in the circumstances and showed the same spirit, in his profession as he had done in his play. Delhi had bade us farewell a month previously in her thousands whose strong feelings could with difficulty be restrained. But the parting from little Mehrauli was no less affecting. We had gone to the little 'Aulia Masjid' and offered our *dugana* of prayers and then returned to the *Dargah* through the bazaar where all the shopkeepers were anxious to offer us some mark or other of their affection and sympathy. At the *Dargah* itself the *Mujawirs* or attendants, who, as is usual in places of pilgrimage, were noted for their pressing attentions with a view to secure the largest offering that they could manage to squeeze, had long before this ceased to worry us and in fact used to press us very often to have tea and the small cakes associated with the Saint to whom they had given the appellation of 'Kaki', were now in tears and could with difficulty be made to accept any offerings. They brought coloured turbans for us which were solemnly tied round our hats in front of the saint's tomb, and bade us a most affecting good-bye. But one incident of Mehrauli we can never forget. Soon after the receipt of the Government of India's orders regarding our transfer to another place and before the police escort arrived, we received a visit from the officer in charge of the Mehrauli Police Station who had only just come to hear of our expected departure for an unknown destination. Hitherto he had never visited us, after the initial visit he had paid us to make our acquaintance, and he now explained that he had purposely avoided us, because he had feared we would have suspected him of spying on us. And now he brought out a Colt's revolver and a purse containing Rs. 200 which he offered to us, remarking that neither this money nor the price he had paid for the revolver when he had bought it formed any part of his police earnings, legitimate or otherwise and with tears in his eyes he begged us to accept these which were all he had at the time out of the proceeds of his private property. We found it difficult to assure him that we had no need of any assistance as we had ample funds which in order to convince him we showed to him and that we placed our trust in Providence much more than in pistols and revolvers. Few incidents in our lives have touched us more deeply than this, and knowing the risks to which a recital of it would obviously expose him, I would not have dreamt of publishing it. But our young friend, who was of a princely family, has now found a better world than our own in which only the fear of God counts with mankind.

One of our greatest troubles on this occasion concerned mother's insistence on accompanying us, and it was with the greatest difficulty that we had succeeded at last in sending her to Delhi after convincing her of the futility of further stay with us when the Police officer who had brought the orders intimating our transfer could give her no assurance that the police escort would permit her to accompany us on our mysterious journey. Great indeed was our surprise when just as our motor car began to move to find another car puffing and snorting and tearing towards us at a pace that seemed impossible and was certainly very risky for a ramshackle thing like it. It stopped near our car and out of it came mother, who had on reaching Delhi managed to send a friend of ours who was our legal adviser to the Chief Commissioner to press him not to withhold his consent to her accompanying us. The Chief Commissioner had said that he had received no instructions on the subject, and could not prevent her following us; but, as for her accompanying us, he pointed out the obvious difficulty of making any arrangements for a *purdah* lady in the only car he had available which the Police escort must of course share with us. Perhaps he believed that this would be an insurmountable difficulty, and had not specified any other objection. But evidently he had reckoned without a woman who was as resolute as she was resourceful, and mother brushed aside his objection by saying that if the police did not mind her, she certainly would not mind them, most of whom would be younger than her own sons, and some perhaps young enough to be her grandchildren. The Chief Commissioner consented, but the odds were that she could not go more than a mile or two in the fastest of carriages before we were whisked off in the police car. The local car repairer had, however, this ramshackle affair in his shop and agreed to hire it out, but guaranteed nothing beyond that. In fact he seemed to be inclined to guarantee a breakdown or two before they had left Delhi half a dozen miles behind. Fortune, however, favours the brave, and mother won the esteem of our escort in reaching us just in the nick of time with the requisite permission from the Chief Commissioner which they found to be in order. Contrary to our expectation we were taken through Delhi itself to a small wayside station on the opposite bank of the river and there took the train which brought hundreds of Delhi men who had seen our car rush through Delhi and took the next train on the off chance of being able to see us. As soon as we had left the limits of the Imperial Enclave, the escorting officer served on us fresh orders which informed us that we were to proceed to

Lansdowne,[15] a small hill station not far from Mussoorie which had no civil population but quartered a garrison of 2/8th Gurkhas and 39th Garhwal Rifles. Additional restrictions were imposed on our freedom such as a censorship over our correspondence and stoppage of all writing for the press.

## END OF JOURNALISM

As a matter of fact about the same time the poor inoffensive *Hamdard* of the tone of which the Chief Commissioner himself had expressed warm approval some time ago, and which had never offended against the Press Act, was singled out for a unique pre-censorship. A highly paid Indian official, who was however entirely innocent of all knowledge of journalism, had been brought over from the Punjab to act as Censor and he had commenced his new career by rejecting such a large proportion of 'copy' that for two or three days no issue of the *Hamdard* could appear at all, and even after that when the Chief Commissioner had been appealed to by the sub-editors in charge, the daily issues contained several columns of blank space, in spite of the fact that much more 'copy' used to be submitted for approval every day than what would have sufficed for a single issue. Partly out of the chagrin and partly no doubt as a test, a rather smart leader-writer dished up an old nursery tale with some queer garniture and submitted it as the next day's leader. When he laughingly pointed out to the Censor that it was the old nursery story with which he must have been familiar from his childhood, the poor man said, 'Yes, I know, but my dear man, I don't know what subtle poison you fellows may have squirted into it, and nursery tales or no nursery tales, I cannot afford to take any risks.' After this naive confession they knew that it was a hopeless task and they confessed to me subsequently that they had never felt so miserable as during the period of that censorship, when an hour's hard squeezing of unresponding brains would not yield a single 'par'. As I have stated once the unfamiliar script was no longer there to act as a damper, the people's enthusiasm for the *Hamdard* began to express itself daily in large increases of circulation and the three machines we had purchased for lithographing it, could with difficulty suffice even when

[15] The Ali brothers were asked to proceed to Lansdowne on 23 June 1915. In his letter to Malcolm Hailey on 15 July 1915, Mohamed Ali protested 'against punishment without even the form of trial and, in fact, punishment without the specification of any offence and without having been given the opportunity of explaining away any circumstances that may have prejudiced you against me'.

worked constantly. That difficulty increased when after the forfeiture of security of the old press, a new press had to be set up and we had a smaller number of machines to work with, though of a larger size. But we had turned round the corner financially, and could afford to purchase more machines, and I was enabled to recoup some of my losses of the terrible days of typography and hoped in another year or two to see a balance sheet that would not send shudders through my frame, but produce quite a different sensation. However that was not to be and after reducing the profits on the monthly sales to zero, and then fast approaching the Figure of earlier losses, I decided to 'Shut up shop'. After all the earlier losses were incurred, we offered to the readers, even though several thousand less, something worth reading. But now there was little worth reading in the *Hamdard,* and in fact little to read at all.

## 'INTERNMENT FINANCE'

Unlike Regulation III of 1918 which made it a statutory requirement to pay to a person on whose liberty restrictions were imposed by the Executive an allowance for himself and his family suitable for a man of his rank, and position, the Defence of India Act had left the detenus entirely unprovided for and both my brother and I had asked for the grant of internment allowance when we were first interned, because on principle we thought it unfair to restrict a man's liberty for any reason short of a proved crime, and not compensate him for any consequent loss of income and at any rate a loss of the means of subsistence as had actually occurred in some cases within our knowledge, when we ourselves offered to relieve some of these fellow-sufferers.[16] But our requests were repeatedly 'turned down' and we had finally given up asking for it. Now, however, the Government came forward, presumably knowing what was soon to follow, with the offer of allowances, which nevertheless were so meagre that the amount fixed for the subsistence of us two and of our families hardly exceeded half the salary of the Censor imported from the Punjab. We were each allowed Rs. 250 a month which comes to less than £ 4 a week that I used to pay to my London typist.[17] As my brother had been anxious

[16] See Mohamed Ali to Malcolm Hailey, 18 and 24 May 1915, in Hasan (ed.), *Mohamed Ali in Indian Politics*, vol. 1, pp. 203–7.

[17] See Mohamed Ali to Ramsay Macdonald, 18 February 1916, in Hasan (ed.), ibid., pp. 227–35. But the letter was not sent. According to an official, 'the letter is interesting—and the writer's atmosphere of the gentle martyr quite amusing, but I certainly agree that it should not be sent to its destination'.

to retire from the public service on any condition, he had readily accepted the small pension offered to him by the Secretary of State as a special case because it was too early yet for him to retire and in fact no pension could be granted under the existing rules. However, since the department was being subjected to sweeping reductions, on account of the agreement with China in 1910 which had doomed the Opium Revenue, and the senior most men were being compulsorily retired on pensions, the Secretary of State had jumped at the offer of a comparatively junior man to retire voluntarily and had driven a good bargain with him. The amount of that pension, meagre as it was, was now deducted from the meagre subsistence allowance, and my brother was granted the magnificent sum of £1–10–0 a week for himself and his family. My brother on retirement from office had established a cotton ginning factory and press at Rampur at the cost of some 1,50,000 rupees, selecting this form of enterprise purposely as it needed his attention only during the cotton season, and let the greater part of the year to him to do his public work as the Secretary and moving spirit of the Servants of Kaaba Society. As for myself the *Hamdard* was enough to provide for my needs and for those of my family. The refusal of Government at first to give any allowance and now their meagreness had no terrors for us at the time. But soon after the *Hamdard* had to close its doors. And my brother also found that unless he could buy and sell cotton himself at and near Rampur it was not possible to establish a new market for that commodity and give a start to a new factory, and this he could not do unless he was free to move about and finance such operations and in fact be on the spot. Consequently before many months were over we had to depend upon such subsistence allowances as Government had granted and it was just as well that my brother had not refused the hundred rupees a month that he had got as the price of his liberty,[18] though in any case we could not make the two ends meet without other resources. Bit by bit we sold off all our landed property of which our mother would not sell an acre during our minority, and we now recalled the grim humour of the contrast that the property earned by the grandfather for assisting the

[18] The Ali brothers were at first given an allowance of Rs. 250. In 1916, Mohamed Ali asked for an increase. On 10 August 1917, Shaukat Ali represented that owing to internment he and his brother had sustained severe business losses, and on 5 December 1917 he wrote again on this point and also on the inadequacy of the subsistence allowance. On 12 January 1918, however, they were told that government could not accept responsibility for business. But the Ali brothers continued to complain of their financial difficulties and the growing needs of their families. On 10 January 1918, the government agreed to an enhanced allowance of Rs. 450 to Mohamed Ali and Rs. 350 to Shaukat Ali.

British during the disastrous days of the Mutiny was lost by the grandsons sixty years later, when they were made 'prisoners of peace', presumably to prevent their assisting the enemies of British.

## PEACE AT LAST

But in spite of the turmoil of war with which the rest of the world was resounding, we found in our deserted hill where a garrison used to be quartered, a 'peace that passes understanding', and we were content with our losses whether of liberty or otherwise, because they brought us the leisure that we needed for a study of our faith. When war that brought all the trouble on us was about to be declared on Turkey, my wife had suddenly been taken ill and an unsuspected heart trouble made her condition so critical that from the very first moment that medical aid had been called, it was not considered possible to leave her for a minute without a doctor in attendance. For three whole nights and the intervening days she had been unconscious and her life hung from a slender thread. But as she had not shown the slightest symptom of improvement, despair had begun to settle down on all, and noticing my own condition the doctors on the third night had insisted on my entire exclusion from the sick chamber to offer me a little change from my restless condition. As the night wore away and the dawn began to streak the East with the first faint glimmer, my mother who had sat up with the doctor and the nurses asked the doctor if I could not now be asked to come down, to have a last look at my dying wife, and realising the hopelessness of the situation he consented. Curiously enough before I had been many minutes in the sick room she stirred and was helped by the doctor to sit up in the bed to ease her breathing, when she began to regain consciousness and for the first time since she had had the attack, recognised my friend the doctor and blushingly expressed her astonishment in finding herself in his arms. Her recovery was a very slow affair, but thank God, the crisis was over and had passed away as unexpectedly as it had come and her life was thenceforward no longer in danger. An hour or two later I was rung up by a member of the Government of India with whom I had for years had the most intimate relations and he asked me about the condition of my wife. When I communicated my happy news to him, he said he had some painful news to communicate, which, however, he had obtained the viceroy's consent to withhold for a day or two if things did not improve with regard to the health of my wife. And he told me that the security of my press was to be declared forfeited, which he knew meant the closure of my press and perhaps the end of my career as a journalist altogether. In all conscience his news was bad enough, but with the glad tidings that my eyes had communicated to me when my wife woke up to receive a shock to her modesty in finding herself in the arms of my friend the doctor, who cared for the Press Act and its forfeiture of securities, for the closure of printing presses and the end of journalistic careers. All that I knew at the time was that I had found a wife that I had all but lost. And now when some eight months later I found myself in a deserted garrison station on a remote hill without friends and companions, without the daily work of my profession, and the wages that it brought me, with my letters to my wife and her letters to me passing through the hands of a stranger and a foreigner and undergoing his scrutiny, I could after reading the Quran in the undisturbed calm of my sequestered retreat, truly say that a compensating Providence had seen to it that in losing almost all else I should at long last find life rich in content and purposeful, the real thing for the first time and no sham or simulacrum.

## OUR FRIENDS

Lansdowne was not only off the beaten track, inaccessible like most hill-stations by railway and connected with a small branch line which terminated some 25 miles away from it at the foot of the hills, but had no civil population at all. And when we were removed to it, even the military were conspicuous by their absence in Europe. Only skeleton depots were kept for purposes of receiving back the wholly disabled from the war, and arranging for the pensions, and enlisting fresh recruits to fill the terrible gaps, and hurriedly training them to become cannon fodder, in their turn. The officers' bungalows were with the exception of ten or a dozen all untenanted and one of these just above the mess of the 2/8th Gurkhas and the Brigade Office had been rented for us by Government, from the widow of a Captain, who had gone back to England. In the barracks of the soldiers were to be found the remnants of these brave battalions of Gurkhas and Garhwalis that had been so mercilessly mown down by the German guns in Flanders and France. Battered and broken men that had once been so agile and were the best of hill-climbers crawled round on the roads. Their ranks were from time to time strengthened by the arrival of fresh apple-cheeked boys enlisted from their homes in far off Nepal, innocent of all clothing except a blanket wrapped round their sturdy young limbs and gaily chattering away like monkeys unconscious perhaps of the doom that awaited them within the next half year. The enlistment in the Garhwal regiment being local was more gradual and not so noticeable. This was, so to speak, a migratory population; but there was besides it another that was almost permanent. These were the women in the married quarters wistfully and often alas vainly looking forward to meeting their husbands and sons on their return. All, indeed, were not grass-widows, for in a very large number of cases these women had nothing to look forward to, except their repatriation in Nepal as the widows of their brave sons who had died in a foreign land, fighting for a foreigner. Autocratic as the East may often be in its governance, it is wonderfully democratic in its social life, and even more so among women than among men. Morning and evening our mother would go out with us in her *burqa* or veiled cloak walking astonishingly long distances for one of her age, and more than age, her sorrows. The strange sight of two men and a boy—my brother's eldest son—not obviously 'Sahibs' and yet very different from the only Indians whom they used to see, the babus or clerks in the Military offices, the Sahib's servants and the few shop-keepers, men with their own complexions but dressed like 'Sahibs' and carrying themselves every whit as if they were 'Sahibs', and that strange apparition of a person in snow white cloak, thickly veiled and slightly bent soon attracted notice. And when mother occasionally lifted her veil when there was no man to be seen on the road and past the men's barracks, and the Gurkha women saw that it was one of their own sex, they were not in the least bit shy, and in spite of an almost complete ignorance of any Indian vernacular they insisted on being visited by her and would clap their hands and beckon to her. How they managed to communicate with her is still a mystery to us; but this much is certain that before we had been a week, intimate social relations had been established between mother and these Gurkha ladies. And when a month or two later my wife and daughters paid us a flying visit, the little ones attracted to our house quite a host of Gurkha girls who would come and dance and sing so beautifully. The local bazaar did not provide a great variety of things with which we could refresh these vigorous little dancers, but walnuts which grew in the hills in abundance were to be had at eight for a pice (or farthing), we could well afford to keep all our coat pockets well filled with them for free distribution during our walks among our numerous little friends in Lansdowne. We did not visit the soldiers, the strange combination of disabled veterans and raw recruits, in the barracks, and an occasional chat with a half-crippled warrior on the road about his wounds and the nature of the fighting in France and Belgium was the limit of our intercourse with them. But we had not long to wait to discover that they were attracted to us and felt a sympathy for us, even though their knowledge of our troubles could not exactly be said to be accurate. For very early after our arrival at Lansdowne, and perhaps the very next day, when out walking in the evening, we were overtaken by a dense mist which began to blot out the outlines of the surrounding hills and made our return to the house we occupied not without some risk for our mother. A Gurkha with a lantern happening to come on the scene, we asked him which way he was going, in the hope that perhaps he may not be greatly inconvenienced if he consented to show us the way. Our astonishment was great when he cheerfully replied that it was all right as he was going to a place very near our house and would see us home. We asked him how he knew where we lived, in answer to which he astonished us all the more by telling us that he knew we occupied 'Kaptan Ishtack's' bungalow and that he was well aware we were Princes ruling over a State from which the English had removed us and hopefully added: 'But, it will soon be all right. You will soon be victorious and get back your raj!' After this if we had extended our friendships from the little Gurkha children to their fathers as well, we would have been perhaps suspected of seducing the soldiers from their allegiance. However our intercourse with them did not go beyond an occasional roadside meeting, and their inviting us and our own children along with their British depot officers, when they celebrated the Dussehra festival.

## FROM GARHWAL TO GONDWANA

But there was a class of people whom we were actually suspected of corrupting, and these were the Musalman servants of the few remaining officers. They used to see us every Friday at the Service in the mosque and had evidently come to know all about us before we had been a fortnight at Lansdowne. Learning that we were among the founders of the 'Servants of Kaaba' Society and that my brother was its Secretary, they began to come to us for enlistment as members, and although my brother had never dreamed of conducting any propaganda in such a place he could not, of course, refuse to enlist such men as came of their own accord to be enrolled as 'Servants of Kaaba', and to obtain, the familiar little badge of the 'Servants', which they openly wore on all occasions. Lord Meston seemed to have been greatly perturbed at this and had orders served on us to desist from such conduct; but my brother wrote back that although he had not made any efforts to enlist such Musalmans as there were in the place, he could not refuse those who offered themselves for enlistment, and since it was a purely religious matter he could not even give an assurance that he would not conduct a propaganda for the purpose if he felt inclined to do so. There was no further development, for this was just towards the end of our stay at this beautiful quiet hill-station, the approach of winter making it necessary for Government to transfer us to the plains, the warmer provinces. 'The world was all before them where to choose our place of rest', and this time they hit upon Chhindwara in the Central Provinces.[19] Being situated on the Satpura Plateau, 2,300 feet above the sea level and surrounded by large forest tracts, it had an excellent climate all round the year and was an ideal place from the point of view of the Government as well. It was, before we came, a dead-and-alive little place without any taint of politics and free from all religious fervour, and though served by a small metre-gauge branch line, was so remote from every place, and sequestered in such a backwoods of Gondwana—the country of the aboriginal Gonds[20]—that few visitors from the outside too could be expected, specially as now additional restrictions were imposed on our freedom even in the matter of receiving visitors. But whether it did or did not suit an over-anxious Government, or furtive political propagandists whose hearts were set on lighting a fiery cross in India, it was, like Lansdowne, the exact spot on earth to which two men anxious to explore the mysteries of their faith and in search of a sylvan solitude could have if they had the freest of free choices betaken themselves. Both at Lansdowne where we stayed only five months of the summer and autumn, and at Chhindwara where we passed three and a half years we had enough leisure and undisturbed peace and quiet to read the Quran and thoroughly soak ourselves in that perennial fountain of Truth that the gathering dust of thirteen centuries has not been able to choke or dry.

[19] The Ali brothers arrived in Chhindwara on 25 November.

[20] The Gonds form the largest tribe of Madhya Pradesh, being concentrated in Chhindwara, Betul, Seoni and Mandla districts. According to the Census of 1921, they were at one time a dominant race in this part of India and the name Gondwana—sometimes given to portions of this state, is derived from them.

IV

# The Discovery

## READING THE QURAN THROUGH

FOR THE FIRST TIME in my life I read it through in an intelligent and comprehending manner. Neither my brother nor I had been able to acquire any real proficiency in Arabic, for we had both commenced our study of it in a school where it was only the 'Second Language'. But the late Maulvi Nazir Ahmad, an excellent scholar of Arabic, the recipient of an Honorary Degree of Doctor of the University of Edinburgh, who was besides a master of the vigorous Urdu idiom of Delhi, which had served him so well as one of the translators of the Indian Penal Code into Urdu, had utilised his leisure on retirement from Public Service to translate the Quran into Urdu. Whatever his own convictions, he had, unlike his friend Sir Syed Ahmad Khan, done nothing to offend the most rigid orthodoxy in translating the Quran, while some of his marginal explanatory notes were the despair of the rationalist. But he had made an entirely new departure in not being so literal as to offend against the Urdu idiom and for the first time Indian Musalmans had a translation which was not only readable, but a pleasure to read, except for an occasional colloquialism hardly in keeping with Divine Scripture. As I have mentioned before, this translation had soon achieved popularity and it was this which had been sent to me to Oxford at my request. It was with the help of this that both my brother and I commenced our first regular study of the Quran and the amount of Arabic we knew was enough to make our daily readings of absorbing interest.

## REVELATION PIECEMEAL

This wonderful book is full of repetitions in spite of being but a small volume, abrupt in its transitions from topic to topic, and I can well understand that Europeans who read it in translations, more or less out of curiosity and are able to go through it in a few days, so often pronounce it to be incoherent and disjointed. But they do not realise that it was not revealed as a complete volume all at once, but piecemeal and in the course of no less than twenty three years of the Prophet's mission. Moreover, they do not realise that even God's Word, when it appears in human language, has to take on the characteristics of the particular language in which it makes its appearance and those who are familiar with the Arabic language and Arab literature know that jerkiness is characteristic of both. In fact it is characteristic of the very mentality of the people whose thought flits from topic to topic with breathless rapidity. Ideas do not continue to glow with a steady light but seem to flash dazzlingly, as it were, through the gloom from time to time. Even in long poems, the same idea hardly runs through more than a few couplets and this peculiarity has made the *ghazal* the favourite metric form in which the metre and the rhyme in the first and second verses and then only in the even verses, 4th, 6th, 8th, and so on are the only marks of continuity, while the topic of each couplet is distinct and unconnected with the rest. Apart from this jerky abruptness characteristic of all Arabic literature, for each fragment of the Quran that was revealed from time to time, the circumstance in which it was revealed, and which in fact necessitated the revelation, supplied a relevance and a context, which are not to be found in the text itself. Moreover, it was not a Book that was meant to be read as most Europeans read it today, sitting comfortably in an arm-chair with their critical faculties specially stimulated, ready to carp and cavil on the least provocation, not altogether unlike a porcupine bristling with quills. It was not revealed for the Arabs as 'literature' designed only to please, though it was admitted by the most inveterate enemies of the Prophet to be superior to any existing literature in the language of which they were so proud that they called the rest of mankind that did not speak it 'Ajami' or dumb. The Quranic revelations made the poetic competitions at the fairs of Ukaz and Majannah a mockery by comparison and the Seven Hanging or Golden Poems suspended in the Holy of Holies, the Kaaba, were removed after the Quran had struck the Arab poets dumb with admiration, and to this day it is acknowledged by Arabic speaking Christian[s] and Jew[s] as well as Muslim[s] as the standard of literary expression. And yet, as I have said, it was not its literary excellence that had the chief significance for those for whom it was revealed in this fragmentary fashion. To them it was Holy Writ, God's Commandment, the Law and the Ethics according to which they had to shape their lives, and a score of years was none too long a time in which they had to learn the lessons it had come to teach them. Our little boys in India memorise the whole book in a few years even though they do not understand a word of Arabic. The Arabs had prodigious memories and the manner in which a large body of ancient Arabic poetry and the genealogy and the traditions of the race had been preserved in an age that was practically innocent of all knowledge of the art of writing bear ample testimony to it. And yet such a devoted Muslim as Umar, the faithful companion of the Prophet,[1] who became his second Khalifa or successor, took no less than eight years to memorise the second Chapter alone. This was because the first Muslims fully understood that it was no use carrying any part of the Quran in their heads unless they could carry it in their hearts as well, and translate it into action in their everyday life.

In fact there are several passages in the Quran which explain why the revelation was so gradual:

And certainly we have repeated (warnings or arguments) in this Quran that they may mind. (17:41)

> And with truth did We send it down
> And with truth has it descended,
> And We have not sent thee but as a herald
> Of glad tidings and a warner. (17:105)[2]

And it is a Quran that we have parcelled out that thou mightest recite (or proclaim, *qara* the same as in Hebrew) unto men by slow degrees and we have sent it down piecemeal (as occasion required). (17:106)

And those that disbelieve say, 'Why hath not the Quran been sent down all at once? 'Thus that we may establish thy heart with it, and we have arranged its revelation piecemeal. (25:32)[3]

For the unbelievers the warnings as well as the arguments were repeated day after day, and through logic, parable and history every facet of the great eternal Truth was presented before their eyes. For the Muslims the fragments that were revealed from time to time were so many messages from their Maker who was watching their daily and hourly growth with more loving care and vigilance than the most anxious parent and helped them every now and then with a word of courage or of caution. His Commandments were not promulgated in the humdrum manner of the laws enacted by human legislators, indifferently received by those that were required to obey them. They descended as occasion required on a people waiting and watching anxiously to conform to them.

[1] Umar Ibn al-Khattab, the second Khalifa. He was converted to Islam in his twenty-sixth year, four years after the Hijra. While the Sunnis revere him as one of the most typical models of all the virtues of Islam, the Shias do not conceal their antipathy to him for thwarting the claims of Ali.

[2] See A.J. Arberry, *The Koran Interpreted*, vol. 1, pp. 314–15.

[3] Ibid., vol. 2, p. 59.

And on His side the ever-vigilant God too, who knew how weak after all was the human creature He had made, did not demand impossibilities from these first believers who had just been weaned off from heathenism with its lax morals. 'Allah casts not on a soul, a heavier load than it can lift' and 'the religion of Allah is easy'. In their probation, the Companions were by degrees habituated to the austere life that Islam with all its abhorrence of anchoritism, expects a Muslim to live. When a visitor, who found that the arrangement of the Quran did not correspond to the chronological order of the revelation of its fragments and after satisfying himself by comparing his own with Aisha's[4] copy that the Prophet himself had so arranged in response to divine commandments, asked her the reason for this, she readily explained that in the beginning the unbelievers were invited only to accept the existence and the unity of Allah and understand His divine attributes, for who would have joined the ranks of the Believers if all the religious duties had been imposed on the neophyte and strict account demanded of his conduct from the very first. It was only gradually that the Muslims were prepared for serving Allah's cause and detached from the evil courses that they had until then been following. But to later generations, most of them born Muslims, the proper order was duties first and an understanding of Allah's essence and attributes as the child grew into the man.

When the commandments were being revealed piecemeal they were engraved, as it were, on the tablets of the Muslims' memories because of the incidents connected with their revelation. A blind man pleads his disability when all Muslims were called upon to bear arms in defence of their faith; a group of men through sheer procrastination tarried behind so long, when the Prophet marched out with the Muslims on an expedition, that they could not catch him up, and became defaulters in their duty as Muslims; or a woman states before the Prophet the pitiable case of her daughters whom Arab custom had totally disinherited while distant relations were succeeding to the estate of their deceased father; or may be her own no less pitiable case when in a fit of anger her irascible old husband with whom she bore up unselfishly partly for his own sake and partly for little children, had used words which according to Arab custom had the effect of a declaration of permanent separation not amounting to divorce. Hostile critics have characterised this as hand-to-mouth legislation; but they have wholly missed the object which would have been defeated if an

[4] She was born at Mecca 8 or 9 years before the Hijra. She was the daughter of Abu Bakr, the first Khalifa, and the favourite wife of the Prophet.

artificial code of laws, like the 'Priestly Code' promulgated after the Babylonian exile by Ezra[5] among the Jews had descended all at once upon the Arabs, many of them uncouth warriors or worse still barbarian nomads of the desert. A Pallas Athene rising ready armed from the head of Zeus[6] would have altogether bewildered such worshippers. Finally, for the Prophet himself, these revelations coming as they did from time to time, provided a Prophet's sustenance, the spiritual food that strengthened his heart and supplied the necessary stimulus throughout a long and arduous mission. And this piecemeal revelation fully served its three-fold purpose. At the most trying moments in his Prophetic career it comforted and consoled him, and at no time did it take on a surer tone in predicting ultimate triumph than when to all outward appearances the Prophet's condition was hopeless. As for the Infidels, unrelaxing repetition and reiteration wore down their prejudice and hostility and truth at last triumphed and falsehood finally vanished from Arabia.

## THE SPEARHEAD OF ISLAM

As for the Believers, whether Arabs like Abu Bakr,[7] Usman[8] or Ali,[9] from the Quraysh of Mecca, or the two Sads from the Ansar of Medina,[10] of the Tribes of Aus and Khazraj, or Ethiopian slaves like Bilal,[11] the *muezzin* of Islam, or Ajamis like Salman,[12] the Persian, Greek slaves like Suhayl, they formed like the Israelites, but without their exclusiveness, a 'Servant People', whom the Lord had chosen to propagate the last of His Gospels. They constituted, so to speak, the spearhead of Islam, and history bears

[5] The Jewish priest and scribe, who played a central part in the reform of Judaism in the fifth or fourth century B.C.

[6] In Greek mythology, the supreme god, equivalent to Jupiter. He is usually depicted with thunderbolt and eagle, and associated with the oak-tree.

[7] He was the first Khalifa. He was chosen by the Prophet to accompany him when he emigrated from Mecca. He was proposed as Khalifa after the death of the Prophet on 8 June 632. He died on 23 August 634.

[8] The third Khalifa (644–55); belonged to the great Meccan family of Banu Umayya. He was appointed Khalifa by a *shura* (council). He was assassinated in June 656.

[9] He was the son of Abu Talib, cousin and the son-in-law of the Prophet and the fourth orthodox Khalifa.

[10] For details, see *Shorter Encyclopaedia of Islam* (Leiden: E.J. Brill, 1974), pp. 482–3.

[11] A slave of Abyssinian origin. He accompanied the Prophet on all his campaigns. He died about the age of 60, in Damascus and was buried there.

[12] Salman al-Farisi was a close companion of the Prophet. His name is associated with the siege of Medina by the Meccans for it was he who on this occasion advised the digging of the ditch by which the Muslims defended themselves from the enemy.

ample testimony to the fact that the penetration of the spear was instantaneous. The 'Flaming Onset' of Islam has had no parallel in the record of human progress. Even those who affect to minimise the value and misunderstand the real significance of this rapid success by asserting that it was only the success of the sword, have got to answer the searching question, 'What was it that gave to that sword so keen an edge?' But fortunately we have the most copious records of the lives of the 'Companions' for our 'Acts of the Apostles', and these 'Acts' are no idealised version of a Luke but plain, unvarnished history. For the purposes of scrutinising and authenticating the Traditions of the Prophet, which constitute after the Quran the most important basis of Muslim Law, Civil as well as Canon, a Science of 'National Biography', so to speak, came into being and the huge corpus that includes the biographical notices of no less than 1,300 'Companions' which resulted from the loving labour of succeeding generations, shows us, as nothing else can, what a revolution in moral and manners, and in fact in all departments of that complex synthesis we call Life, had been brought about by the teaching of the 'most successful Prophet'.[13] To deal only with one aspect of it, and by a no means unimportant aspect, for 'greater thing can no man do than lay down his life for his friends', when the first call to arms was sounded to meet at Badr[14] the Quraysh assailants who would not leave in peace even at Medina refugees whom they had driven out from Mecca after thirteen years of the most cruel and ceaseless persecution, and the Prophet was anxious to learn what response would be made to such a trying call, Miqdad gave expression to the sentiment of the 'Servant People' that the Lord had chosen for His service and said, 'O Prophet of God! we are not like unto the Israelites who said to Moses, when he wanted them to march onward to the conquest of the Promised Land, "Go thou and thy Lord and fight; we sit here"'. And when in the following year the Meccans returned to avenge the defeat at Badr[15] and the Prophet was encompassed on all sides by assailants at Uhud where victory had, through the indiscipline of a few Muslim archers, been turned almost into defeat, it was not only men that sacrificed their own lives to save his but women also rushed into the breach at the imminent risk of death.[16] There was none to deny him in

[13] To quote the exact words of Professor Noldeke, 'that most successful of all Prophets and religious personalities' (*Encyclopaedia Britannica* XV, p. 898, 11th edn.).

[14] Badr, or Badr Hunayan, a small town south-west of Medina. Here occurred on 17 Ramazan, 2 A.H. or 17 March 624, the first great battle of the Prophet of Islam.

[15] Site of the Prophet's first encounter with the Meccans.

[16] For a brief description of the Battle of Uhud, see *Shorter Enclyclopaedia of Islam*, p. 400.

the hour of peril three times before cock-crow. It was on this firm rock that the Church of Islam was first erected, and if it has endured through so many and such strange vicissitudes, it was because truth had trickled down on the early Muslims drop by drop and soaked them through and through. Throughout the day the 'Companions' used to be in attendance on him, some to jot down on paper and skins, on tablets and bones and palm branches shorn of leaves, the Word of God as the official scribes of the 'Illiterate Prophet' the moment he recovered from the trance-like condition in which he used to receive the revelation, and others to memorise it for their own use both as lessons for their lives and for liturgical purposes. Those whom business did not permit to be in attendance every day and who did not lead the ascetic lives of the 'Companions of the Suffa (or Platform)', which enabled them with help of the ever-ready hospitality of their co-religionists to remain constantly within the mosque of the Prophet, paired with others and thus arranged with them to be in attendance by turns. Thus not a syllable of Holy Writ was lost or confounded with human utterance and the chief topic of conversation among the thousands at Medina used to be the day's revelation, which, along with the explanatory comments of the Prophet, were treasured in the most retentive of memories. They loved to read and to recite over and over again the portions of the Quran already revealed and men like Abdullah, the son of Amr bin al-Aas,[17] Conqueror of Egypt, would go through the whole of it in the course of each day and not be content with it. But the Prophet, knowing the divine purpose, insisted on a less rapid reading so that what was read could be easily assimilated. It was this kind of teaching which produced the first evangelists of Islam, men of whom the Quran only too truly says:

Ye are the best community that hath been raised up unto mankind. Ye enjoin the right and ye forbid the wrong and ye believe in Allah. (3:109)

But when they had won divine approval by the 'Pledge under the Tree', in the great crisis of the Hudaibiya[18] pilgrimage and had sworn, whilst themselves almost unarmed, to avenge the rumoured death of their envoy, Usman, regardless of the tremendous odds against them which could not be contemplated but with utter hopelessness, the Quran also describes how gradual was the growth of such valiant

[17] One of the most wily politicians of his time, his fame rests on his conquest of Egypt. In 640, the Greeks were defeated; in 641 Babylon was occupied by the Arabs; in 642 Alexandria lay in their power. He founded Fustat, which was later called Misr and in the tenth century al-Kahira.

[18] About 7 miles from Mecca. The Prophet collected his followers at the sacred tree of Hudaibiya and demanded the oath of fealty from them.

and noble characters. Citing earlier scriptures it compares these men to 'the seedling that putteth forth its sprout, then strengtheneth it so it groweth stout, then straighteneth itself upon its stem, rejoicing the husbandman that He may enrage the unbelievers through them'. (48:29)

## OUR DAILY READINGS

When we commenced our study of the Quran, we wisely decided to read only a little everyday, so that it took us no less than eight or nine months to finish our first reading of it, and although I am now able to obtain equal pleasure in reading four or five times as much in the same space of time, I still prefer to keep up the old rate of progress and to supplement the knowledge I have already acquired with additional information to be obtained from commentaries. In reading so little everyday the repetitions do not produce the same effect as they are apt to do if one reads the whole book, say, in seven days which many Muslims do to this day, and in still less time as is customary with them, when they fast in the month of Ramazan, and no part of the freshness of the Quran is thus lost. A classic has been well described as literature which reveals a fresh charm every time it is read and one is never tired of reverting to it. Judged by this standard the Quran is the greatest classic for the charms it reveals seem to be inexhaustible. How often have we not felt as if the passages we happened to he reading on a particular day were revealed only that instant in response to our own prayer or to settle some point about which we happened to be undecided and uneasy. My brother would call out to me from his room and recite to me a verse, or I would do the same to him pointing out how apposite it was to the question we happened to be debating only a little before. And these 'coincidences' were of such frequent occurrence that by degrees a habit of expectancy was formed, and we began to expect all unconsciously a response from the day's reading of the Quran to unexpressed references to Heaven!

## FRESHNESS OF THE QURAN

This never-fading freshness of the Quran and its responsiveness was illustrated on a historic occasion more than thirteen centuries ago. At the battle of Uhud, the death of the Muslim standard-bearer Musab bin Umayr,[19] that miraculously successful missionary of Islam who had brought about the first conversions at Medina and had thus paved the way

[19] He belonged to one of the Quraish (Kurayash) families. He met his death at the battle of Uhud.

for the famous migration [*hijrat*] from which Islam commences its new era, led his Meccan assailant to proclaim that he had killed the Prophet, for Musab resembled his great Chief. This caused such a consternation in Muslim ranks that some of the bravest fled from the field of battle, and even of those that remained, some like the stout-hearted Umar, threw down their arms in despair and disgust with life and awaited the end. It was only when another Muslim who learnt the cause of this change in the attitude of Umar, and said that if the Prophet had died fighting, it befitted them to do the same and avenge his death before they died, that fighting was resumed by the Muslims and their new resolve was rewarded by seeing the Prophet alive though wounded and encompassed all round by relentless assailants. When the great crisis was over, and the Meccans, content with saving their face after the previous year's defeat at Badr and escaping another disaster almost after the eleventh hour, had hastily retreated homewards, and the Prophet had returned from the expedition on which he had proceeded on the following day to meet the Quraysh again outside Medina, if they thought they had broken down the strength of the Muslims, some sixty verses of the Quran were revealed. The incidents of the great battle were reviewed, and those Muslim archers were rebuked who had disobeyed the Prophet and leaving the opening in the mountain at the back of the Muslim force unguarded, had joined in the plunder of the defeated enemy, thus enabling the brilliant Khalid,[20] to seize the unexpected opportunity and all but turn the tables on the victors. Those Muslims also came in for mild rebuke who had given up the fight when they were led to believe that their chief had been killed. These verses constitute one of the most moving and impressive portions of the Quran, and the lesson they taught was never forgotten. And yet, when seven years later the Prophet lay dead in the lap of his beloved wife, Aisha, the news of his death produced such a consternation among his devoted followers that they expected the heavens to burst open and the earth to cleave asunder and wondered how long it would be for the end of the world to come. The loving Umar was entirely besides himself and so hateful to him was the very idea of the passing away of the Prophet that he could not bear to hear of it and his irrepressible emotions led him to unsheathe his sword and to proclaim that he would make of him a dead man then and there who dared to say that the Prophet was dead. It was on a scene of such

[20] He was an outstanding Muslim general. In the battle of Uhud, he commanded the right wing of the Meccan forces. His intervention decided the battle in favour of the enemies of the Prophet. As a reward the Prophet gave him the title of honour 'Sword of God'. He died in the year 641–2.

stormy emotions that the tender-hearted but ever tranquil Abu Bakr arrived from the suburb of Al-Suna where he lived. He went inside his daughter's chamber, kissed the cold brow of his Chief and his oldest friend, now in another world than his own, and resigning himself, as the Quran had declared of a Muslim, to the will of his Maker, he came out and asked Umar what all that meant. And when he learnt, what he could well believe, that the 'Companions' who had for half a life-time looked up to the Prophet for help in every difficulty, personal as well as public, and who could not conceive of an existence without that never-failing aid, refused to believe that this prop of their lives stood no more as it used to do, and that the Prophet was no longer among them, he said to the assembled crowd with that sureness of conviction that had won him the title of *Siddiq* or verifier:

> O Men! he who worshipped Muhammad, let him know that verily Muhammad has already passed away; but he who worshipped Allah, let him know that verily Allah is living and shall never die.

And then he recited one of the verses of the Quran revealed after the battle of Uhud:

> And Muhammad is no more than an Apostle; other apostles have already passed away before him; if he die, therefore, or be slain, will ye turn upon your heels? And he who turneth upon his heels shall not injure Allah in aught; and Allah will assuredly reward the grateful. (3:144)[21]

The authentic Tradition that pictures this momentous scene goes on to say that this allayed all doubts and fears, and a great tranquillity ensued. People who had constantly read and had repeatedly heard recited in prayers the verse that Abu Bakr so appositely quoted, and were thoroughly familiar with it, stated that when he recited it on this memorable occasion, it seemed as if it had just been revealed!

To us, therefore, who read such small portions of the Quran everyday, even when for the first time we had abundant leisure, it never seemed to lack freshness, and its repetitions and the variety of ways in which its main theme was presented to us day after day, as it had been presented to the Arabs thirteen centuries ago, only served to enable us to learn a much needed lesson that we were apt to forget and even ignore in the distractions of the world. Ever since, this book which so many European critics pronounce to be incoherent, disjointed and dull, has had the invariable effect of intoxicating us, with its simple grandeur, its intense directness and its incessant flow of motive power for the manifold activities of life.

[21] See Arberry, *The Koran Interpreted*, p. 91.

And long before I had read it through, Eureka! I had found a new meaning in life and in this world and an entirely new significance in Islam. I had been familiar enough with the main tenets of Islam; but they had been little more than a bundle of doctrines and commandments each for a particular department of life or situation, though, of course I had looked upon them as superior to the dogmas and ethical codes of other faiths. Now, however, they acquired a new coherence and, as it were, fell suddenly into place, creating an effect of unity such as I had never realised before. They were no longer a bundle of doctrines but a single divine Purpose running through all creation from the remote genesis of the world to the very minute of our present existence. But it was not a 'far off divine event', nor had we to wait for the Advent of a Messiah and the realisation of a millennium when God's kingdom was to come. It had *already* come. Nay, there never was a time when it was not there. *This* was God's Kingdom and *every* man was a 'Servant of the Lord' and His Anointed brought into the world for one human function—the service of his Maker and the fulfilment of His divine Purpose. Nothing stood apart; nothing was alien; nothing could exist for itself unrelated to others. The entire universe was one. The unity of the Creator postulated the unity of His Creation and all was one vast Theocracy with Allah for its King and Man for his earthly Vicegerent. Man made in the image of his Maker, was not the sport of chance and slave of destiny, but master of his fate. Of all His creatures in the world, we know Man alone had been endowed by the Creator with a will of his own, and was to that extent responsible for his actions and fit to be God's deputy or Agent on earth. But, nevertheless, man made a voluntary and complete surrender of himself and became the rightless slave of his Creator, or rejecting the purpose for which he was created, he chose to surrender himself to another Master than God, what the Quran calls *Taghoot*, or Satan, whether that other master was an earthly potentate, a father, mother, or wife, or one's own low desires. The keyword of the Quran was 'Serve' and while man was free to serve whom he would, his inborn inherent faith, the nature with which his Creator had endowed him at his creation told him that he was to serve none but the One God, the Creator, Sustainer, and Developer of all Creation, and this 'revelation' of his own soul supported by the testimony of all Nature was finally confirmed by the teaching of those whom God had given a more acute intuition, the Prophets on whom had descended a yet more impressive revelation than his own. Once he chose to serve none but God and surrendered himself wholly to his Maker, he could not accept for himself a position of inferiority to any other Creature of God. This rightless slave of Allah became free for ever and the equal of Kings and Emperors in the greatest of all Republics, and even superior to them if they presumed to resist the Will of God, when he had identified his own will with God's. Then as the Vicegerent of God he had the full force of the universe at his back, and had the entire Omnipotence of his Master, at his beck and call. He could now use it whenever, and wherever His Divine purpose necessitated its use though he was no more than a poor weak biped whenever his own will asserted itself in any other direction and was no longer in opposition to the Divine Will.

This was my unique discovery in that small volume revealed more than 1300 years ago to an Arab of the desert whose name I bore—unique to me even though thousands, tens of thousands and hundreds of thousands of other Columbuses had discovered the same New World in each succeeding generation, after the first revelation to the solitary worshipper in the cave of Hera one night towards the end of the month of Ramazan. Nay, the first revelation was in fact far earlier. It was in that infinitely earlier epoch that people call the Genesis when God revealed Himself to the first Man. If a savage, removed from some inaccessible recess of Australia or from the heart of the Dark Continent, who had known nothing beyond his own savage horizon, were to be placed all by himself in a boat, and it could drift on endlessly till at last it touched the shores of America, now surpassing in the maturity of its development even the most progressive regions of the Old World, would it not be to this savage rediscoverer of Columbus', find as New a world as ever it had been to Columbus himself four hundred years and more ago? Nay, on the contrary it would be even newer to him for while the civilised Spaniard had only discovered an almost empty Continent, our savage rediscoverer would discover it with the added richness of a civilisation in full bloom. His would be a double discovery, the discovery of a civilisation as well as that of a new Continent, and his astonishment and joy would be twofold. And such was mine. I had discovered God and in discovering Him and His message to mankind I had discovered myself. I had found a new meaning and a hitherto unrealised fullness in life contrasted with which my previous existence which I had thought to be crowded enough for a rather somnolent sub-continent of the East like India, appeared to be empty and barren.

But did I want this New World all to myself, to 'corner' it and make it my own particular perquisite and monopoly, a secret pleasure and joy which not a single soul should share with me or as much as dream of? No, a thousand times no, for however selfish I may still have been in other things—and I lay no claim to more than a very modest amount of altruism—the moment that this eternal Truth had dawned upon me in all its refulgence I was too full of it to keep it to myself, even if I could have desired it. I was literally bursting with my new discovery and felt impelled to shout it to all and sundry, to everyone at home, to the servants, to the passers-by on the road, to the very cats and dogs of the place and the trees and shrubs that covered the hill side. Years ago I had read the 'Preaching of Islam', a work of patient and industrious research by my old tutor at Aligarh, Sir Thomas Arnold. He introduces the theme on which he writes with a quotation from the lecture of Max Mueller[22] delivered in Westminster Abbey on the day of intercession for Missions in December 1873, in which Max Mueller distinguishes Missionary from non-Missionary religions and defines a missionary religion as one 'in which the spreading of truth and the conversion of unbelievers are raised to the rank of a sacred duty by the founder or his immediate successors'. He goes on to say, 'It is the spirit of truth in the hearts of believers, which cannot rest, unless it manifests itself in thought, word and deed, which is not satisfied till it has carried its message to every soul, till what is believed to be the truth is accepted by all members of the human family.' I remember that when I had first read this passage I had greatly admired the force and nobility of its restrained rhetoric. But now with my own individual experience of the explosive force of Truth it sounded so tame, and, far from appearing rhetorical, it looked as if it was a dull, staid and rather prosaic description of the reality. A man in possession of the secret of Truth, with head and heart at bursting point, with his pulse beating 150 to the minute and his blood tingling in every vein of his body, felt more like a bomb ready to explode and subject to another's will than a human being who could deliberate and decide and control his actions and speech. Yes, he *could* talk 'in season and out of season' of his new faith, and it did not need any such explanation as Doughty's about the Musalmans, that it is not 'hypocrisy' that makes them talk continually of their religion. Hypocrisy? Why, it should be sheer hypocrisy *not* to talk of it continually! And conversion was not so much felt to be a 'sacred duty' as an inalienable and indefeasible *right*—nay, a compelling necessity of man's entire being to declare the Truth that all may share it. I could now understand the

[22] Friedrich Max Mueller (1823–1900), comparative philologist and religious writer. He was educated at the universities of Leipzig and Berlin and was elected a Fellow of All Souls in 1858. In 1875 he undertook the edition of *The Sacred Books of the East*, a series of translations of eastern religious classics in 51 volumes, over 30 of which are devoted to the religions of India.

eagerness of Jesus (on whom be peace) to take advantage of the Jewish custom, which, outside the Temple at Jerusalem which had a clergy of its own, permitted the first comer to stand up in the Synagogue on a Sabbath to give the lessons of the day *(parasha* and *haphtara)* and add there to a *Midrash* or entirely personal commentary in which he expressed his own ideas:

And they went into Capernaum; and straightway on the Sabbath day he entered into the Synagogue, and taught.

And they were astonished at his doctrine; for he taught them as one that had authority, and not as the scribes. (Mark, 1:21–2)

Yes, he had authority, the authority of the Truth that must be declared and not merely the tradition of the scribes handed down mechanically from generation to generation. It was all the difference between one who had something to say, and others who had to say something. Similarly, I can now imagine the force of the impulsion that led the Last of the Prophets (on whom be Allah's benedictions and peace) to call from the height of Mount Safá the leaders of the Quraysh, family by family and name by name, as if to warn them of the approach of an enemy and then to tell them that their infidelity was a far greater danger, to invite his family to dine with him and at the end of the repast to tell them in spite of their sneering scepticism, that the faith he offered for their acceptance was a richer gift than ever a kinsman offered to other kinsmen. I can now understand what drove him, after his rejection by the bulk of his own fellow-townsmen and tribe and their cruel persecution for a whole decade, to the fertile oasis of Táif in the hope of getting a hearing from the Bani Thaqeef and the Hawázin, and what impelled him, when rejected once more with contumely by the nobility and stoned and whipped with their approval by the slaves and the boys in the streets, instead of giving up a task that was apparently so hopeless to await the season of the pilgrimage when but once a year recurred the possibility of securing an audience within the Holy precincts of the Meccan sanctuary, and what made him wander from one group of pilgrims to another, regardless of humiliation, and ask them, with a tender and piteous appeal in his tone, whether they would listen to him if he talked of Allah and the latter day. Tennyson[23] says truly of a poet that like the linnet he sings because he must. He who has any particle of truth to share with his fellow-beings is under the same compelling necessity, because truth is not truth if it is not self-propagating.

[23] Alfred Tennyson (1809–92), the great English poet.

'Paid Missionaries' indeed! Why the true missionary would pay with his last farthing on earth, nay with his life-blood itself, for the inestimable boon of a hearing.

I must, however, confess that the fear of being smitten with religion is even worse than being smitten with love; for no ardent lover could be so eager to recite to any kind of audience his latest sonnet on his mistress's eyebrow than a new convert to any faith is to inflict on all and sundry his latest sermon. And I am not sure if to the heart—whole crowd of sane and sober people with settled convictions, however hazy or open to serious dispute, and busy with their own absorbing affairs of daily existence, to whom sonnets and sermons are alike distasteful, the sermoniser is not a greater nuisance than the sonneteer. Looking back to those green days of my conversion after the few years that have passed and in the light of more settled convictions which still glow, but have no longer the appearance of a bonfire, I can afford to smile, though I am thankful to God, not to laugh at that early enthusiasm of the convert-preacher.

But this compelling necessity which gives to Truth its explosive character is also accompanied by an exhilarating sense of freedom. Truly was it said that:

'The Truth shall make you free', specially the basal truth that in serving the purpose of Allah one is serving an Omnipotent Master who never forsakes his servitor:

> Say 'Truth hath come and falsehood hath vanished. Verily falsehood is evanescent!' (17:81)

> There is no compulsion in religion. Now is the right way made distinct from error; whoever, therefore, shall reject Tághout and believe in Allah, he will have taken hold of a strong handle in which is no breaking off; and Allah is Hearing, Knowing. (2:256)

The greatest falsehood is fear, and only too often is it the motive behind human action. Once the fear of God—or call it the love of God, for true knowledge of God must be comprehensive and must include both—enters a heart, it turns out every other fear, just as the love of God makes one independent of every other love. The knowledge that we are serving Him begets the completest confidence in His ever-ready succour. 'Eli, Eli, lama Sabachthani' is no cry for the possessor of Truth, unless it means that owing to our human frailty we ourselves lost for a time the hold we had taken on the strong handle that knows no breaking; and when Truth came once more to our rescue, we gave utterance to our confession of the weakness of a moment ago in a half-petulant half-plaintive wail: 'My

God, my God, why didst Thou forsake me?' As a Christian writer who rejects the translation of *Sabachthani* as 'hast forsaken me', says: 'It is over now. The relief is come. But it was utter forsaken abandonment while it lasted. "My God, My God, why *didst* Thou . . . ?"' And this is only logical. As the Quran says, 'There is no *compulsion* in religion'. We have a free choice whether we should serve God or the Devil. Convictions are not things that can be forced. Whatever compulsion there is, is not *in* religion but *of* religion. Once 'the right way is made distinct from error' and faith and belief have taken a firm grip on the strong handle of the truth that service is due only to the Supreme Ruler and the Omnipotent Creator, Sustainer and Developer of all Creation, how can mistrust make us waver and hold ourselves back in His Service? He is Hearing, Knowing. If He has further need of our service, we shall of a surety be rescued in good time. If, on the other hand, it serves His Divine Purpose that we should at a given moment completely spend ourselves in a cause that is dear to Him, how can we hold back anything, even if it be life, from Him, who gave it to us not for our petty purposes but for His Own Supreme Purpose? The author of the fourth Gospel seems to have grasped the true meaning of this fulfilment of Divine Trust when he makes Jesus say: 'Never is my soul troubled; and what shall I say? Father save me from this hour: *but for this cause came I unto this hour.* Father glorify Thy name' (John, 12:27–8). No, there is no alternative but to say what Jesus said at Gethsamane[24] [*sic*]: 'Thy will be done.' We are human after all, even though we be the Vicegerents of God on Earth, and even to a Prophet it is permissible to say before the Will of the Lord is finally declared: 'If it be possible, let this cup pass from me' (Matthew, 26:39). But when that declaration *has* been made it does not beseem us to say aught but what Jesus did say, 'Not as I will, but as Thou Wilt!' In fact, there is then no difference between the two wills. 'I will' is the same then as 'Thou wilt', or rather there are no two wills then, but only one, and when the hour comes God's Deputy and Agent hands over to the Principal all that which had been entrusted to his care in life: 'Into Thy hands I commend my spirit' (Luke, 23:46). 'The long days' task is done. It is finished' (John, 19:30). It is only when the right way has not been made distinct from error, when conviction that cannot be compelled is *not* complete and perfect faith is still wanting that the falsehood of fear comes to us in all sorts of disguises. But when the right way has been made distinct from

[24] It refers to the garden of Gethsemane, the garden where Jesus retired with his disciples after the Last Supper and which was the scene of his betrayal..

error, no disguise even if it be the love of our friends can serve the purpose of fear. If the Temple of Truth has to be cleansed, even though one's own life-blood be required for the purificatory rites, it must be done. We have not to spare but to spend ourselves in the cause we have espoused. We see this in the life and teaching of Jesus. He had evidently, soon after the commencement of his short ministry, the presentiment that his denunciation of the scribes and the priests would ultimately lead to Calvary and the Cross. He had not *sought* trouble, and had in fact avoided it so long as he could avoid it, while still continuing the work for which he had received a clear call. But 'it came to pass, when the time was come that he should be received up, he steadfastly set his face to go to Jerusalem' (Luke, 9:51). He had already begun to make his disciples understand the drift of things and we find it recorded while he was at Cæsarea Philippi,[25] that 'from that time forth began Jesus to show unto his Disciples how he must go unto Jerusalem and suffer many things of the elders and chief priests and scribes' (Matthew, 16:21) all culminating in Calvary. What could be more natural then for Peter, who was with his brother Andrew, the very first to follow him when he called and who loved the Master with all the heartiness of an impetuous simple fisherman, even though it was he who denied him on the night of his capture three times before cock-crow, what could be more natural for him than to wish that he would not let things come to such a pass? Then Peter took him and began to rebuke him, saying, 'Be it far from Thee, Lord, this "shall not be unto Thee"' (Matthew, 16:22). Jesus could not have misunderstood what the well-meaning Peter had said, but he no doubt realised that it is the love of friends that is only too often apt to make us fear the foe and to hesitate when we should steadfastly set our face to do what duty demands. And he was not going to be tempted after the test through which he had already gone at the commencement of his ministry. The talisman that can make the Devil disappear is no other than the creed of mankind from its cradle. 'Thou shalt fear the Lord Thy God and serve Him and shalt swear by His name' (Deuteronomy, 6:13).[26] 'Thou shalt fear the God thy Lord; Him shalt thou serve and to Him shalt thou cleave and swear by His Name' (Deuteronomy, 10:20). As the Psalmist had said: 'The fear of the Lord is clean enduring for ever'. Was he who had once put the Devil to flight in the temptation,

[25] In Macedonia, the first of the Churches founded by St. Paul in Europe.

[26] The book, which contains Moses' final utterances on the east side of the Jordan before his death.

out there in the wilderness and drawn the angels to himself to minister unto him by giving expression to that reverential trust in his God and hatred of all evil, no matter in what consequences it involved him,—was he going to suffer himself to be tempted again? The old talisman was still effective 'Thou shalt worship Thy God and Him only shalt thou serve' (Matthew, 4:10). He had to teach a lesson to his disciples and by his timely sternness prepare them for future sufferings if they were to propagate the Truth. So 'He turned and said unto Peter, Get thee behind me Satan; thou art an offence unto me; for thou savourest not the things that be of God, but those that be of men. Then said Jesus unto his disciples, If any man will come after me, I let him deny himself, and take up his cross and follow me. For whosoever would save his life shall lose it and whosoever will lose his life shall find it. For what shall a man be profited if he shall gain the whole world and lose his own soul, or what shall a man give in exchange for his soul?' (Matthew, 16:23–6). His yoke was no doubt easy, and his burden light but not in the sense that the coward would take it. He had made that perfectly clear when he had instructed the twelve and sent them forth:

Behold I send you forth as sheep in the midst of wolves. . . . But beware of men; for they will deliver you up to the councils, and they will scourge you in their synagogues; and ye shall be brought before governors and kings for my sake for a testimony against them and the gentiles. . . . And the brother shall deliver up the brother to death and the father the child and the children shall rise up against their parents, and cause them to be put to death. And ye shall be hated of all men for my name's sake; but he that endureth to the end shall be saved. . . . The disciple is not above the Master, nor the servant above the Lord. . . . Fear them not therefore, for there is nothing covered that shall not be revealed and hid that shall not be known. What I tell you in darkness that speak ye in light; and what you hear in the ear that preach upon the house tops. And fear not them which kill the body, but are not able to kill the soul, but rather fear Him which is able to destroy both soul and body in hell. Are not two sparrows sold for a farthing? And one of them shall not fall on the ground without your Father. But the very hairs of your head are numbered. Fear ye not therefore ye are of more value than the sparrows. . . . Think not that I am come to send peace on earth; I came not to send peace, but a sword. . . . For I am come to set a man at variance against his father, and the daughter against her mother, and the daughter-in-law against the mother-in-law. And a man's foes shall be they of his own household. He that loveth father or mother more than me is not worthy of me and he that loveth son or daughters is not worthy of me. And he that taketh not his Cross and followeth after me, is not worthy of me. He that findeth his life shall lose it, and he that loseth his life for my sake shall find it. (Matthew, 10:16-39)

And yet if the story of the Gospels is an authentic record of facts, Calvary took the twelve by surprise and it was only later on that they showed by their own patiently borne sufferings that they did not deem the disciple to be above the Master and proved worthy of him. But what are we to say of the later generations, that while professing to exalt Jesus to nothing short of Divinity have yet rediscovered the old heathen values in ties of blood and even of political relationship?

V

# The Secular Outlook in Europe

## RENAN'S 'MODERN' INTERPRETATION OF CHRISTIANITY

RENAN IS NO FAVOURITE of the Church of Christ today and in fact confesses himself to be outside the pale.[1] But he is nevertheless so ardent an admirer and in a sense so devoted a follower of Jesus that few professing Christians could excel and not many could even equal him. And in what I am about to cite from his *Life of Jesus,* he has the whole Christendom in progressive Europe at least with him in practice even if here and there a few unimportant persons may be reluctant to accept the theory in all its nakedness. Now to Renan it appears that in teaching all this, which must be regarded as the commonplace of all true religions, Jesus 'boldly preached war against nature and total severance from ties of blood'. This is not merely in reference to his apparent preference of a monastic ideal of life and the complete renunciation of the world which he prescribed in the case of his disciples and those who would similarly attach themselves to him. One can well understand that some of those dicta of his were in all probability misunderstood by the evangelist *authors* of the Gospels as wholly unqualified when they were obviously meant to be subject to qualifications or as commandments of universal application, when they were unusually bitter doses of medicine prescribed only for particular pathological cases. Renan is frankly the modern progressive worldly European to whom the Kingdom of God is merely a Utopia to be patronised with a little faint praise and then passed over, not a world-order to be established as the one practical concern of mankind. He cites all these and many other similar passages from the Gospels and it is precisely in reference to these that he thinks 'a strange ardour animates all these discourses'. He remarks their 'entirely Utopian origin', their 'exag-

[1] Ernest Renan (1823–92); French philosopher, theologian and orientalist. His most widely known work, referred to by Mohamed Ali, was *Vie de Jesus*, published in 1863. In this book he repudiated the supernatural element in Christ's life, ignored its moral aspect and portrayed him as a charming and amiable Galilean preacher. Its publication created a sensation in Europe. Two years after the publication of the book, he was removed from the professorship at the College de France.

gerations' and 'excesses' and in his view they would 'reduce everything to a frightful wilderness'. 'In these fits of severity', as he calls them, he says 'Jesus went so far as to abolish all natural ties. His requirements had no longer any bounds. Despising the healthy limits of man's nature, he demanded that he should exist only for him, that he should love him alone. . . . The harsh and gloomy feeling of distaste for the world and excessive self-abnegation, which characterises Christian perfection, was originated not by the refined and cheerful moralist of earlier days, but by the sombre giant whom a kind of presentiment was withdrawing more and more out of the pale of humanity. We should almost say that, in these moments of conflict with the most legitimate cravings of the heart, Jesus had forgotten the pleasure of loving, of seeing, and of feeling.' It is with reference to one of the finest things, not only in the Gospels but in all literature (Matthew 16:24–6) ending with 'What is a man profited if he shall gain the whole world and lose his own soul' that Renan says Jesus employed, 'still more unmeasured language'. He of course rejects it as unhistorical, because they 'clearly illustrate his defiance of nature', the two anecdotes which provided for Jesus the occasion to lay down the axioms of all religion: 'Let the dead bury their dead; but go thou and preach the Kingdom of God', and 'No man having put his hand to the plough and looking back, is fit for the Kingdom of God', and then comes out the core of all his trouble, which lays bare the worldliness of modern Europe. 'A great danger,' says he, 'threatened the future of this exalted morality, thus expressed in hyperbolic language and with terrible energy. By detaching man from Earth the ties of life were severed. The Christian would be praised for being a bad son or a bad patriot if it was for Christ that he resisted his father and fought against his country. The ancient city, the parent republic, the State or the law common to all, were thus placed in hostility with the Kingdom of God. *A fatal germ of theocracy was introduced into the world.*' No wonder, that after pronouncing a characteristically modern judgement on such unlimited requirements of religion 'Commonsense revolts at these excesses', and after declaring that 'the Gospel man would prove a dangerous man', Renan turns with delight to that piece of clever casuistry when the Pharisees[2] who had taken counsel 'how they might entangle him in his talk' sought to compromise Jesus and bring him into collision with the Roman authority. When they flatter his frankness and courage regardless of consequences and ask him, 'Is it lawful to give tribute unto Caesar[3] or not?' he perceives their

[2] 'Separated one's', a Jewish religious party.

[3] The word, which was virtually a title of the Roman emperors in the first–third centuries, occurs several times in the New Testament.

wickedness and makes them show him the image of Caesar and the superscription on the Roman Conqueror's coin which not even the Pharisees ever hesitated to have and to board. 'Render,' he is stated to have said, 'Render unto Caesar therefore the things which are Caesar's; and unto God the things that are God's' (Matthew, 22:21). Renan at once bursts into a paean of praise: 'Profound words which have decided the future of Christianity. Words of perfected spiritualism and of marvellous justness, which have established the separation between the spiritual and the temporal, and laid the basis of true liberalism and civilisation.' One knows not whether to drown this colossal insanity characteristic of the fanaticism of laic France in a thundering guffaw of laughter or cry one's eyes out at the imbecile misinterpretation which while establishing the 'separation between the spiritual and temporal' excludes God from the world He had created and, while laying down 'the basis of true liberalism and civilisation', lays the axe at the root of all religion. Earlier in his *Life of Jesus,* he is no doubt more cautious and careful in his praise and qualifies it with some mild criticism. But even there his outlook is entirely secular. 'His submission,' he says, 'to the established powers, though really derisive was in appearance complete.' He paid tribute to avoid disturbance. Liberty and right were not of this world, why should he trouble his life with vain anxieties? Despising the earth and convinced that the present world was not worth caring for, he took refuge in his ideal kingdom; he established the great doctrine of transcendent disdain, the true doctrine of liberty of souls, which alone can give peace. . . . The true Christian enjoys more real freedom; here below he is an exile. What matters it to him who is transitory governor of this earth, which is not his home? Liberty for him is truth. . . . By the sentence 'Render unto Caesar the things which are Caesar's and to God the things which are God's', he created something apart from politics, a refuge for souls in the midst of the Empire of brute force. 'Assuredly', he adds, 'such a doctrine has its dangers'; but the dangers he specifies are the least significant in a religious sense and utterly secular. 'To establish as a principle', says M. Renan in his most critical mood, 'that we must recognise the legitimacy of a power by the inscription on its coins, to proclaim that the perfect man pays tribute with scorn and without question, was to destroy republicanism in the ancient form and to favour all tyranny. Christianity in this sense has contributed much to weaken the sense of duty to the citizen and to deliver the world into the absolute power of existing circumstances.' But he is not without excuses and explanations even here. 'In constituting an immense free association which during three hundred years was able to dispense with politics, Christianity amply compensated for the wrong it had done to civic virtues.

The power of the State was limited to the things of the earth; the mind was freed or at least the terrible rod of Roman omnipotence was broken for ever. . . . As an austere republican or zealous patriot, he (Jesus) would not have arrested the great current of the affairs of his age; but in declaring that politics is insignificant he has revealed to the world this truth, that one's country is not everything and that man is before, and higher than, the citizen.' Now a Biblical scholar has already remarked that 'Renan has a charming genius for neglecting all facts that disturb an artistic arrangement of his subject'; but even that could have hardly prepared one for his dealing so sovereignly with the facts of history. Howsoever 'the terrible rod of Roman omnipotence' may have come to be broken, it was with a view to restore that omnipotence that after three hundred years of being 'able to dispense with politics', Christianity was invited by a Roman Emperor to his Council Board and in secularising it, he enabled it in after ages to play a part in the politics of the Roman Empire that was neither good for politics nor for Christianity. But that is another story. Here it may only be remarked that we are not so much concerned with the wrong done to 'civic virtue' as with the wrongs done to the conception of virtue itself and that the destruction of 'republicanism in its ancient form' matters much less than the destruction of religion in every shape or form. And that is precisely what such a conception of religion as M. Renan's must inevitably do. For a Frenchman in the latter half of the nineteenth century to talk of this earth as not a man's home but a place of exile, to ask what matters it to man who is the transitory governor here, and to pretend that politics is insignificant is sheer cant and hypocrisy; specially after the unshamed secularism of the remark that 'it required more than a century for the true Christian Church—that which has converted the world—to disengage itself from this little sect of "latter-day saints" and to become a framework applicable to the whole of human society.' It was this little sect of 'latter-day saints' who had at least come to understand what Christ meant by the Kingdom of God that realised the only scrap of Truth in all the apologia of M. Renan that 'one's country is not everything, and that man is before and higher than the citizen'.

## CONFLICT BETWEEN GOD AND CAESAR

M. Renan has referred to the 'derisiveness' of Jesus' 'submission to the established powers'; but surely his derision was directed rather towards the acquisitiveness of the Jews who hungered after the Conqueror's coin, and would dispute only his title to it, in the form of tax, than towards his own submission. Jesus and his disciples had no wealth to worry about; but those who had, who found nothing in their exacting and inflexible code of religious laws against hoarding money that bore the image and superscription of Caesar, should not scruple to share some of it with Caesar. They had cleverly put a poser to him; but the good who are generally simple are not necessarily such simpletons as the wicked imagine them to be, and he turned the tables upon those that sought to 'entangle him in this talk'. However, the affair of the coin was obviously purely incidental and ought by rights to have been forgotten even in the generation of Jesus. Nobody would be more astonished than he to know that when so much else that he must have taught would be strangely neglected and consigned to oblivion, this trivial incident would be preserved for 1900 years, and it is not difficult to imagine his sore vexation at learning that his deft answer intended to shame those whose religion had come to be divorced from life, would be used as a proof text to justify the separation of the spiritual and the temporal and to nullify religion and the Kingdom of God that he had come to proclaim. Not that the dictum of Jesus is devoid of permanent value. By no manner of means. But the emphasis is not on the first part that requires one to render unto Caesar what is due to Caesar, which would have sufficed as an answer to the question asked. The emphasis is rather on the latter part, on the *obiter dictum,* so to speak, in which he demands what is due to God. If it is not to be a receiver of stolen goods for one to receive coin from the mint of Caesar, why should money paid as taxes into Caesar's treasury be stolen money as the Jews for the most part regarded? If you accept his sovereignty you must submit to it. But though Caesar could mint money he could not mint men. Man was not made in the image of Caesar but of his Maker, and his soul bore no superscription other than God's. All that we had received from God must be returned to God when He desired it. Caesar, if he demanded aught of that, was a mere interloper.

## H.G. WELLS' CONCEPTION OF THE KINGDOM OF GOD[4]

How refreshing it is to turn from the 'modernism' of Renan to the 'Modern religion' of one still more 'modern' and one who is even more outspoken as a critic of the Christian Church than M. Renan. H.G. Wells' purpose

[4] Mohamed Ali was supposed to meet the English novelist, scholar and writer in April 1920, but could not do so.

is, as he tells us, not primarily to shock and insult any more than M. Renan's, but he is more zealous to liberate himself from the shackles of dogmas which he regards as 'the imperfectly embalmed philosophy of Alexandria',[5] and even though it is incidentally and because it is unavoidable, he candidly attacks doctrinal Christianity. But in attempting to restore Theocracy in modern Christendom, who can say he is not nearer to Jesus than Renan and in fact nearer to him than most of those who unlike him still profess Christianity and are indeed the pillars of the Christian Church? Let us see what his 'Mr. Britling', after losing a son, sees through the mud and blood of French and Belgian battlefields in which the 'civic virtues' of M. Renan's nationalists culminated and hear what his rebellious Bishop—a Bishop with a soul—has to say of Caesar and God of Theocracy, which to M. Renan is 'the negation of civil society and of all Government' and of his 'liberalism and civilisation'. 'Religion', finds Mr. Britling, 'is the first thing and the last thing, and until a man has found God and been found by God, he begins at no beginning, he works to no end. He may have his friendships, his partial loyalties, his scraps of honour. But all these things fall into place and life falls into place only with God. God who fights through men against Blind Force and Might and Non-Existence; who is the end, who is the meaning. He is the only King. . . . And before the coming of the true King, the inevitable King, the King who is present whenever must men foregather this blood-stained rubbish of the ancient world, these puny Kings and tawdry Emperors, these wily politicians and artful lawyers, these men who claim and grab and trick and compel, these war-makers and oppressors, will presently shrivel and pass—like paper thrust into a flame.' And the Bishop is shown by an Angel the vision of the world as a whole, in which he could see on the sphere of the earth great countries like little patches and at the same time that he saw the faces of the men upon the highways, he could also see the feelings in men's hearts, and the thoughts in men's minds, and whispers 'So God perhaps sees it'. China and Japan and Turkey, India, South Africa and Russia, England, Norway and Germany all pass in a sort of review before his uplifted gaze and everywhere he meets with evidence of the growing feelings that God as conceived by narrow nationalists was 'perhaps only the last of a long succession of blood-stained tribal effigies—and not God at all'; that the 'very children in the

[5] In size and importance, Alexandria in Egypt was the second city of the Roman Empire. The foundation of the Church there is traditionally ascribed to St. Mark. The city was surrendered to the Arabs in 642.

board schools are turning against this narrowness and nonsense and mischief of nations, creeds and kings', that 'the world is all flashing and flickering—aquiver with the light that is coming to mankind', that 'it is on the verge of blazing even now into the one Kingdom of God' and that men all over the world are 'all coming to the verge of the same salvation, the salvation of one human brotherhood under the rule of one Righteousness, one Divine Will'. And then the Bishop is shown his church and sees it in the light of this vision plainly 'for the little thing it is'. 'The world saw a light, the nations that were sitting in the darkness saw a great light, even as I saw God. And then the Church began to forget and lose itself among secondary things. As I have done. . . . It tried to express the truth and lost itself in a maze of theology. It tried to bring order into the world and sold its faith to Constantine. These men who professed the Invisible King of the world, shirked His service. It is a most terrible disaster that Christianity has sold itself to Emperors and Kings. They forged a saying of the Master's that we should render unto Caesar the things that are Caesar's and unto God the things that are God's. . . . Who is this Caesar to set himself up to share mankind with God? *Nothing that is Caesar's can be any the less God's.* But Constantine Caesar sat in the midst of the Council, his guards were all about it, and the poor fanatics and trimmers and schemers disputed nervously with their eyes on him, disputed about homoousian and homoiousian and grimaced and pretended to be very fierce and exact to hide how much they were frightened and how little they knew, and because they did not dare to lay violent hands upon that usurper of the Empire of the world. . . . And from that day forth the Christian churches have been damned and lost. Kept churches. Lackey churches, Roman, Russian, Anglican; it matters not. My church indeed was twice sold, for it doubled the sin of Nicaea[6] and gave itself over to Henry and Elizabeth, while it shammed a dispute about the sacraments. No one cared really about transubstantiation any more than the earlier betrayers cared about con-substantiality that dispute did but serve to mask the betrayal.' And the first fruits of this vision of the world, 'as perhaps God sees it', was this address of the Bishop to the young people assembled for the Confirmation service—the last sermon he preached before he quitted the church for good. 'All ceremonies', he began, 'all ceremonies grow old. All ceremonies are tainted even from the first by things less worthy than their first intention, and you my dear sons and daughters,

[6] Now Iznik, this was the venue of the first Oecumenial Council (325) summoned by the Emperor Constantine within few months of his conquest of the Eastern Provinces.

who have gathered today in this worn and ancient building, beneath these monuments to ancient vanities, and these symbols of forgotten and abandoned theories about the mystery of God, will do well to distinguish in your minds between what is essential and what is superfluous and confusing in this dedication you make of yourselves to God our Master and King. For that is the real thing you seek to do today, to give yourself to God. This is your spiritual coming of age, in which you set aside your childish dependence upon teachers and upon taught phrases, upon rote and direction and stand up to look your Master in the face. *You profess a great brotherhood when you do that, a brotherhood that goes round the earth, that numbers men of every race and nation and country, that aims to bring God into all the affairs of this world,* and make Him not only the king of your individual lives, but the king—in place of all the upstarts, usurpers, accidents and absurdities who bear crowns and sceptres today—of a united mankind. This, my dear children, is the reality of this grave business today, as indeed *it is the real and practical end of all true religion.*'

I have made these large extracts from the views, about Christianity and the Christian Church, of two European writers, neither of them a Muslim and yet neither a professing Christian because it would be easier after this to understand what I have to say of my own faith as I found it to be in the Quran. There is much in Mr. Wells' *God the Invisible King*, which he would have to outgrow before he could become a Muslim; but in the main theme of all the three books of his, which I have named, and which I was given to read, during my internment, by a Muslim friend to whom I had only too eagerly given an exposition of Islam as I discovered it for myself is the creed of Islam, and it is, as one could now easily judge, the diametrical opposite of 'liberalism and civilisation' of M. Renan, which would reduce religion to a limited liability Company. The main theme of the life and teaching of the Arabian Prophet was the same as in the case of the life and teaching of his predecessor of Palestine, as I shall presently show. They both wanted man to realise himself as a member of the Kingdom of God and, identifying himself with the Great Divine Purpose in Life, serve Him day and night, waking and asleep and serve none but Him. If today the professing Christian does not share the ideas and ideals of the professing Muslim or as Europeans call him, Muhammadan, it is due to the differences of the theologians and not to those of the original teachers who had drunk deep from the same perennial source—the fountain of Eternal Truth.

## 'THE HELLENISTIC GRAFT WHICH CHANGED CHRISTIANITY OUT OF RECOGNITION'

But then what Europe called Christianity was not the teaching of Jesus of Nazareth but of Saul of Tarsus,[7] an Asiatic no doubt like Jesus himself and no more gentile than Jesus, but one who was steeped in the Hellenism of Alexandria. He had never known the teacher of Galilee,[8] never heard him preach; and when Jesus had disappeared after the tragic scene of Calvary, Saul had taken a leading part in persecuting his followers. The story of his conversion to the faith of Jesus rests on his own authority; but when once he is Paul, he outstrips the disciples who had lived throughout his ministry in the company of the Master who would fulfil the law and reform Israel. Whether it is the zeal of the new convert or some other motive that drives him, it is needless to speculate here. But what is certain is that apart from the infinite extension that he gave to the field for the Christian missionary effort the 'apostle of the gentiles' as he calls himself, was responsible for the transition of Christianity from its Jewish to its gentile form. This transition was not a mere enlargement of its field by the abolition of particularist barriers. His valuation of the law which Jesus said he had come not to destroy but to fulfil was a thing altogether new and startlingly original. He had acute differences with the Galilean apostles and they were not concerned merely with the extent of the Gospel message, but also, and in a higher degree, with its quality. Paul had no knowledge of the words and acts of Jesus such as the disciples alone possessed and alone could impart, and its absence, which must have appeared to another mind a tremendous handicap, seemed no disadvantage or drawback to that of the new evangelist, the author of a Gospel not of Jesus, but as Biblical scholars, in order to mark the difference, have termed, a gospel *about* Jesus. In his Epistle[9] hardly an event in the life of Jesus except his supposed death and scarcely a word of his teachings is ever mentioned, and as Professor D.D. Bacon, of Yale, says, 'it is probable that when at last three years after his conversion he went to Jerusalem, "to get acquainted with Peter", the story he was interested to hear had even then more to do with that common apostolic witness of resurrection appearances reproduced in 1st Corinthian XV:3–11 than with the sayings and doings

[7] Capital of the Roman province of Cilicia in 67 B.C. It was the birthplace of St. Paul.

[8] Constituted one of the Roman divisions of Palestine.

[9] In Christian worship it was customary for two passages of Scripture to be read or sung at the Eucharist; the former came to be known as the 'Epistles'.

of the ministry.' As to this Paul preserves, as we have seen, 'an almost unbroken silence'. With the significant indifference to the story of Jesus and to his words, for which the only authority we have are the Petrine traditions believed to have been embodied in the Gospel according to St. Mark,[10] and the Mathian Logia and Syntagina similarly believed to have been incorporated in the Gospel according to St. Matthew,[11] he had depended entirely upon his own inner consciousness to evolve his peculiar Christology.[12] It rests more upon his subjective insight or gnosis of Christ than upon any objective reality, and naturally it differed from that of the disciples who had known and lived with Jesus. Indeed he opens his Epistle to the Galatians[13] by not only revelling in his independence but in repeatedly cursing those who dared to differ from his view of the nature and doctrine of Jesus. 'But though we or an angel from heaven', he writes, 'preach any other gospel unto you than that which we have preached unto you, let him be accursed'. 'As I said before, so say I now again. If any man preach any other gospel unto you than that which you have received, let him be accursed. . . . But I certify to you, brethren, that the Gospel which was preached of me is not after man. For I neither received it of man, neither was I taught it, but by the revelation of Jesus Christ.' Contrasting his career as a persecutor 'beyond measure' of 'the Church of God', with his spiritual condition after his conversion he proudly adds, 'Immediately I conferred not with flesh and blood. Neither went I up to Jerusalem to see them who were apostles before me'; and even when he writes of his visit to Peter, he makes it clear that he did not condescend to see any other apostle 'save James the Lord's brother!' Well, the Christology, that was thus evolved and differed so radically from that of the disciples and companions of Jesus during his ministry, was still further developed by the unknown author of the fourth Gospel, known as the Gospel according to St. John. This theological dissertation is admittedly part of controversial literature produced in the second century A.C. to meet the menace of gnosticism. The affinity between the epistles of Paul and the fourth Gospel with regard to questions which it is alleged did not arise for consideration and discussion until the second century and which

[10] The noted evangelist who set out with St. Paul on their first missionary journey. The Gospel of St. Mark was known in the first century. He is said to have drawn his information from the teachings of St. Peter.

[11] Apostle and Evangelist. His name occurs in all four lists of the 12 Apostles.

[12] The study of the Person of Christ, and in particular of the union in Him of the Divine and human natures.

[13] Refers to the Galatian converts of St. Paul.

yet forms the main subject matter of the Epistles, what is called 'a very radical and revolutionary theory', has been attracting attention in some quarters and has Professor Van Mennen of the University of Leiden, for one of its leading exponents. Of course some of the epistles that have for centuries passed as Paul's are now universally regarded as the work of others falsely attributed to him; but according to this theory, *none* of the Epistles ascribed to Paul are his, but were written by others in his name some time during the second century. But whether they be Paul's and written in the first century or the works of others and like the Fourth Gospel written during the second, they show one common characteristic. Their Hellenism is beyond dispute. When the author of the Fourth Gospel began to combat the Hellenistic extravagances of the Gnostics with the help of Hellenism itself, as often happens both in polemics and in warfare, orthodoxy took up the very weapons of Heresy to fight it and the philosophy of Pythagoras[14] and of Plato[15] which had little kinship with the simple faith of Jesus of Nazareth, but which at Alexandria had already been adopted by his older contemporary, Philo,[16] to serve the purpose of later Judaism, was now similarly adopted by the disciple of the 'Apostle of the Gentiles' to serve the purpose of this new doctrine. In the heathen markets of Greece the heathen coin of Hellenism was offered, and once having entered Europe through the gateway of Salonika,[17] Christianity or Paulinism or whatever other name may be given to this amalgam of Hebraic and Hellenic cultures, gradually made its way throughout that continent. But who can say whether the victory was that of Jesus of Nazareth or of Plato and Pythagoras; whether European mentality made its submission to Asiatic spirituality or capitulated to a conqueror with the familiar features of ancient Greece? What is certain is that for all the slurring over of St. Luke,[18] who claimed to be writing true history in the Acts of the Apostles and would have us believe that nothing but harmony prevailed, Paul and the disciples of Galilee had acute differences, and even if a truce was patched up for the sake of unity, whatever the terms of

[14] Greek philosopher and mathematician. Known for the Pythagoras theorem—a mathematical proposition that in any right-angled triangle, the squares on the hypotenuse is equal to the sum of the squares on the other two sides. The converse of the theorem is also true.

[15] (*c*. 427–347 B.C.) Athenian philosopher. He was a disciple of Socrates, who appears in most of Palato's 35 dialogues. He founded his own Academy at Athens. His influence has been universal, extending through his pupil and disciple, Aristotle.

[16] *c*. 20 B.C.–*c*. A.D. 50, Jewish thinker belonging to a priestly family of Alexandria.

[17] Or Thessolonica, founded in *c*. 315 B.C.

[18] According to tradition the author of the Third Gospel.

the compromise, the *teaching* of Paul reflects little submission to the views of the 'Judaizers' whom he openly denounced in his outspoken epistles as 'false brethren,' 'super extra-apostles' and 'ministers of Satan.' And it is *his* doctrine and not theirs that won the victory in Europe. They had obviously conceded much to the more masterful 'gentile of the apostles' but even after hoping to succeed by agreeing to the principle of 'live and let live' they did not long survive. The Church of Jerusalem was at first still the Church of the Nazarenes, as the Jewish converts were afterwards called, but even here in their very home they were soon overwhelmed by the increasing multitude of converts from among the gentiles who at length refused them the toleration that the Judaizers had conceded to them in the earlier days. The ruin of the Temple, of the city and of the public religion of the Jews was severely felt by these Nazarenes with whom their affinity was found to involve them in trouble. They retired from the ruins of Jerusalem to the little town of Pella beyond the Jordan where their ancient church languished for two generations. But they could still revisit the Holy City. 'The desperate fanaticism' of the Jews as Gibbon calls it, filled up the measure of their calamities and under the reign of Hadrian,[19] their repeated rebellions were punished with unusual rigour. A new city under the name of Aelia Capitolina[20] was founded on the Mount Sion[21] and the severest penalties were prescribed against any of the Jewish people who should dare to approach its precincts. The Nazarenes[22] had now only one way left to escape the common proscription, namely, to elect for their bishop a prelate of the race of Gentiles and having done that the large majority of the congregation was persuaded by him to renounce the Mosaic law the practice of which they had preserved above a century. The remnant of the Church of Nazarenes, who refused to accompany their Latin bishop to the Church of Jerusalem on Mount Sion, the congregation of which now had its union firmly cemented with the Catholic or Gentile Church, was branded with heresy while they still preserved their former habitation of Pella, spread themselves into the village adjacent to Damascus and formed an inconsiderable church in Aleppo. In reference to the poverty of their condition, characteristic of the disciples of Jesus whom they followed,

[19] Hadrian I (d. 795). Pope from 772.

[20] The new city which Hadrian built in *c.* 130 on the site of Jesusalem (destroyed in A.D. 70).

[21] Or Zion, the citadel of Jerusalem, taken by David from the Jebusites.

[22] The term has been applied in various senses. In the New Testament Christ is called 'Jesus the Nazarene'. Jesus was brought up and lived in Nazareth till the beginning of his ministry.

they assumed the name of Ebionites,[23] which was soon turned by the now orthodox or Catholic Church of the Gentiles into a term of contempt indicative of the poverty of their understanding. Jesus is stated in the Gospel to have said that 'Salvation is of the Jews', but now the vast majority of the followers of Jesus denied that a man who, although he acknowledged Jesus as the Messiah, still continued at the same time to observe the Law of Moses which Jesus had said he had come not to destroy but to fulfil, could possibly hope for salvation. These Ebionites, rejected from one religion as apostates, and from the other as heretics insensibly melted away into the Gentile Church or reverted to the synagogue and the only trace of the Christianity of the disciples of Jesus and of members of his family left after the 4th century was to be found in certain Jewish rites like circumcision practised in Abyssinia. One cannot say, but maybe it is some little affinity to the parent church of the Nazarenes at Jerusalem that accounts for the description of the Negus of Abyssinia at whose court the first Muslim exiles from Mecca took refuge, and who died a Muslim, as 'those who say we are Nazarenes' in the Quran. The net result of the contact of Hellenism and Hebraism was that Christianity came, in course of time, to be identified with Europe. This was in spite of the remarkable strength and even predominance of the African Church of Carthage[24] in the first few centuries and of the leading part that the Egyptian Church of Alexandria, and to a smaller extent the Asiatic Church of Antioch,[25] took in the terrible controversies that wrought so much havoc in Christendom before the Muslim conquests in Asia and Africa in the 7th century. But although Christianity survived to some extent in these continents and the toleration of the Musalmans has made it possible for the heretic churches of Nestorians[26] and Jacobeans,[27] Maronites[28] and Armenians[29] to live to this day, there is this distinct division that the Hellenistic doctrines of Paul while they prevailed all over the Gentile continent of Europe, were

[23] The name given by modern scholars to an apocryphal Gospel supposed to have been used by the Ebionites.

[24] The early ecclesiastical Council were held at this place.

[25] Antioch in Syria was the third city of the Roman Empire. The Council of Antioch was held on the occasion of the consecration of Constantine's 'Golden Church'.

[26] They believed that there were two separate persons in the incarnate Christ, the one divine and the other human, as opposed to the orthodox doctrine that the incarnate Christ was a single person, at once God and man.

[27] The body of Syrian Monophysites who rejected the teaching of the Council of Chalcedon (451) on the Person of Christ.

[28] A Christian community of Syrian origin, the greater part of whom still live in Lebanon.

[29] The Armenians were the first nation to embrace Christianity officially.

'never accepted south of the Tawrus Range'. Can we wonder after this that the fact of Jesus' Asiatic lineage and local habitation has not helped the East and the Easterns to secure a more sympathetic treatment for themselves from Christendom? The Jews are certainly more oriental in their mental outlook in spite of the fact that Dispersion sent them in such large numbers out of the East. But, even such of them, as have now begun to affect a territorial patriotism foreign to their old ways of thought, are, as a rule, looked down upon in Europe as Asiatics and while they may dominate the realm of international finance and may even dictate in the realm of international politics, as the *Morning Post,* the *National Review* and last but not least Chesterton Brothers[30] would have us believe, they seem still to exist on sufferance, as aliens, more or less undesirable. Jesus had spiritually succeeded Moses and the Prophets of Israel and a genealogy of very doubtful genuineness eagerly claimed for him descent from David.[31] Yet today the followers of Jesus are more and more coming to look upon these heroes of the Old Testament as possessing little merit of their own, and like John the Baptist[32] useful only as the heralds of the Messiah. While the laity[33] has even learnt to sneer at them in many cases, the clergy too does little more than patronise them as not entirely devoid of certain elements of Divine truth! All this is the result of that Hellenistic graft upon Hebrew religion and well may the Jews say that the day on which the first step was taken towards Hellenism, and the Old Testament was translated into Greek by the Seventy was 'as fatal to Israel as the day on which the golden calf was made at Horeb!' Islam also came into contact with Greek dialectics which powerfully reacted on Muslim dogma. But, except for a short period of uneasiness, when Mamun-al Rashid and two of his successors, Al-Wasiq[34] and Al-Mutasim,[35] were led by the leaders of the Mutazila[36] schism to insist on conformity to some of their doctrines

[30] Gilbert Keith Chesterton (1874–1936). British, critic and novelist. He became a Catholic in 1922, and thereafter wrote mainly on religious topics.

[31] The first king of the Judean dynasty. In Hebrew tradition, his name came to occupy a central position. He made Jerusalem the political and religious centre of his kingdom. He was succeeded by Solomon.

[32] Fore-runner of Christ. He is said to have appeared as a mission preacher on the banks of the Jordan demanding repentance and baptism from his hearers in view of the approach of the Kingdom of God.

[33] Members of the Christian Churches who do not belong to the clergy.

[34] Abbasid Khalifa. He died at the age of 32 in 847.

[35] (1212–58), the last Abbasid Khalifa of Baghdad. He was executed by Hulagu in February 1258.

[36] Name of the theological school which created the speculative dogmatics of Islam.

to institute a sort of inquisition and punish the dissenters for the first time threatening the individual consciousness by a word from the throne, the only results of this contact of Islam with Greek Philosophy were the growth of Muslim scholasticism and the revival in Europe as well of a study of Aristotle. The Arab mentality reasserted itself and the pure and simple faith of the Arabian Prophet survived the peril.

VI

# The New Zeal

## A WELCOME GIFT

It was about this time that a kind friend sent to us a gift than which nothing could be more acceptable, a copy of the Quran for my brother and one for myself, printed most exquisitely from blocks that reproduced in facsimile the elegant *Naskh,* together with an austerely faithful translation in English and copious footnotes based on a close study of commentaries of the Quran and of such Biblical literature as could throw light upon the latest Holy Writ.[1] This was the work of my learned namesake, Maulvi Muhammad Ali, of Lahore, leader of a fairly numerous religious community, some of whose members were doing missionary work in England and had located their mission at the Mosque in Woking, Surrey.[2] The translation and the notes which supplied the antidote so greatly needed for the poison squirted in the footnotes of English translators of the Quran like Sale,[3] Rodwell,[4] and Palmer, the fine printing, both English and Arabic, the India paper and the exquisite binding in green limp Morocco with characteristic Oriental *Tughra* or ornamental calligraphy in gold, all demonstrated the labour of love and devoted zeal that so many

[1] This refers to Mirza Yaqub Beg. The Quran was sent to Mohamed Ali in early February 1918. See Mohamed Ali to M.Y. Beg, 23 February 1918, in Hasan (ed.), *Mohamed Ali in Indian Politics*, vol. 2, pp. 83–7.

[2] He was the founder of the Ahmadiya Anjuman-i Ishaat-i Islam, an organisation formed after the death of Mirza Ghulam Ahmad (of Qadian in the Gurdaspur district of Punjab) in 1908. The difference between his 'Lahore Party' and Nuruddin, the Khalifa, was that the former regarded the Mirza as a reformer (*mujaddid*) while the latter considered him to be a Prophet. The Lahore Party was involved in extensive missionary work in Great Britain and Germany. Maulvi Muhammad Ali published an English translation of the Quran with a critical commentary and, besides other work, a voluminous treatise on *The Religion of Islam.*

[3] The eighteenth century brought translations made directly from an Arabic original by George Sale into English (1st published in 1734). Although he was hostile to Islam, his translation was not supplanted for some 150 years. This was the Quran for all English readers almost to the end of the nineteenth century. According to Arberry, his translation was superior to that of his forerunner, Ross. See Arthur J. Arberry, The Koran Interpreted (London, 1955).

[4] See Arberry, The Koran Interpreted, pp. 14–15, and J.M. Rodwell, *The Koran*, Introduction by G. Margoliouth (London, 1909).

willing workers had obviously contributed. This beautiful book acted like the maddening music of the *sarod* [a musical instrument], according to [a] Persian proverb, on the mentally deranged, and in the frame of mind in which I then was I wrote back to my friend who had sent these copies of the Quran that nothing would please me better than to go to Europe as soon as I could get out of the 'bounds' prescribed by my internment and preach to these war maniacs from every park, and at every street corner, if not within the dubious precincts of every public house, about a faith that was meant to silence all this clamour of warring nations in the one unifying peace of Islam. As I shall explain, the theocracy of Islam naturally condemned the narrow prejudices that created nationality and killed humanity, for to God, the Universal King, there could be no distinction of Arab and Ajam, of Aryan and Semitic, of Anglo-Saxon and Teuton, and from the very outset, I had seen in this terrible war the natural consequence and culmination of nationalism.

## CONTACT WITH MOHAMMAD IQBAL[5]

About the same time there came to us, separated by a rather distressingly long interval as appeared to me in my greed for more of such exquisite and yet forceful literature, two slim volumes of poetry by my friend, Sir (then Dr.) Mohammad Iqbal, M.A., Ph.D., Barrister-at-Law, to give him his full professional and academic titles.[6] I had known 'Iqbal'—as he was to me and even to hundreds of thousands of Muslims in India who did not know him—for many years and latterly I would inflict my company on him and claim his hospitality whenever business took me to Lahore, where he was earning at the bar just as much as would suffice to maintain him on a very moderate scale so that he could smoke his *hooqa* in peace, study his favourite subjects of literature and philosophy, and above all, galvanise Muslims with his powerful poetry. Others had come to recognise Iqbal's genius years before I had read a single verse of his, but I may claim this much that when once I had come under his spell I made some

[5] See Mohamed Ali to Iqbal, 5 April 1913, in Hasan (ed.), *Mohamed Ali in Indian Politics*, vol. 1, pp. 56–7.

[6] Mohammad Iqbal (1876–1938), the outstanding Urdu and Persian poet. He was an extremely popular poet with Mohamed Ali and his friends. 'We loved Iqbal the Revolutionary', recalled Choudhry Khaliquzzaman, 'calling upon his people to rise to action, the Iqbal who introduced Muslim heroes in their true glory, the Iqbal who by his own interpretation of Quranic injunctions put life into what had been stale by philosophical pondernigs'.

amends for the time I had lost by reading over and over again everything of his fugitive verse that I could secure in the Urdu periodicals and newspapers and by sharing my intense pleasure with the readers of my own newspapers. Ghalib, perhaps our greatest Urdu poet,[7] not excluding the older Mir,[8] to whose genius he himself repeatedly pays homage, had never before been quoted so often in journalism as the readers of the *Comrade* could testify, and now Iqbal, who was perhaps born after Ghalib had died, came to share 'the honours' in the columns of the *Comrade,* and of course of the *Hamdard* to which he several times contributed. He was the poet of Islam's reawakening in India in the 20th century, and to no man does Muslim India owe a greater debt than to this modest, shy and retiring barrister of the Punjab. His name was a household word throughout the Urdu-speaking Muslim world, and of course I was an ardent admirer and devotee. But if there was one man who not only equalled my enthusiasm for Iqbal, but surpassed it, and that too by a generous margin, it was my brother whose speeches during his propaganda were so full of Iqbal's poetry which he would chant in his ardent love of it, that my ill-suppressed jealousy found a good opportunity of chaffing him for I used to say that he would whip up the enthusiasm of his audience with his copious quotations from Iqbal when his own laboured and drowsy eloquence could do little more than rouse it to a jog-trot. But when he found that this time Iqbal had written verse in Persian which needed a little brushing up of all he and I had learnt of that language in the *maktab* of our red-bearded pedagogue at Rampur ages ago, he swore with full-throated ease at his favourite. Nevertheless, we started reading his *Asrar-i-Khudi*[9] *or 'Secrets of Self-Realisation', and gradually his anger was appeased for we soon realised that this was even greater and more enduring than what Iqbal had so far written and that it made a wider appeal to the Muslim world for which Urdu would not have sufficed. Compared with the molten lava of his Urdu verse this appeared at first to*

[7] Mirza Asadullah Khan Ghalib (1797–1869), the greatest *ghazal* poet of the nineteenth century. Notice the following couplet:

> I filled the blood-stained pages with the story of my love
> And went on writing, even though my hands were smitten off.

[8] Mir Taqi Mir (b. 1723–1800), also a great Urdu poet. He once wrote:

> Don't think me a mere poet—no my verse
> Is made of pain and grief more than you know.

[9] The *masnavi* written in the style and meter of the famous Persian poet, Maulana Jalaluddin Rumi. Iqbal held that the Indian Muslims had been corrupted by the influence of Persian pantheistic ideas and had forgotten everything of true Arabic Islam and its ideals.

*be colder and more 'monumental'. But when once Iqbal had shed the philosophy of the earlier part, in which he gradually unfolded his theme and familiarised the Oriental readers with the new meaning of old terms like Khudi* and the technique of his philosophy and was no longer a 'Ph.D.' but a poet, we could see that in the veins of the marble too a fiery fluid was flowing. I had already heard him recite fragments of it while it was being written, during my frequent visits to Lahore on account of the *Comrade* security case before the Chief Court of the Punjab. But, just as in the case of the Quran, here too I had not been able to see the forest, so to speak, for the trees. Now the complete scheme gradually came into view, and I experienced an exquisite thrill of delight when I found that the Poet and Philosopher was, in his own inimitable fashion, giving expression to the self-same basic truth of Islam, which I had in a blundering sort of way discovered for myself. Here let me explain that it was a commonplace of Muslim religious literature that Islam meant submission to God's Will and that He was the Supreme Ruler of the Universe, but this truth had been allowed by the theologians to sink into the insignificance of a truism, so that we all passed it by, thinking we were fully familiar with it, when in fact, we were entirely ignorant of its true valuation. It had been allowed to fall out from the foreground. A new stressing, a far greater emphasis was needed to restore to it its older value. The entire perspective had to be changed before Musalmans could realise the great Life Purpose and learn to live as true Muslims. This is what I had in my own way by now fully realised and here was Iqbal forcing the door of Muslim mentality, and securing once more an entry into it for the Theocracy of Islam. How much such a revaluation was needed can well be understood when I state that in the second volume Iqbal had to explain and almost declared on oath that every word he uttered was based on the Quran and was not German philosophy—as the *ulama* had begun to think! This second little volume *Rumuz-i-Bekhudi* or 'Secrets of Self-Annihilation' provided a broad pathway once the earlier volume had accomplished the laborious pioneer work, and it was now easy-going for the meanest intelligence. Life, according to Iqbal, was a wilderness unless a definite purpose cleared a pathway through it, and man's realisation of his self was the discovery of this life purpose. This was nothing else but the Divine Purpose for which Theocracy existed on the Universe, and once man identified his life purpose with God's Purpose running through all His creation, he set to work to demolish all the intervening obstructions. The realisation of the true self and its assertion was the same as the annihilation of the untrue self, and the fretfulness of the life-force with its inevitable militancy emerged into the abiding peace of Islam. In the course of his exposition of Islam's message and the main features of its ethical code, he too had condemned the nationalism which narrowed human sympathies and divided man from man.

## H.G. WELLS[10]

To clinch matters, there arrived at our quiet retreat in the Gondwana backwoods, a friend who was reading Mr. H.G. Wells' latest novel, *Mr. Britling Sees It Through*, and when he had recovered from the effects of my gushing sermons on Islam, he asked me to read the book he had just finished. I confess I had read little of Wells, but as my friend and comrade in journalism, the late Ghulam Husain, was passionately fond of his writings, I had arranged to meet him when I was in England in 1913, in connection with the Kanpur mosque and other affairs to which I have already referred. I found him on acquaintance most charming and very sympathetic about India and Islam, which no doubt prompted him to extend his hospitality to me during one of his brief visits to his London flat. When in the following year war broke out, I recalled some scraps of conversation at dinner in which I had seemed at the time to detect the usual anti-German feeling of the patriotic Englishmen of those days. Mr. Wells was certainly very furious with Germany in those fateful days when the attitude of England towards the hostilities that had already commenced on the continent was the subject of universal interest, and I had reproduced in the *Comrade* the whole of his controversy with Vernon Lee in the columns of the *Labour Leader*. So when I took up his latest novel, which seemed to give an exposition of his own psychology during those early years of the war, I found in it little that I could not guess he was bound to write. He is always full of ideas and his phrases even when they lack polish have a freshness that always suggest to me bread hot from the baker's shop, so that *Mr. Britling* could not exactly be dull reading. But I often caught myself wondering why he had written this book, and whether it was not itself a series of 'the third leader' of the *Times* of those days of which Wells had made Mr. Britling the author. It was late on the second or third night that I neared the end, and then Mr. Wells startled me with a powerful passage in which I learnt why after all he had written the book.

[10] Herbert George Wells (1866–1946); novelist. *The Time Machine* (1895); *The Stolen Bacillus* (1895); *The Invisible Man* (1897) were some of his novels. The novel Mohamed Ali refers to was published in 1916. It was a justification of the war on religious grounds, as was *God the Invisible King* (1917), though Wells afterwards recanted his religious beliefs.

Mr. Britling in the poignancy of his sorrow on the loss of his young son—of course a 'casualty' had suddenly stumbled into religion and discovered God, and to me, who had not been prepared for this by the earlier writings of Mr. Wells, it seemed that he too had just then made this discovery. But I now understood why my friend had asked me to read that book after a series of my lay sermons, because Mr. Wells' God was not only God, but the One and only King! Mr. Wells was not a patriotic Englishman who must as such hate Germans for he detested such nationalism. He was no doubt a republican but he was not a republican like so many others who find royalty too medieval for these progressive days. He was a republican because he was a believer in theocracy—the most ancient of all forms of Government. A few days after this interesting discovery, I read a long review in a newspaper of a later book of his, than the one I had just read, a book called, *The Soul of a Bishop*, and also read that he had written yet another book, *God the Invisible King*, and I immediately ordered both, and, in fact, received two copies of the latter, as I had, in my eagerness to obtain it, written for it to two of my friends both of whom managed to procure it for me. The conclusion of *Mr. Britling* and these two books, as I said, clinched the matter finally, and I felt an unconquerable craving to go to Europe and preach Islam to these heathens who had set up races and nationalities and states as idols to worship in the temple that should have been dedicated to the one God, the ruler of an undivided mankind, who waited for our submission and in return gave us peace. I wanted to go to Europe, not that there was no room for religious reform in India itself, and in my own community. God knows that there was and still is only too much of it, and if preaching is charity, as it is no doubt, it should by rights begin at home. But on the other side there was to be said that the corruption of the best is the worst, and undoubtedly in a thousand ways Europeans and Americans were immeasurably superior at present to the Asiatics and Africans. If to their progressiveness, Europe and America could only add that essentially necessary element of all real and enduring progress, a true religious outlook, they could accomplish so much which Asia and Africa could net for a long while yet hope to do. It was indeed a true instinct which made Indian Musalmans rejoice a generation ago at the conversion of an American, Mr. Alexander Russell Webb, and of an English solicitor of Liverpool, Mr. Quilliam, and which made them more recently entertain great hopes of the conversion of large numbers in Japan to Islam. Moreover, the East is sure to benefit greatly from any change in Western mentality that could bring the West to take a greater interest in Eastern life and modes of thought and not look upon the Orient only as a portion of God's earth, destined for ever to provide raw materials for Western factories and a dumping ground for Western manufacturers and upon the Orientals as indelibly branded by an *Occidental Kismet* as permanently and inherently inferior, fit only to be exploited as so much cheap labour and to be ruled as 'subject races'. And what could effect such a change better than an awakening to Islam, and recognising that it was an Arab of the desert as much an Asiatic as hundreds of millions of subjects of Western Powers in the East and hewers of wood and drawers of water for Western nations, that had been chosen by the Ruler and Creator of Mankind to convey His last Message to man? It is true that such an Asiatic had been Jesus of Nazareth.

If the West could be brought to study and understand this faith, it would, I felt, be the surest solvent of its race and colour prejudices and East and West would both greatly benefit. And Muslim states, those remnants of the vast temporal power of Islam and, barring China or Japan, the only survivors of the new deluge of the West, would secure a fresh lease of life, and the opportunity they need so badly of instituting a thorough-going reform. Turkey, Iran, Egypt and Morocco all had been administered during their long continued decline by some of the worst rulers that history has known, and had they lost their independence in the reign of some such tyrant, every right minded Muslim would have acknowledged the historic justice of it. But that they should lose it just when the people had been roused at long last to insist on a reform of the administration was the negation of all justice and the Muslim mind was everywhere revolting at it. What added to the bitterness was the undeniable fact that the religious prejudices of Christendom fought on the side of the land-grabbers. Not that those who sought the dissolution of these Muslim states were, except in very rare cases, impelled by such prejudices. As a Muslim, who is plainly told by the Quran, what any school boy could easily understand, that there is no compulsion in religion, I abhor from the bottom of my heart the cruel futility of forcing convictions down peoples' throats. The thing is absurd and as degrading for humanity as, say, idol worship. But in the light of modern warfare with unspeakably base and sordid motives that lead to it, I confess I would any day welcome a real live Crusader who would lead Christendom even against my co-religionists. Peter the Hermit,[11] on his ass, blowing the enthusiasm of the superstitious into the white heat of passion by his uncouth oratory, is by

[11] (1050?–1115). He was one of the most eloquent preachers of the First Crusade.

comparison with the sanctimonious war lords of today, a noble figure. They too, occasionally, talk of Crusades, but, alas, theirs is a Crusade without the Cross and instead of Peter the Hermit it is, as a rule, some bloated profiteer safely seated in a Rolls-Royce that today leads millions to their death. But religious prejudices exist among his dupes, and he is not loath to fan them into flame. Christendom had given to the Muslim as bad a name as to the dog in the proverb, and even when Christianity as a living faith is on the wane, and can no longer provide Christendom with sufficient motive power for a Crusade, it still adds a peculiar zest to the effort of Christendom when it sets out to kill the Muslims.

## INJUSTICE TO THE TURKS

When I had gone to England in 1913, in connection with the Kanpur mosque case and the anti-Turkish policy of England which had insisted on the surrender even of Adrianople by the Turks *before* they had lost it, and was then alone in insisting on its return to the Bulgarians when the former had won it back, I had been invited by the President of the Positivist Society to speak on a paper which he read before it in which he dealt with the Eastern situation. In the course of my comments on it I had pointed out that the Turks had almost lost the Balkan War before it had been declared, for it was not fought on the battlefields of the Balkan, but in the editorial sanctums, and on the public platforms, in the pulpits, in the clubs, and in the drawing rooms of Western Europe. The Turk was unspeakable mainly because he was a Muslim whose religion permitted polygamy and divorce without the intervention of the law courts, with all their paraphernalia of co-respondents and chambermaids peeping through key-holes and private detective agencies. And this unspeakable person who had a *harem*—with fewer females, incidentally, who were his spouses than the average Western man mates with promiscuously,—had the still more unspeakable obduracy not to accept even in theory the doctrine of turning the other cheek which the good Christians themselves had never converted into practice. What then could be more natural than all Europe 'Cutting the Turk's head' in its politics as it pretended to do in its sport. And so long as he had for his capital the city founded by the first Christian Emperor of Rome whose name it still bore and instead of the church bells ringing the *muezzin's* chants called the faithful at dawn of day to prayer and to salvation from the minarets of St. Sophia, what could be more agreeable than to turn him out 'bag and baggage'?

## THE EVIL OF NATIONALISM

But although Christianity is on the wane and the Church repels today, every good Christian of the old days does not become a profiteer and there are some who have even escaped the epidemic of an earth-grabbing Imperialism. It is these men to whom an appeal might, I thought, successfully be made by so rationalistic and natural a faith as Islam, and although even after discarding most of the church dogma they have not shed all their anti-Islamic prejudices, they are people to whom reason cannot long appeal in vain. The Armageddon,[12] as it was at one time the fashion to call the terrible war in Europe, did not proceed very long before people saw its sheer godlessness. The church of each nation blessed its flag and whatever may have been its inner private belief, publicly prayed for the national victory, as if each conscript carried the sword of Gideon, the sword of the Lord. Every church shouted its appeal to the God of Hosts, but when Israel was so hopelessly divided and tribe fought against tribe, it became clear to not a few that Jehovah could only be an indignant neutral. He knew only too well that the appeal of each contending tribe was, in reality, not to Him, the Lord God of Israel, but to the heathen deities that each had taken up, to Baal[13] and to Ashtoreth, to Molock[14] and to Mammon. And before long many of the warriors too began to realise this for tinselled falsehood could not long pass for truth when shots and shells were tearing everything to pieces. Human sanity was beginning to return at last, and many began to recognise that there was some such thing as a human brotherhood in spite of those contradictions in terms, the 'National Churches' which continued to work as the willing tools of National Governments. It seemed to me that long before the West would know the truth about the 'Great Illusion', which was not war, but the Nationalism that was bound to lead to wars, and symptoms of what the Nationalists and Imperialists called Defeatism were not wanting. When towards the close of the War the American President[15] began to assert himself and to voice the opinion of this class of people a new hope began to dawn. Phrases like 'a peace without victory' began for the first time to

[12] A place mentioned in the New Testament as the site of the final cosmic battle between the forces of good and evil in the last days.

[13] Used especially of the Semitic deities who were held to produce agricultural and animal fertility.

[14] This refers to Moloch. In the Bible, a god of the Canaanites and other peoples, in whose cult children were sacrificed by fire.

[15] The reference is to Woodrow Wilson (1856–1924), elected Democratic President in 1912 and 1916.

lend significance to the cant of an earlier day about 'a war to end all wars', and I felt that when such a peace came, that would be the psychological moment to go and entreat the West to try and understand the faith that judged by any standard has proved undoubtedly the best solvent of race and colour prejudices. Modern Christianity that still laid so much stress on the Fatherhood of God had apparently forgotten all about the Brotherhood of man, or had come to whittle down its claims by such qualifications as those of that fugitive politician Lord Rosebery[16] who in my Varsity days, had told a British audience that man was no doubt a brother, but not necessarily a citizen! I felt that the least that one could prophesy with safety as one of the consequences of this war would be that the post-war Europe would not be the pre-war Europe, and after the terrible nightmare of this war it could be easily awakened into a recognition of the Kingdom of God in which every man would be a brother and a fellow-subject of God, the sole Sovereign of His Universe. And I had made a vow to myself that as soon as the war ended and we were once more free, I would go to Europe with this the latest and yet far the oldest evangelic, which God had Himself preached to the primeval man.

## MAN PROPOSES, GOD DISPOSES

But the war went on merrily for some time more and so did our own internment. In fact, the armistice that put an end to all hostilities still left us the same 'prisoners of peace' as the war had made us. Through Mahatma Gandhi's[17] intervention a Committee was appointed by the Viceroy to examine the question of our release, but although it consisted of two Judges of the High Court [B. Lindsay], one of whom was an Indian[18]—and incidentally an ardent political opponent of ours—there was nothing judicial about the inquiry. At our request it forwarded to us a number of very brief and indefinite statements which were supposed to be the reasons for our internment,[19] but curiously enough they did not include the most important and definite statement that had been heard about a great deal

[16] (1847–1929). British statesman and Liberal Prime Minister (1894–5).

[17] Gandhi first met Mohamed Ali in 1915, and wrote to him on 9 January. Soon thereafter, he took up the cause of the release of the Ali brothers. 'I dare not,' he wrote to the Private Secretary of the Viceroy on April 1918, 'shirk an obvious duty regarding Ali brothers. Their internment has soured the Muslim section. As a Hindu I feel that I must not stand aloof from them.'

[18] Abdur Rauf, a judge of the Punjab High Court.

[19] See Hasan (ed.), *Mohamed Ali in Indian Politics*, vol. 2, pp. 115–16.

during the whole of the previous year, namely, that we had written to His Majesty the late Amir of Afghanistan, a letter urging him to attack India which His Majesty had, of course, forwarded to the Government of India with a special envoy and that my brother had written during our internment a letter to our spiritual adviser [Maulana Abdul Bari] telling him that it was now necessary to resort to violence and to organise an armed rebellion against the British Government.[20] In the autumn session of the Imperial Legislative Council, at Simla, in 1917, a Muslim member had asked Government with regard to the release of Mrs. [Annie] Besant[21] and her two fellow-workers and lieutenants from internment and had been informed in terms so general as to appear applicable to us also, that Government contemplated the release of *detenus* if she could be satisfied on certain points. A supplementary question was then asked with regard to our release which elicited the reply that it too was under consideration. And before we could read these proceedings of the Council, the Director of Criminal Intelligence[22] sent from Simla a police officer[23] under him to obtain from us certain undertakings. Immediately after him came the Hon'ble Raja Sahib of Mahmudabad,[24] who was also a representative of the Musalmans in the Imperial Legislature and he interviewed us by arrangement with Government. Not aware of the Raja Sahib's intended arrival, we had already given the undertakings required only after altering the form slightly in two places, with a view to prevent any inference even by implication of any impropriety in our conduct in the past and to safeguard our religious freedom. The Raja Sahib felt completely assured by

[20] This Report was submitted by the committee which was appointed to enquire into the cases of the Ali brothers. The charges were sent to them on 13 November 1918 and their written replies were received on 2 December 1918. On 6–7 December Lindsay and Rauf interviewed the Ali brothers in Chhindwara. These details are set out in Part I of the Report, while Part II refers to Mohamed Ali's objection that the Defence of India Act, 1915, was *ultra vires* of the Indian Legislature, and that if the Act was *intra vires*, 'the rules made under it . . . were made without authority'. Part III of the Report produced here in an abridged form deals with the history of the *Anjuman-i-Khuddam-i-Kaaba*.

[21] Annie Besant (1847–1933), herself a victim of government repression, campaigned for the release of the Ali brothers.

[22] Sir Charles Cleveland. He joined the Indian Civil Service as Assistant Commissioner in 1887. He was Inspector-General of Police before his appointment as Director of the Central Intelligence Department in 1910.

[23] Abdul Majeed.

[24] Mohammad Ali Mohammad (1889–1931) was a patron of 'Young Party' activities; supported them 'with a clique of noisy and aggressive Muslims . . . who make the Raja's house their headquarters and live and agitate at his expense'; President of the Muslim League, 1915–19.

what transpired at the interview and wired to Simla that he was satisfied. Soon after Mrs. Besant and her companions were released, but no orders were received with regard to us, though we were flooded with telegrams from all parts of India congratulating us on our release, or anxiously inquiring if we too had been released. Mrs. Besant was then elected to preside at the forthcoming session of the Indian National Congress to be held at Calcutta and a similar honour was done to me by the All-India Muslim League of which I was one of the founders. But although Mrs. Besant occupied the Presidential Chair I was not destined to do so. When our release was still delayed a question was asked by the same member[25] in the Council at Simla and in reply Government announced that it did not intend to release us like Mrs. Besant. It was then that we heard about these two letters, and in fact the letter of my brother to our spiritual adviser was alleged to have been written *after* our undertaking had been given but *before* the final announcement made by Government some weeks later! It was then freely talked about that but for the two documents and particularly for the latter which fell into the hands of the Criminal Intelligence Department just in the nick of time we too would have been released. When we came to know of this we denied the authorship of both and requested Government to enable us to see the forgeries.[26] That request, however, was never complied with, but when a year later the question of our release came up once more for consideration and the Committee after perusing our written statements came to interview us in December 1918, we naturally asked why those two documents did not figure in the statement of reasons for our internment and its continuance, specially when many matters comparatively trivial and far less definite had been included. The only answer we received was that the Criminal Intelligence Department had made no mention of them, and it was even suggested that we had been misinformed about their existence.[27] It may here be added that when subsequently I visited England in 1920, I wrote to the Rt. Hon'ble Edwin S. Montagu, Secretary of State for India,[28] on the subject of these two letters and in an interview subsequently pressed him for a reply, which he

[25] Syed Raza Ali (1882–1949), an Aligarh graduate, lawyer and later member of the Viceroy's Council; member, UP Legislative Council, 1912–25, and led Muslim delegations to the Viceroy over Turkey in 1922 and 1923.

[26] See Mohamed Ali to James DuBoulay, 24 October 1917, in Hasan (ed.), *Mohamed Ali in Indian Politics*, vol. 2, pp. 69–70.

[27] See ibid., n. 4.

[28] Edwin Samuel Montagu (1879–1924); M.P., 1906–22; Parliamentary Under-Secretary of State for India, 1910–14; Secretary of State for India, 1917–22.

at last promised after communicating with the Government of India. I do not know what reply he received from Government. All I know is that I waited in vain for months and finally sailed for India in September 1920, without the promised reply. To resume the thread of this narrative, the Committee, as we had all along expected, justified the internment when it had been ordered but reported in favour of immediate release.[29] Nevertheless we were kept waiting for months even after that and although we understand that the Secretary of State favoured it, the Director of Criminal Intelligence refused to be responsible for the peace of India in the event of our release. The final result was that we were informed we could not be released so long as the peace negotiations with Turkey still continued. A year previously Mrs. Besant had on her own release interviewed the viceroy, Lord Chelmsford,[30] and other members of the Government of India, and had been assured that it was our sympathy for Turkey that prevented our release during the War; and now when hostilities had ceased, our sympathy for Turkey prevented our release during the peace negotiations. But, as we had more than once made it clear, our sympathy with Turkey was not political or territorial but religious, for the Sovereign of Turkey was the successor of the Prophet and the Commander of the Faithful. It was our religious duty to prevent the further disintegration of the temporal power of the Khilafat which was indispensable for the defence of our faith, to maintain the inviolability of the sacred regions of Islam and to see that the dying injunction of the Prophet with regard to exclusive Muslim sovereignty over *Jazirat-ul-Arab* (or the Island of Arabia including Syria, Palestine and Mesopotamia) was not disregarded.[31]

[29] At the insistence of H.D. Craik, the Government communicated the proposed reply by William Vincent to questions asked by G.S. Khaparde regarding the cases of the Ali brothers. The Government refused to release the report of the Committee of Enquiry (submitted on 20 December 1918), but summed up its findings. The Committee concluded that the Government of India was 'fully justified in imposing restrictions upon their liberty', adding that 'the contact of the brothers since their internment has been sufficient justification for the refusal to release them during the period of the war'. The Committee, however, recommended the release of the brothers because 'there is no longer occasion to apprehend that any views or activities of theirs can interfere with the relations between Great Britain and Turkey'.

[30] (1868–1933); Viceroy of India, 1916–21. In October 1917, Annie Besant went to Simla, following her conditional release from internment, with the intention of discussing with the Viceroy the release of the Ali brothers.

[31] 'The mandate of Jazirat-ul-Arab', declared Mohamed Ali, 'has been given to us by the Prophet. No Christian or Jew can be the mandatory. The order to us is to expel the Christians and Jews from Arabia.' The Jazirat-ul-Arab, according to Mazharul Haq, 'touches the deepest religious sentiments of the followers of Islam. This country must remain under the suzerainty of the Muslim Khalifa.'

Moreover, it was our right as British subjects to put such pressure upon our Government as we lawfully could to respect our religious requirements on the satisfaction of which alone our political allegiance rested. But of this right we were still being deprived, and then came on top of this grievance the grievance of the whole Indian people after the terrible happenings at Amritsar.[32] It was then that we decided in order to mark our protest against all this, to break, after giving due notice to Government, some of the internment regulations that Government had prescribed, such as the submission of our correspondence to scrutiny by the district magistrate, and thereby invite the penalties attached by law to their breach. We expected our arrest and trial; but although the arrest came some weeks later, the Government avoided the publicity of a trial by confining us as state prisoners under Regulation III, which more than a hundred years ago, the East India Company had enacted while India was still being added little by little to the British Empire. Early one morning,[33] well before day-break, we were removed from our house at Chhindwara which armed police had surrounded, and, escorted by two high police officials and some armed policemen, we were driven in motor-cars to Betul, some 80 miles distant, and lodged in the gaol.[34]

## END OF INTERNMENT AT CHHINDWARA

It is true as, unlike the Old Testament story, the Quran tells us, that Joseph had preached the finest little sermon that was ever preached to two of his fellow-prisoners on the text of God's sole sovereignty, when they had betrayed to him their fear of Pharaoh, the only Lord they knew and served and regarded as the master of their fate and had asked him to interpret their dreams well known to every reader of Genesis.[35] I had, therefore, a Prophet's precedence for preaching on the same text even in my prison-

[32] The Amritsar massacre, in which government troops fired on a peaceful gathering and killed 379 and wounded abut 1,200 (according to official reports). This occurred at a park—Jallianwala Bagh—on 13 April 1919. The troops were commanded by General Reginald E.H. Dwyer.

[33] 8 June 1919.

[34] In June 1919, the government issued orders under Regulation III of 1818 for the detention of the Ali brothers at Betul in the Central Provinces. This was done, according to a notification, because 'the Government of India have ample evidence that the brothers are pursuing an active campaign of hostility against the Government and having advocated assistance to the Amir of Afghanistan. They are also satisfied that the restrictions hitherto imposed upon them at Chhindwara under the Defence of Indian Act are not sufficient to prevent them from inciting loyal Muslims to discard their attitude of loyalty.'

[35] The opening book of the Old Testament, and the first of the five Books of the Pentateuch.

house, and my experience of more than one Indian prison has amply confirmed Shakespeare's view that 'There is a soul of goodness in things evil'. And although I may just as well state at once that I delivered no set sermons to my fellow-prisoners, there was many a heart to heart talk with some of them on the subject of our spiritual experience which may, I trust, prove as helpful to them as it has already proved to me. The Betul gaol population was no less intelligent and receptive than I had found many of the townspeople of Chhindwara or the village folk that used to visit us so often during our three and-a-half years' internment there.[36] Of course we were not permitted to take part in any public meeting, and when we had first come to Chhindwara few people indeed knew what fearful wild fowl it was. But they were all eager to listen to us and the anniversary of the Prophet's birthday in the lunar month of Rabi I, which has come to be celebrated in India as a festival and a ceremony, provided the requisite opportunity. On these occasions more or less trained reciters read in a singsong fashion from printed books or manuscripts copied from their set discourses in very ornate and often rhymed prose, as a rule much above the intelligence of the audience. They contain legendary accounts of genesis of the world and traditional accounts of the Prophet's birth and of his famous 'Night Journey' from the Kaaba in Mecca to the Temple in Jerusalem which are based in the majority of cases on the less reliable Traditions, or on such interpretations of authentic Traditions as favour the miraculous element. This ornate prose is literally garnished with verse in which the panegyrics of the Prophet are chanted by the reciter along with three or four other companions with more fervour than musical talent. Beyond rousing religious emotion, these celebrations do little spiritual good and in fact the custom to stand up as a token of deep veneration when the reciter comes to the prose passage or verses announcing the birth of the Prophet has led a few of the more ignorant and superstitious to entertain a vague sort of notion akin to the Christian notion of the presence of Jesus at the Eucharist, which naturally gives great offence to the 'Non-conformists' or *Ghayr-Muqqalids* of Islam, generally known as *Wahhabis*[37] or followers of that aggressive puritan, Mohammad ibn Abdul Wahhab of Nejd,[38] who are opposed to such

[36] From 23 November 1915 to 8 June 1919.

[37] This name was given by its opponents. The community called itself Unitarians following the school of Imam Hanbal, as interpreted by Ibn Taimiya, who attacked the cult of saints in many of his writings.

[38] Nejd, on the Yemen border and the eastern Hejaz near Mecca.

celebrations altogether.[39] But on rare occasions learned *ulama* conduct the celebrations themselves and then the religious discourse is *ex tempore* and while it deals with a few prominent events of the life of the Prophet, it is more in the nature of a sermon in which the moral is enforced by copious illustrations from the Prophet's more authentic Traditions. When it was suggested to my brother and to me that we should address the assembly on this occasion we agreed and I decided to cram my discourse with as much of the Prophet's biography as possible, of course to eschew every tradition that had not been fully authenticated and was not, in the truest sense of the word, historical.

I had myself an open mind on the subject of miracles, but I felt that it would serve no purpose to include in what I said anything that was generally interpreted as a suspension of the law of causation in nature particularly as, unlike Christianity, no part of our faith rested on belief in a miracle. I must confess I was at first afraid that for the simple folk of Chhindwara, most of whom were illiterate. I was providing very unfamiliar fare. It may be a 'feast of reason' right enough, but it would be tasteless and insipid by comparison with the rhymed though unintelligible prose and the fervently chanted 'poetry' of the usual reciters. But my mind was set at rest when I learnt that we would not monopolise the entire celebration but that the familiar figure of the reciter would still be there and that in fact he would begin the proceedings. But whatever doubt I had felt before was soon dissolved, for I found the audience unusually interested and the celebration lasted well past midnight. More than that, we were invited to another celebration which one of the audience then and there decided to hold at his own expense on the following evening, and in fact several others followed. This led to my planning a regular series of discourses dealing with the entire life of the Prophet and his teachings and the history of his times, together with a discourse or two on the results of that teaching as exhibited in the lives and times of his Companions who succeeded him as Khalifas. It was only when I began to carry out my plan that I realised not only the eagerness of the people to listen to such discourses but the difficulty of avoiding stories that could be regarded as above the suspicion of being apocryphal. There was no biography of the Prophet in Urdu that did not contain stories of doubtful authenticity. This I had known for some time, and it was this that had made me urge on my old tutor, the late

[39] (1703–87); his general aim was to do away with all innovations which were later than the third century of Islam. The Wahhabi doctrine was introduced into India by Saiyid Ahmad of Rae Bareli (1786–1831). He acquired a large following in India, and established a permanent centre in Patna, where he appointed four *Khalifas*, and an *Imam*.

Maulana Shibli, as a great grievance, during a visit of his to me at Baroda, ten years earlier, that even a historian of Islam like him, who had written the life of Mamun al-Rashid in his 'Heroes of Islam' series had not gone beyond a biography of the great Umar, and had left the life of the greatest Hero of the World, the Prophet himself, unchronicled. And it was then that he had explained to me that the task was far from a light one, for in no language did such a biography of the Prophet exist as I and a hundred thousand others today desired. There were large tomes in Arabic no doubt, but they were all in the nature of material for a Life of the Prophet, and would have to be threshed and winnowed by a biographer before such a life, as a proper critical standard required, could be published. Nevertheless he recognised not only the importance of such an undertaking but the immediate urgency of it, and before long he announced his intention to take the work in hand.

With the ever-ready financial assistance of Her Highness the Begum of Bhopal,[40] Shibli and the ardent disciples whom he had gathered around himself completed the Prophet's biography just before the hand of death removed him from our midst. But at the time when I needed such a work it did not exist. The first volume came out while we were still at Chhindwara, and in Betul gaol I was privileged to read the proof-sheets of the second volume as they were being printed off. Several other volumes are yet to be published, and even while I am writing this in midsummer of 1923, I am still awaiting the issue of the third volume. As I have confessed before, never having acquired such a knowledge of the Arabic language as to be able to read Arabic books with ease, I had to be content with such poor material as existed in Urdu and of course in English, though I have to admit it was my own ignorance that prevented my having access to the Urdu translations of all the six noted compilations of Traditions known as the *Sihah-Sitta*,[41] some of which I was subsequently enabled to purchase second-hand at Chhindwara itself. In the first year of our residence at Chhindwara only one *Meelad* celebration had taken place and we had assisted only as members of the audience. In the next year no less than eight celebrations took place, and in the following year they were as many as seventeen. Naturally my next study after the Quran itself was the

[40] Bhopal was a princely state in central India. It was founded by an Afghan soldier of fortune. Among its well-known rulers were Sikandar Begum (1844–68), her daughter Shah Jahan (d. 1901), and Sultan Jahan Begum.

[41] The compilation of *Hadith* (*Hadis*) by Bukhari (810–70). In his selection of Hadith, Bukhari showed the greatest critical ability and in editing the texts sought to obtain the most scrupulous accuracy.

biography of the Prophet and with additional impetus supplied by the ever-growing enthusiasm of the people of Chhindwara, I pounced upon every scrap of such literature that was within the range of my linguistic capacity, so that while I became more and more acquainted with the teachings of him whose life was the best commentary on the Quran and supplied as much theology as one needed to be a good Muslim, I was also enabled to make my discourses at those *Meelad* celebrations of some utility and profit to my eager audience. In the gaol at Betul these meetings were out of the question though I see no reason why they should not be encouraged by the authorities and see good reason why they should be. But such intercourse as we could have with our fellow-prisoners was not, as I have already said, without its opportunities of offering such spiritual aliment and sustenance as we could to our comrades in confinement.

But Europe, which to my mind needed nothing so much as a clearer knowledge of Islam and of the Prophet who had brought to the world the Last Message of God, was still a far cry. However, after we had added seven months of confinement as State Prisoners inside a gaol to four years of internment and exile, came all of a sudden a 'clear the line' telegraphic message from the Government, towards the end of December 1919, and within a few hours we found ourselves once more free and travelling with all speed towards Amritsar, where the Indian National Congress, the Muslim League and the recently organised Khilafat Conference were already holding or were about to hold their respective sessions.[42]

## KHILAFAT DELEGATION TO EUROPE

We had not been two days at Amritsar when my brother who had been elected to preside at the Khilafat Conference broke to me the startling news that the organisers of that conference insisted on my heading a Khilafat delegation[43] to Europe, and lo and behold! before scarcely a month had passed since our release I was out on the sea travelling with three companions on what used to be an Austrian Lloyd Steamer bound for

[42] On 27 December 1919, the government decided to extend the benefit of amnesty to the Ali brothers. This was probably done at the behest of the Home Member who considered that their release was desirable 'in order to placate Muslim feeling which would be irritated by their exclusion as contrasted with indulgence shown to Punjab and other political offenders'.

[43] The delegation sailed for Europe on 1 February 1920. It was received by Fisher, the minister, on behalf of Montagu, the Secretary of State for India. For the full text of the discussion, see Hasan (ed.), *Mohamed Ali in Indian Politics*, vol. 3, pp. 12–26. For Mohamed Ali's itinerary in Europe, see Afzal Iqbal, *Life and Times,* pp. 217–23.

Venice. Only a few of those who are fairly familiar with our names as propagandists perhaps know how deeply we love domesticity, for all the publicity that has fallen to our share, and I must confess even my missionary zeal did not seem equal to the task of tearing myself away from my family so soon after our restoration to freedom. Strictly speaking, the expression 'tearing myself away from my family' did not accurately define the position, for even the month that I spent in India after the release from Betul jail was mostly spent in travelling across the country, with barely three or four days thrown in at Rampur, and even while there the number of visitors that we received made us more or less complete strangers to the family circle itself. I learnt what baggage I was taking with me only when on board the ship my old servant, who had been my companion since childhood and my school fellow [Mohammad Husain] for some time, gave me the keys of the boxes and a list of the things *he* had thought I would need in Europe, and it was startlingly unpleasant to realise as I did on the receipt of my first letter in England from my daughters that I had not been able to have a single meal with 'my little suffragettes' even during the few days that I was at home! However, it seemed that I had been taken at my word and Europe was soon enough before me filling the pews of my Church and awaiting for the new message from the pulpit! But in reality that was not so. It was certainly not politics that had lured me this time to Europe. The impulse was purely religious and one of my companions, Maulana Syed Sulaiman Nadvi, the disciple of Shibli and the Head of the Shibli Academy of Authors, who was editing the Prophet's life by his Master and had never taken any part in politics, was there to prove it.[44]

Nevertheless long before I reached the mission field that I had been pining for, I had fully realised that my propaganda was to be of a greatly restricted nature. Although by no means confined to them, our appeal was in the first instance to be addressed to the governments that dominated the Peace Conference, and where governments come in, freedom such as a missionary needs cannot be completed. Diplomatic decorum may suggest nothing more irksome than silk-thread; but the coils of that thread mean to the ardent preacher just as much captivity as fetters of steel that leave surest marks on the wrists and ankles of a galley slave. Knowing something of the way in which I had been 'bitten' by religion, several of my friends

[44] Syed Sulaiman Nadvi (1884–1953); educated at Phulwari Sharif and the Madrasa Imdadiyaa in Darbhanga, Bihar, and the Nadwat al-ulama in Lucknow. He was one of Shibli Numani's favourite disciples and founded the Dar al-Musannifin at Azamgarh in 1914; member of the Khilafat delegation to Europe (1920), and of delegation to the Hejaz in 1924–5.

in England advised me to avoid all mention of religion in the advocacy of our cause. But how could we do that? We were not Turkish Nationalists fighting for a little space in which their race could breathe and live. We were Indians and subjects of the King of England who had been at war with the King of Turkey. But as we were Muslim subjects of a Christian Sovereign to whom we had tendered our temporal allegiance on the clear understanding that he would respect our religious obligations, and it was only our religious obligations that had compelled us to voice our protest against the annihilation of a temporal power which our religion required to remain unseparated from the spiritual head of the Islamic world. Religion, therefore, was the one thing that gave us a *locus standi* in the councils of the Allied and Associated nations dictating terms of peace to their fallen foes. Moreover, I had already seen, as I have stated, that at the back of the minds of most people in these nations, who hated the Turks was their detestation of the Turk's religion which they regarded as a confused jumble of spiritual tags plagiarised from the older Semitic creeds of Moses and Jesus, and of oriental licentiousness, intolerance and tyranny. The Turk could not, therefore, hope for justice at the hands of these nations before Islam had been better understood by them. Nevertheless, people do not easily come to meetings in Europe, however extensively and efficiently they may be advertised, in order to be preached to and converted, particularly, to 'pagan' creeds. And in any case, however much religion may loom in the background, the foreground has necessarily to be occupied by politics as the principal figure.

It is not possible for me to judge what religious effect our propaganda produced on our audiences, but I cannot help recalling the pleasurable sensation I experienced at discovering that a most representative gathering of organised Labour at the Annual Convention at Scarborough,[45] was not half as averse to hearing about my religion as I had been warned by friends that I would find such an irreligious body as Labour to be. The five minutes that the committee had finally, and after several unsuccessful efforts on my part, allotted to me owing to a very crowded programme previously fixed upon which the convention had anyhow to get through, had expanded into something like twenty, and when the chairman found the audience so eager to be chaffed on its reputed irreligiousness by a pagan evangelist as to protest more than once against the Presidential bell that sounded the summons to resumption of silence. And in France too, where the laic law has its fanatics that are as intolerant of all religions as the Inquisitors of

[45] See Hasan (ed.), *Mohamed Ali in Indian Politics*, vol. 3, pp. 107–10.

Spain were of heresy and heretics,[46] every fresh meeting that we held attracted a larger audience than the one before it, though unlike the public meetings in England these were open only to those who had been invited or had procured invitation cards from the organisers. Perhaps nothing was so indicative of an awakened interest in an exposition of Islam as the compliment paid us by that well-known senator and publicist M. Victor Bernard, by entering the lists as a doughty combatant.

## AN UNKNOWN VISITOR

The incident that proved most encouraging to me, however, was the visit that I received one day from a gentleman in London with whom I had not been previously acquainted. I learnt that although a layman he was a keen student of religion and an able expositor of Anglican Christianity and an intimate friend of many distinguished Churchmen on Church dignitaries. The attitude of that Church during the peace negotiations had proved as hostile to the cause that our delegation had come to advocate as the non-conformist conscience itself; but I found my visitor to be extraordinarily gifted with imaginative sympathy which is, oddly enough, perhaps rarer in his imperial race, than continental nations without anything like the same number of imperial possessions outside Europe. He had evidently read a good deal of what we had published and had been sufficiently interested by what he had read to pay us a visit, and become still more intimately acquainted with our views. In the course of my exposition of the institution of Khilafat I had occasion to explain the Theocracy of Islam and the significance of the Kingdom of God as understood by a Muslim, and at the end of it I was naturally gratified to learn that I had not really bored my all too patient listener. As a matter of fact, I soon received a still more gratifying assurance which I could not take as mere politeness and a desire not to betray boredom to one's host at his drowsy discourse, for he invited me to prepare on the subject of our conversation a small volume which he had arranged to get published and enclosed a contract form for me to sign if I accepted his all too kind offer. I would have signed it then and there were it not for the fear that preoccupied as I then happened to be, I might not be able to fulfil the contract within the time specified. However, the offer was too tempting to be refused and I carried the contract form in my attaché case for some months hoping to be able one of these days to muster sufficient confidence to sign it and commit myself finally

[46] The delegation left for Paris on 28 May 1920.

to a task that had at one time appeared so congenial to me. But, alas for the vanity of human wishes! I left the shores of Europe just towards the end of the period that I had been allowed for writing that little volume, and even the contract form had remained unsigned.

## BACK TO INDIA: HOME ON WHEELS

In October, 1920, I was back in India, but as my wife and children soon found, it was not to my home that I had returned. Mahatma Gandhi, my brother and I were constantly on the move touring all over India and I can hardly remember two or three consecutive days during many months in which I was in one place. The railway train became my home as it had become my brother's when I had left for Europe. Once it so happened that I was within an ace of sailing again to Europe without the least previous notice just when I was about to step into a waiting taxi at Delhi bound for the railway station where my wife had already preceded me with the intention of accompanying me to Aligarh, and sharing with me my professional apartments at the National Muslim University. The Government of India had arranged to send some nominees of its own from among the Indian Musalmans to place their views on the Khilafat question before the Prime Minister and one of these was the President of our Central Khilafat Committee. He had agreed to go only if another member of the Committee was also nominated by Government, and Mahatma Gandhi asked me to proceed. I was most reluctant particularly as I expected little good would result from such a representation; but I could not refuse. I, however, consented to go only if my friend, Dr. Ansari of Delhi, who had been the Director of the All-India Medical Mission to Turkey during the Balkan War, was also one of the party and to this all agreed. But then I suggested that Dr. Ansari could himself suffice and pressed that I should be spared; and luckily for me I managed to escape the second exile almost within a year of the first and to catch the train for Aligarh just as it was about to start. When in the train I told my wife of my lucky escape, she took a warning from it and after that, like a wise woman, decided to share my home on wheels as well as my modest professional apartments at Aligarh. She said she had had enough of grass widowhood, and next time if I was ordered again to proceed to Europe on such short notice, Mahatma or no Mahatma, she intended to be present to put her foot down or at least insist on accompanying me—at public expense! Well, I have not gone again to Europe and she has not therefore had occasion to travel in strange lands so far from the usual horizon of an oriental woman which had for centuries been bounded by the four walls of her home, however spacious, but she has travelled long enough I should think—at public expense. For when she began to accompany me she disdained to be a useless appendage and being a far better book-keeper than myself and certainly as good an organiser at least in her own circle of women, she started a lively enough propaganda among Indian women and collected for the Khilafat Fund such large sums that they soon invited her to travel on their behalf. We passed several months in this fashion together, flitting from place to place and province to province, touring with Mahatma Gandhi and a small party of fellow-workers and secretaries when on the 14th September, 1921, I was arrested at the railway station of Waltair, when we were travelling on our way to Madras and the disturbed area of Malabar. We parted company once more, but it has been a source of consolation to me, not unmixed with some amusement, that my wife is still travelling—at public expense—with our nephew and son-in-law [Zahid Ali][47] as secretary and has collected large amounts for the Khilafat Fund and for the National Muslim University. Mahatma Gandhi had insisted more than once on her addressing a few words to gatherings of ladies and had assured her at the end of her speeches that she was a better speaker than myself, and since my arrest it is not unoften that large male audiences have had their enthusiasm whipped up by the stirring address of a veiled Muslim woman who had never dreamt some years ago of addressing even an audience of women outside the *harem* or *zenana.* In a nomadic life such as I have described writing even a booklet was out of the question, for much as I envied the equanimity and placid calm of my chief who filled his two reviews week after week with crisp fresh matter from his own pen, while trekking in noisy, smoky and jolting fast trains across the extensive sub-continent, I could not, with my own more excitable temperament, ever hope to imitate his example.

## ARREST AT WALTAIR AND THE KARACHI TRIAL

The arrest at Waltair on a warrant notifying that the Magistrate of the District which I had never before even visited demanded security from me for good behaviour and keeping the peace, was, as events subsequently proved, only an expedient to detain me pending the arrival of another

[47] He was the son of Shaukat Ali and Mohamed Ali's son-in-law. Before launching the Urdu newspaper *Khilafat* from Bombay, he had been the manager of the *Comrade* and *Hamdard Press*. He died in 1968.

warrant from far-off Karachi, and before I could reach Madras, not to mention Malabar, I was lodged in the local gaol and three days later the proceedings were withdrawn, only to enable the Police Officer from the Bombay Presidency to arrest me on the Karachi warrant as I came out of the gaol. This fresh warrant had been issued because of a resolution passed at a Khilafat Conference held at Karachi over which I had presided. My brother and I were charged along with five other co-workers, one of whom was a Hindu and a religious dignitary of great eminence, with conspiring to seduce Muslim troops from their allegiance and we expected the sentence of transportation for life. But the Jury, which consisted of one European, two Goanese Christians and two Hindus, gave a unanimous verdict of Not Guilty on that charge. However, on the minor charge of publishing a statement *likely* to have that effect, the Judge sentenced the six Musalmans to two years' rigorous imprisonment and discharged the Hindu co-accused. It was then at long last that I found a haven of refuge in the prison at Karachi where no doubt from the point of view of Government, 'the wicked cease from troubling', and from that of 'the wicked', 'the weary have some rest!'

## AUTHORSHIP

During the long winter nights there it occurred to me that even after the day's labour in the gaol I could have some leisure, and the peace and calm that I needed for writing, and accordingly I applied for sanction to have my own books and purchase writing material at my own cost for the purpose of indulging in a little authorship. When I had done about four or five months of my 'time' in gaol I received the necessary sanction and some months later the list of books too was sanctioned and gradually I began to get most of the books that I needed. But estimating my capacity for serious mental work after the drudgery of my gaol task far more liberally than experience subsequently showed it to be, I had thought of compiling a Life of the Prophet as well as an exposition of the message he had brought for mankind. This Life was in the main to be based on Shibli's monumental work, though differing in its arrangement on account of the difference in the classes of readers for whom the two were intended. As it happened I decided to commence the larger work first, and began to read for it in the evenings. This was a congenial enough task, though the difficulties of a prisoner in communicating with the outside world and other restraints greatly delayed the supply of the books I needed. But when more than a year of my sentence was passed I realised that the preparation of such a work as the Life of the Prophet in the circumstances in which I found myself was an impossibility. No volume of Shibli's *Life,* after the first two, had been issued and it was neither possible to get the manuscript from the Shibli Academy even if it was safe to send it all that distance. In its absence, access to a much larger library than I could get together in the existing circumstances was a *sine quo non* and, above all, constant consultation with literary friends better acquainted with Arabic than myself. So I gave up all idea of that and fell back on the much less ambitious task of preparing an exposition of Islam which would be far more personal than a Life of the Prophet could have been. About the same time I received from England from my sympathetic visitor who had arranged for the publication of a small volume on this subject, his own latest booklet on the reunion of Christian Churches. Evidently he had not forgotten the conversation at our first meeting. During our trial at Karachi, in which our plea was that we must follow God's law in preference to any man-made law if the latter conflicted with it, a letter had appeared, in a weekly review, of the Khilafat situation, published in London over initials which were perhaps his, in the course of which the writer had alluded to a conversation he said he had with me from which he could understand that such would be our plea, and he had aptly cited the similar plea of the Apostles Peter and John, when prosecuted before the Sanhedrim: 'Whether it be right in the sight of God to hearken unto you more than unto God, judge ye' (Acts 4:19) and 'We ought to obey God rather than men' (Acts 5:29). His kindly thought in sending me his latest book had on me the effect of a reminder, and I took up the task that I had so long neglected. The spirit was willing but, alas! the flesh was weak. Diabetes had undermined my bodily strength and during the excitement of the trial at Karachi had given me a clear enough "notice to quit" in the shape of a nasty carbuncle in the neck not far from the jugular vein. The absence of all worry and excitement and the strict dieting in the gaol coupled with my ten or twelve days' fasting every month in addition to the ordinary fasts throughout the month of Ramazan which was obligatory, had warded off further attacks of Glycosuria but I had not recovered sufficient strength enough to sit up and do much writing work after the day's gaol task. And the absence of a chair and a table and better lighting than what a single hurricane lantern provided, added to my difficulties. I have little hope that even this volume that I had hoped to be able to prepare well within the period of my imprisonment will be finished, or even well advanced before I am discharged. But since I have already commenced this task, I continue it and trust to the Shaper of our destinies to enable me one day to complete it.

Since I first commenced the study of the Quran I have read a fair amount about Islam from the point of view of Muslims and also of their critics; but nothing that I have read has altered the significance of Islam for me on which I had stumbled in the first few months of our internment eight years ago. The main theme of the Quran and, as I subsequently discovered, of the sayings of the Prophet as perceived in authentic Traditions is the Kinghood of God and the Service of Man as His Agent and vicegerent, and everything that I have since read only serves to strengthen the theocratic character of Islam. As I said at the outset of this account of my individual experience I am not an expert writing for experts but still a mere "man in the street" writing "for the man in the street," and I have every hope that an unbiased non-Muslim who would study Islam as I have done would come to share my individual experience. I am no theologian and the average non-Muslim who is likely to commence a study of Muslim dogmatics with a readiness to resist the dogmatiser will not, I hope, take up this book too in a similar spirit. But one thing must be made clear. I am no heretic with an unheard of theory of Islam and passing off something which is peculiarly my own creation for the faith of hundreds of millions of men who are Muslims. I am intimately connected with orthodoxy and it not only does not look askance upon me but has on the contrary taken me gladly enough to its bosom. Only it had, unfortunately, stressed during the decadence of Islam that which was less important and not laid enough emphasis on that which was more. Moreover, it had answered as best it could such questions as had arisen in the past, whether as a result of genuine curiosity or scepticism, or merely of an intellectual itch to question for the sake of questioning with the help of the science and philosophy of the period, and it had seen no reason not to rely on the supernatural in which the whole world believed as the readiest interpretation of what was uncommon and unprecedented. But its science as well as its philosophy were the ancient heritage left by Greece, with the help of which Muslim orthodoxy had fought such heresy as Hellenism had introduced into Islam. The result was a scholasticism which as a European and Christian theologian [D.B. Macdonald] truly says, 'with its formal methods and system, its subtle deductions and needless ramifications of proof and counter-proof, drew away attention from the facts of nature. The oriental brain studied itself and its own workings to the point of dizziness.'

VII

# Islam: Whence and Whither?

## THE FIRST REVELATION

As is well-known that Muhammad following an Arab custom—'a right natural custom,' as Carlyle calls it,[1] 'a praiseworthy custom which such a man, above all, would find natural and useful'—had been wont to retire specially during the month of Ramazan, into solitude and silence. It had been his wont to betake himself, sometimes with his family, at others alone, for prayer and meditation, to a cave on the Mount Hira, 'a huge barren rock, torn by cleft and hollow ravine, standing out solitary in the full white glare of the desert sun, shadowless, flowerless, without well or rill'.[2] In this cave three miles from Mecca he would pass many consecutive days and nights, returning home only to replenish the little stock of provisions when he had exhausted them, and several months in each year would be spent in this Tahaunuth when plunged in profoundest thought he would endeavour to elevate his mind to the contemplation of divine Truth. The Quran gives a glimpse to us of the simple, yet profound meditation of his ancestor the Patriarch Abraham to whose faith Muhammad was, with divine grace, destined to bring his posterity. In Chaldea, where the worship of the Creator had in course of time come to be confused with that of His creatures, the sun, moon and the stars, this is what Abraham was cogitating during a night and the following day spent in contemplation of Nature that encompassed him all round:

And thus did we show Abraham (the Government of the) Kingdom of the heavens and the earth that he might be of those who are confirmed in belief. So when the night overshadowed him he beheld a star. 'This,' said he, 'is my Lord!' So when it set, he said, 'I love not those that set!' Then when he beheld the moon rising, he said, 'This is my Lord!' So when it set, he said, 'If my Lord had not guided me I should surely be of the people who go astray.' Then when he beheld the sun rising, he said, 'This is my Lord, this is the greatest.' So when it set, he said, 'O my people verily I am clear of that which ye associate with Allah. Verily I have turned my face to Him who hath originated the Heavens and the Earth, following

[1] Thomas Carlyle (1795–1881); Philosopher, critic and historian.

[2] The mountain some three Arabian miles from Mecca in a north-east direction.

the natural faith, and I am not of those that associate aught with God'. (6:75–8).

Who can tell us what reflections were the companions of his descendant in the solitude of the 'uncultivable valley' which at God's command he had selected for the local habitation of part of his posterity? Carlyle attempts to probe into the Prophet's heart and soul and says, 'From of old a thousand thoughts, in his pilgrimage and wanderings had been in this man: What am I? What *is* this unfathomable Thing I live in, which men name the Universe? What is Life; what is Death? What am I to believe? What am I to do? The grim rocks of Mount Hira, of Mount Sinai,[3] the stern sandy solitudes answered not. The great Heaven rolling silent overhead, with its blue glancing stars answered not. There was no answer. The man's own soul, and what of God's inspiration dwelt there, had to answer. '

His loving and beloved wife Aisha, perhaps the most intelligent and understanding of so many venerating Boswells who have left to us a most copious record of the Prophet's words and deeds and the smallest details of his life, is the only original authority for the authentic Traditions in Bukhari's[4] most carefully prepared collection that tells us of the earliest revelations. They began with dreams during his sleep and she tells us in her expressive language that he never saw anything in a dream but it would come true 'like the bursting of the dawn'. Then it was that solitude became a passion with him and the Cave of Hira became so frequently his retreat. It was in the solitude of one of these Hira nights in the month of Ramazan, that subsequently became the most sacred month of the Muslim calendar, devoted to fasting and prayers and charity, that the revelation took another form and the first tiny fragment of the Quran was revealed. One of the very earliest revelation refers to this night, the night of Majesty or Power:

Verily We sent it down on the insight of Power. And what shall make thee comprehend what is the Night of Power?

The Night of Power excelleth a thousand nights. Therein the Angels descend and the spirits by the permission of their Lord for every affair. Peace! It is till the breaking of the morn. *(Sura* xcvii)

In another chapter of the Quran, its first revelation is associated with the

[3] This is where God revealed himself to Moses, and is said to have made a covenant with Israel by giving Moses the Ten Commandments on tablets of stone.

[4] (810–70); a leading compiler and interpreter of the *Hadith*. He is highly rated among the Sunni Muslims.

month of Ramazan and that is all we know, except that Tradition locates the night as one of the odd nights in the last ten of that sacred month, and there is a more or less general consensus that it was the 27th. Appropriately enough in the additional voluntary prayers, that the Prophet used to love to offer on Ramazan nights, Muslims who have memorised the Quran recite it as the main part of the liturgy, and often the *Hafiz*, or 'Preserver' of the Quran as the memoriser who leads these prayers on such occasions arranges the recitation in such a manner that the last chapters are recited on the anniversary of the Night of Power. In a few days when the new moon becomes visible, the period of daily fasting and the extra nightly prayers ends, and on the following morning Islam celebrates all the world over the *Id al-Fitr*, or Feast of Bairam as the Turks call it.

## WHAT IS THE SPIRIT?

The Quran tells us that the Prophet was asked 'What is the Spirit?' (16:2) which according to the context and parallel passages in the Quran elsewhere obviously refers to inspiration or revelation, or what the Christian would call the Holy Ghost. And the Prophet is instructed to say nothing more than this that 'The Inspiration is by the Commandment of My Lord.' If we are still curious, as many would no doubt be, the immediate sequel should suffice, for it says: 'And you are not given aught of knowledge but a little' (17:85). No amount of curiosity can lift or penetrate the veil that the Lord of the Spirit has deliberately let down. But this is nothing exceptional. In fact it is the general law observed to be working in all nature. We have not the intelligence to comprehend the mode of divine activity in any of its workings. Do we comprehend how the bee learns the trick of making her wonderful habitation, of culling sweets from different flowers and making the honey and then storing it in the comb? There is a chapter of the Quran to which the humble bee gives its title and it seems that a comparison not only between the selective process by which honey is made and the 'Last word in religion', as Islam claims to be is subtly suggested, but a hint is also apparently thrown out that just as the bee does not have to wait for the slow working of the evolutionary processes before she can satisfy the first physical necessity of her life and begins from the very outset as an expert, so too a prophet who has to satisfy the most claimant and spiritual needs of the community to which he may be sent or of mankind in general is independent of the acquisitive characteristics of humanity and his soul takes at the appointed time a leap into light and floods the world with the radiance of divine

Truth. The ordinary man reasons, and proceeds step by step to his final judgement. The premises are more or less logically conceived and then comes the inevitable conclusion. But the Prophet does not reason. The intermediate steps are missing and the conclusion stands revealed. It would seem that nature thus completes a circle, from the bee to the man and from the man to the superman, the apostle or Messenger of God.

But while the mode of God's activity may not be within our comprehension we can perhaps understand something of the subjective experience of the Prophet as the result of that objective activity. But at best it will only be the outer shell.

So far as God's activity is concerned we must rest content with the dictum of *Hafiz* that 'none has solved and none shall solve this riddle through philosophising'. As for the experience of the prophets themselves our understanding of that too must be limited. As a merry poet of Delhi has said, 'How can I tell thee, O ascetic, the joys of wine? O, luckless man, thou hast never tasted it.' However, there is an authentic Tradition in Bukhari's collection in which according to Aisha the Prophet answering Hareth son of Hisham, who questioned him on the subject, describes the various forms in which revelation descended upon him. He said: 'On some occasions revelation comes as the tolling of a bell, and in this form I experience great hardship. When I have learnt what is revealed, this sound ceases.'

'On other occasions the angel takes the shape of a man and addresses me and I learn what he tells.' In relating this Aisha says: 'I have noted revelation descending on him on the coldest day and when it was over, sweat would pour down from his brow.' There are other reports which confirm the testimony of Aisha. The Camel of the Prophet on which the Prophet would be riding would kneel down whenever revelation descended upon him while he was out riding, and a Companion on whose knee the knee of the Prophet happened to be resting on one of these occasions relates that he felt an almost unbearable weight while the descent of the Spirit lasted. From the beads of perspiration and the sound as of a bell ringing in his ears, European critics have rushed to assure the world that this trance-like condition was nothing but an epileptic fit, and of course it is only a short step from this pathological inference to conclude that the victim of this disease was an impostor who skilfully utilised his fits to palm off his carefully prepared compositions on his Arab dupes as the Word of God.

I remember the statement of one of these writers with regard to the utility of such diseases to some persons living among ignorant and superstitious neighbours, and he could not help referring to the 'epileptic fits' of the Prophet which he facetiously declared to have been worth a mint of money to him. That this kind of humour should still be indulged in when dealing with one, who, apart from other considerations, is to about a fifth of the world's population the object of such great veneration, is a sad reflection on the present day boasts of toleration and imaginative sympathy with other peoples' views. One can hardly deal with such specimens of humour seriously and I may perhaps be permitted to relate here a pictorial story from a very old issue of *Punch*. At the corner of a street where stood the inevitable *gin-palace,* so significant of modern progress, a man had on a midsummer morning reeled down and collapsed near a lamp post which lent him a little support in his helpless condition. An old lady with a very large 'gamp', who had just turned the corner happened to see him in his distress, and being a sympathetic old lady, she went up to him and exclaimed: 'Poor man, he is very ill.' Nearby was the cab-rank and one of the 'Cabbies', a specimen of mankind, with a robust health, ready wit and some thirst, alas, now likely to become very rare, if not altogether extinct like the Dodo, who had evidently a more extensive experience of such cases, indulged in the Cabby's usual 'aside' which is as a rule fairly audible and said with a sigh, 'I wish I 'ad 'arf 'is disease.' Considering what influence for good the 'Epileptic' of Arabia has exerted during thirteen centuries over so large a population of mankind, one could well say about such critics of his as these: 'I wish they had half his disease!' But to look at the matter more seriously it is a wonder that these European critics reject without the least hesitation the barest possibility of Divine revelation in the Prophet's case and yet the majority of them accept without demur that it was God that had revealed Himself to Moses in the burning bush; that both Elijah[5] and Elisha[6] were bodily lifted to Heaven; that an angel visited Zacharias[7] to announce that his barren wife shall conceive and he shall be turned dumb for a time; that an angel announced the virgin birth of God's only begotten Son to Mary; that when Jesus was born, wise men came from the East to Jerusalem to worship him because they had seen his star in the East and when they went to Bethlehem it went before them till it came and stood over the infant Jesus, that an angel announced his birth to the shepherds in the field keeping watch over the flock by

[5] Traditionally held to be the greatest Hebrew prophet.

[6] Hebrew prophet and the successor of Elijah.

[7] The father of St. John the Baptist. A Jewish priest, he received a vision promising him and his aged wife a son, who would be 'filled with the Holy Ghost, even from his mother's womb'.

night and gave them sign that he would be found wrapped in swaddling clothes in a manger; that the Holy Ghost revealed to Simeon[8] in Jerusalem that he should not see death before he had seen the Lord's Christ.

## SCHOLASTICISM IN ISLAM

Baconian induction[9] has changed the face of the world, and even the East could not remain unaffected. Muslim orthodoxy naturally resisted at first the results to which it led and clung to Greek syllogisms[10] with unverified premises as if what Muslim scholasticism had only borrowed from Hellenism and that too to combat its fatal tendencies, was peculiarly Muslim and sacrosanct. Controversy generated passion and heat, and the fury of theologians is proverbial. But slowly and imperceptibly things underwent a change that has truly been revolutionary and orthodoxy, although it has made no formal renunciation and will not perhaps be willing even now to make it, is not so insistent as before on the acceptance of everything that it had inherited from the pious scholasticism. Tacitly it has accepted a new valuation and does not denounce those who do not take the high *a priori* road as infidels or even heretics. In fact it is anxious that such temporal power as is still left to Islám would avail itself of the results of science which could never had been achieved but for the departure made in Europe by Baconian induction. This practice has reacted on theory also, and far from condemning a Muslim who shares its love of Islam and is willing, if need be, to suffer for it, and would yet support Islam with arguments not unacceptable to modern science, as it had supported it for centuries past with the help of arguments not unacceptable to Greek philosophy, it is on the contrary quite gratified to avail itself of this new coadjutor and ally. Without examining its own consistency too strictly, it has moved on, and there is very hope that if not tactlessly stirred

[8] One of the Hebrew patriarchs. In the New Testament, the aged and devout Jew who took the infant Christ in his arms in the Temple at Jerusalem.

[9] Induction (in Logic). The process of reasoning whereby a general law or principle is reached from the observance of particular instances. The philosopher Francis Bacon (1561–1626) had argued that by inductions from the simple facts of experience man could reach forward to the discovery of fundamental principles, which in turn would issue in beneficial practical results.

[10] A deductive argument containing two premises. *Categorical* syllogism contain subject–predicate sentences, as in 'Some dogs are chihuahuas, all chihuahuas are small; therefore Some dogs are small'. *Hypothetical* syllogisms contain conditional sentences: 'If roses are red, then violets are blue; If violets are blue, then carnations are pink; therefore If roses are red, then carnations are pink'.

into opposition it will in another decade closely scrutinise its armoury of arguments, and discarding such as are obsolete, unsafe and harmful, would make formal renunciation as well of a mildewed scholasticism based on the improved and now disproved premises of Greek philosophy and thus set itself right with the progressive world of science, and what is still more important, set itself right with itself. Islam was unchanging and has remained unchanged in more than thirteen centuries that have passed over, but Muslim theology, so discouraged by the leaders of Islam in its best days, has, since its coming into existence, constantly moulted its skin. If the student of Muslim theology makes a rapid survey of its history, he will find many a half-way house from the early days of Hasan al-Basri,[11] Wasil bin Ata,[12] and Malik bin Anas,[13] through those of Ahmad bin Hanbal,[14] Al-Jahiz (d. 255 A.H.), Al-Kindi,[15] Al-Ashari,[16] Al-Jubbai (d. 305 A.H.), Al-Tahami (d. 331 A.H.), Al-Maturidi,[17] Al-Baqillani (d. 403 A.H.), Avicenna (Ibn Sina, d. 428 A.H.), Ibn Hazm,[18] Imam al-Haramayn (d. 478 A.H.), Al-Ghazzali,[19] Ibn Tumart (d. 524 A.H.),[20] Ibn Bajja (d. 533 A.H.),[21] Ibn Tufayl (d. 581 A.H.),[22] Averroës (Ibn Rushd,

[11] He was a prominent figure in the first century of the Hijra. He had a great reputation as a transmitter of tradition and was widely respected for his strength of character, piety and learning. He exercised a lasting influence on the development of Sufism.

[12] Born in Medina in 699–700, he migrated to Basra where he belonged to the circle of Hasan al-Basri. He wrote several books or pamphlets on the theological and political questions of his day. He died in 748-9.

[13] He was one of the most prolific traditionalists, though Abu Hanifa, it is said, refused to acknowledge his authority in matters of tradition.

[14] (780–855) celebrated Islamic theologian was brought before the inquisition. The Hanbalities were widely spread in the Islamic countries until the ninth century.

[15] Born in the middle of the ninth century in Kufa, al-Kindi was a leading Arab philosopher, astrologer, translator or editor of Greek philosophical works in the Abbasid court of Mamun and Mutasim. He was a Mutazalite. He died in 260 A.H.

[16] Abul Hasan Ali Al-Ashari (b. 873–4), born in Basra, was a distinguished theologian. He is said to have written 300 books and is regarded as the founder of orthodox scholasticism (*kalam*). He spent the closing years of his life in Baghdad and died there in 935.

[17] Titular head of the Maturidite School of theology which, with the Asharite School, form orthodox Sunni Islam.

[18] Abu Muhammad Ali (b. 994), a Spanish-Arabic scholar, famous theologian, and prominent poet was born in Cordoba.

[19] Abu Hamid Al-Ghazzali (1058–1111), theologian, jurist and mystic. His best-known work is Ihya ulum al-din, an attempt to integrate the major disciplines of Islamic religion—theology and law, ethics and mysticism.

[20] A celebrated Muslim reformer in Morocco.

[21] Philosopher, mathematician and astronomer. He wrote commentaries on several works of Aristotle.

[22] A celebrated philosopher of the Maghrib. He was also called al-Andalusi (the Spanian).

d. 595 A.H.),[23] Fakhruddin Razi,[24] Ibn Arabi,[25] down to the times of Ibn Taimiya.[26] The Crusades had greatly disturbed Islam in Western Asia, and it had hardly recovered from their effects when Hulagu[27] and his Mongols wrought terrible havoc in Baghdad, and indeed throughout the Islamic world. Although the victors were soon vanquished by Islam and became its champions, Islamic letters could not so easily be revised, and a century later Tamerlane's[28] world conquest led to a stagnancy which has lasted until very recently. But with the 18th century of the Christian era, while Arabia produced a stern Puritan in Muhammad ibn Abdul Wahhab, whose theology led to a great deal of bloodshed and destruction, India produced a theologian of a very different temperament, and though perhaps a non-conformist as the Central Arabian Muhammad ibn Abdul Wahhab and far more advanced than any that have been named, was then and has, since too, been universally respected by all classes of Muslims. This was Shah Waliullah of Delhi. And when the dust of controversy is laid a little more, Islam in India would recognise the worth of Syed Ahmad Khan, who dominated the latter half of the 19th century. His militant rationalism, even if it gave rise to violent controversy, roused the Muslims out of their stagnant complacency. About the same time Egypt produced Mufti Muhammad Abduh[29] and helped by the support which the spread

[23] This great Arab philosopher of Spain was born at Cordova in 1126. He wrote, among other works, commentaries on Aristotle, on Plato's Republic and criticisms on al-Farabi's logic.

[24] (1149-1209), famous theologian and philosopher and a leading Shafite and Asharite scholar.

[25] Abu Bakr Muhammad (1165–1240), a celebrated mystic of pantheistic doctrines, styled by his followers al-Shaikh al-Akbar. In Spain he was also called Ibn Suraka.

[26] (1263–1328), noted Arab theologian and jurist. He was a bitter enemy of innovations, attacked the cult of saints and pilgrimages to tombs. He was particularly critical of the Sufis and thinkers like Al-Ghazzali. 'The Sufis and the *mutukallimun* are from the same valley', he declared.

[27] (1217–60), a Mongol conqueror and founder of the Mongol kingdom in Persia. He ransacked Baghdad in January 1258. The Khalifa Mustasim was forced to make an unconditional surrender. Ten days later he was put to death with several members of his family while the town was plundered and set on fire.

[28] (1336–1405). In 1369, he ascended the throne at Samarkand, subdued nearly all Persia, Georgia and the Tartar empire, and conquered all the states between the Indus and the Ganges (1398). He won Damascus and Syria from the Mamluks of Egypt, then defeated the Turks at Angora in 1402.

[29] Leading Muslim theologian and founder of the Egyptian modernist school. In 1872, he came into contact with Jamaluddin Afghani. The two founded a society called *al-Urwa al-wuthaka* and published a paper with the same name. In 1899 he attained the highest clerical post in Egypt, that of state mufti.

of modern Western Education lent to them, they have exercised on the younger generation of Islam an influence that has been incalculably great.

As I have said Islam is unchanging and has remained unchanged, but theology has moulted its skin from time to time. The answers that it furnished to questions raised at the time, based though they were on the science and philosophy of the period, were superseded by others based on later and perhaps better science and philosophy or simply ceased to be asked and were replaced by others. God's Word was uncreated and everlasting and, therefore, remained the same, but men's words—*quot homines, tot sententiæ*—were their own creations, limited in time and space, and became obsolete. As the Arab poet has said of his lady-love: 'Our descriptions vary, but thy beauty is the same' and perhaps none of these descriptions of ardent lovers, enthusiastic as they were, did justice to the beauty of the beloved. It would, therefore, be foolish for the greatest modern rationalist in the Muslim world to claim that his word alone will share permanency with God's. No such claim is even thinkable to one so ignorant as myself. But it is this very recognition of my ignorance that makes me careful not to attribute to the mind of the Divine Author of the Quran that which belongs only to the mind of so human and fallible a reader as myself. I know it is not quite uncommon a practice of exegetes to discover statements, doctrines and allusions in Scriptures as in other works of classic antiquity which have no existence in their pages and to torture and mangle simple phrases till at last they are made to yield their assent to ideas foreign to the whole of the text. Particularly is this the tendency of those who have to reconcile science with religion. It has been frequently observed that at first science is categorically declared to be false; but when it is found to be winning, lo and behold! the text is made to yield a meaning in conformity to science and the inspired record is 'dovetailed into every latest crinkle of scientific fact or fancy'. A writer quotes, in this connection, an excellent story popular in the middle of the last century. There seemed to have been some sort of a plan to marry Garibaldi,[30] who was in those liberal days so deservedly popular in England, to a wealthy English lady. But it was discovered that Garibaldi had a wife already and she was still alive. When faced with this difficulty Disraeli[31] is said to have dryly remarked that 'Gladstone[32] could be easily

[30] Giuseppe Garibaldi (1807–82), Italian patriot, who joined Mazinnini's 'Young Italy' movement, and was condemned to death for participating in the attempt to seize Genoa.

[31] Benjamin Disraeli (1804–81) was twice Prime Minister of Great Britain (1868, 1874–80).

[32] William Ewart Gladstone (1809), British Liberal statesman and Prime Minister (1868–74, 1880–5, 1886, 1892–4).

got to *explain her away*'. Well, expositors of religions are not above *explaining away* such inconvenient features in the religions they favour, and Le Tourneau with the triumphant sarcasm of the scientist says: 'The interpreters of skilful, the sacred text obliging, the metaphysical theories ductile, malleable, flexible. Courage! We must be very narrow-minded indeed not to recognise in the first chapter of Genesis a succinct exposition of the Darwinian theory!' Now, no one is wholly proof against an unconscious bias of this nature, but knowing that a strong tendency of this sort exists in the human mind, I have, from time to time, turned the searchlight inwards to see that I was not taking similar liberties with the sacred text.

## SCIENCE AND RELIGION

But where the struggle of science and religion is concerned, I could afford to be serene, for I recognise no possibility of conflict between the two and there is nothing to reconcile. Religion as the interpretation of Life cannot be said to have no connection with science, but its province is merely to encourage it and to leave it untrammelled and free. It is concerned with its progress and with the use that is made of the results achieved by it, so that it benefits the whole of mankind and in fact all God's creation. But it does not set out to teach science to mankind. It is the Sovereign and can do no wrong; and the responsibility of mistaking fancies for facts is that of the minister and the subject, which is science. The Quran certainly does not aim at teaching us how the world was created, and even when it talks of mankind as made of clay and of the *jinns* or devils or Satan as made of fire, it is not making a scientific chemical analysis of man or the devil in man, but merely using the current coin of the realm and of the reign to indicate the normal human characteristics and the fiery impulses that lead to transgression and sin. No one will today belittle the importance of Science, and yet when compared with the importance of Religion, it seems petty and trivial, for Religion is the Science of Life, and the quintessence of all sciences and philosophies. Since Islam does not set out to teach biology, it has nothing to explain away, nothing to torture or mangle, bend or beat into shape, and while it will grieve to find people so lazy and inert as to remain unaffected by progress, and still swearing by the first chapter of Genesis when such a person as Darwin has put forward a theory like that of Evolution, it still refuses to set its seal on Darwin and Evolution as the last word in scientific truth. But there are passages in the Quran, often similar to those in the Bible or in the Rabbinical literature of the Jews, which the old commentators who, with little or no critical restraint, accepted both on their face value readily, and even with avidity interpreted in the light of the two and supplemented the Quranic text with Jewish and Christian embellishments. It is, therefore, no sin against the Holy Ghost for a Muslim today to reject such interpretation and supplementation when it involves an absurdity or a needless supposition of supernatural happenings and to put forward another interpretation which is rational and entirely within the domain of the natural. Nevertheless I have no reason to reject the supernatural as impossible to God, for to Him all is possible. Beyond this freedom of interpretation that every man must reserve for himself, I claim nothing, and I hold it to be the most deadly sin in a mortal, as the Quran gives me warrant to hold, to add anything of his own to God's Word, to alter it or take anything out of it under the fiction of interpretation.

## THE ART OF FABRICATION AND ITS APOLOGISERS

Higher Criticism of the Bible has exposed the pseudonymity of only too many books of the Old and the New Testament, and the supplementations that had taken place from time to time in such a fashion as to approximate to geological stratification. But even while exposing these pious frauds and forgeries, Biblical scholars have seldom condemned the gross immorality and sinfulness of such conduct. In fact, only too many have condoned the offence on the ground of geographical and historical standards of Ethics—the difference between literary morals of those times and places and our own. Some have not been content only with explaining and justifying the practice but have gone the entire length of extolling it, and that too with an artistry that makes the fabrication a most touching form of self-effacement. For instance, Mr. J.W. Chadwick, in his *Bible of Today*, writes:

> There is this at least to be said for those who put forth their own writings as the writings of illustrious men who had lived long before. It was not for themselves they desired the honour which could accrue from such a course; no, but only for the word they had to speak, the cause they wished to serve. If only this might prosper, they were willing to remain for ever in obscurity. And there they have remained until this day. . . . They denied to fame that Israel might live for righteousness and for the honour of her God.

One wonders whether it has ever occurred to such apologists that the same justification, or rather glorification of the fabricator of Holy Writ, might well be applied to the cases of those clever rogues 'behind the scenes' at Delphi[33] who were equally 'willing to remain for ever in obscurity' if only the cause of their oracle might prosper and who have equally remained there until this day. They too died to fame that their people might live for the sort of righteousness that they had evolved for themselves and for the honour of their 'gods'. Nay, what is there to prevent this eulogy being pushed to its logical conclusion in order to extol the cleverness of every forger of a cheque, every manufacturer of currency notes, and every counterfeiter of coins, provided only that the motive of such self-effacement and impersonation was the presumed benefit to other people as well. Either we must accept for all cases the formula that the end justifies the means or one's judgement of these pious frauds must be independent of the *motive* of fabrication. The doctrine of St. Paul on the subject is stated with a curious naïveté, in Romans 3:7. 'For if the truth of God hath more abounded through my lie unto His glory, why yet am I also judged as a sinner?' But the Quranic doctrine is very different. It condemns the end and the means alike: 'Woe, then, unto those who write the book with their own hands and then say, "This is from Allah", so that they may gain a trifle thereby (Lit. buy therewith a small price); therefore woe unto them for what their hands have written and woe unto them for what they gain' (2:79). To assign Divine Infallibility to a fallible human document is an offence far worse than any forger's and counterfeit-coiner's, no matter what end there may be in view. Such fraud upon human conscience is indeed woeful and no less woeful is the petty purpose that the perpetrators of such frauds have in view compared with the Divine purpose of transcendent importance running through God's revelations. Feeling on the subject as I do, I shudder at the very thought of my liberty of interpretation degenerating into license and leading me to read into the infallible divine text my own mortal's fallible ideas for which in fact there is no warrant. But on the other hand it must be remembered that I have as much right to interpret God's message as any other man except the infallible Messenger who brought it, though it is obvious that the *qualifications* of various interpreters for the task as apart from their *right* to interpret must vastly differ.

[33] Renowned throughout the ancient Greek world as the sanctuary of Apollo and the seat of his oracle.

## NO 'THEOLOGY BY COMMITTEE'

Islam had no apostles, no Church, and no Church Councils like Christianity to dictate his creed to the believer. It has not even a clergy and the whole spirit of Islam is consistently and relentlessly opposed to such a thing as 'experts' in religion. It wants all alike to know their faith, and religion should be the province of all the faithful. That is why, unlike Christianity, it has had no 'Theology by Committee', as Mr. H.G. Wells aptly calls it. The Roman Catholic Church does not depend for its doctrines merely on the Scriptures but relies also upon Church Tradition and to that dependence it has added the doctrine of the infallibility of the Pope. The Protestant Churches too have Articles of their dogma to which they demand the adherence of their members. But Islam demands no such adherence to any man's interpretations of God's word, except of course, the infallible Prophet's. But in the latter case the believer has to be satisfied about the authenticity of the Tradition or *Hadith* that contains such an interpretation and so searching is the test of authenticity that a *Hadith* must satisfy, that the great Imam Ahmad bin Hanbal discredits certain classes of traditions as being 'baseless' and these include *tafseer* or exegesis of the Quran attributed to the Prophet as well as *maghazi,* or the accounts of the Prophet's expeditions from which Christian critics of the Prophet have almost entirely furnished their armoury.

This judgement, according to the later scholars, is not perhaps meant to be as sweeping as it looks, and they specify in particular the famous exegesis of Kalbi and the biography of the Prophet by Waqidi, on whom the European assailants of the Prophet's character so largely rely. The result of this latitude given to the individual Muslim to interpret God's Word may be given in the words of Carra de Vaux, writing in the *Encyclopædia of Islam:* 'In Islam as a matter of course an official redaction of the dogmas of faith has never existed, the Islamic theory precluding the appearance of personalities like apostles of Christianity composing a creed with help from above.' Thus Islam has nothing like the so-called 'Apostle's Creed', which incidentally was not formulated in its final form until about 700 A.C. and was developed out of a creed favoured in Rome and evidently triumphed at the end of the 8th century over all other forms through the imperious desire for conformity of that champion of Latin Christianity and Papacy, Charlemagne, the founder of the Holy Roman Empire.[34] It has nothing like the Nicæan creed which was framed at the

[34] (742–842). He defeated the Arabs in Spain, and took control of most of Christian Western Europe.

Council held at Nicæa, in 325 A.C. and attended by an equally ardent Imperial seeker of conformity, Constantine, who had embraced Christianity mainly in order to strengthen and consolidate his Empire. This, it may parenthetically be added, was very much 'Theology by Committee', since it was a compromise between two parties that constituted the majority who suspended their disputes and agreed on the use of the mysterious Homoousian, which, as Gibbon[35] tells us, 'either party was free to interpret according to their peculiar tenets'. Nor has Islam anything like the Athanasian creed[36] which damns the heretics, but which Athanasius,[37] although the most persistent and vigorous leader of what subsequently became Christian Orthodoxy, never framed, and which 'does not appear to have existed within a century after his death'. Islam has had no Council of Trent[38] from which its orthodoxy derives its theology today, nor has it a Pope that can help it to evolve new dogmas based on infallible authority. It possesses no Confession of Augusburg,[39] and no Westminster Confession[40] either, nor has any Parliament passed for it an Act of thirty-nine Articles.[41] As I have already indicated, in its earliest days its leaders, commencing with the Prophet and his immediate successors known as the 'Truly Guided', sternly discouraged theological speculation, and the Muslims in those days were indeed too busy *living* an Islamic life to contemplate life and speculate about it. There was no racial inclination in the Arab in that direction and many of the Arabs had not yet reached a stage of intellectual development to make dialectics an agreeable occupation. 'The Golden Age' of the Abbasids had yet to come, but even under the Umayyads, Arabs made a remarkably rapid progress in letters considering that the Quran spoke of them in the days of the Prophet as *ummia* or unlettered.

A regal court at Damascus could not fail to attract literary talent and partly through the toleration inherent in Islam and partly through the religious indifference of some of the Umayyad *Khulafa* many non-

[35] Edward Gibbon (1737–94); British historian and author of *The Decline and Fall of the Roman Empire*, in six volumes.

[36] A profession of faith widely used in Western Christendom.

[37] St. Athanasius (*c.* 296–373), Bishop of Alexandria.

[38] (1545–63). This Council was the most impressive embodiment of the ideals of the Protestant Reformation.

[39] The Confession of Augsburg (1530). The Lutheran confession of faith which was presented at Augsburg to Charles V.

[40] The profession of Presbyterian faith set forth by the Westminster Assembly.

[41] The set of doctrinal formulae finally accepted by the Church of England to define its dogmatic position in relation to the controversies of the sixteenth century.

Muslims soon began to hold important positions under them. Professor Margoliouth[42] can see little of Islamic tolerance in such features of Muslim rule and would use them as indications of Muslim incapacity to do without Christian and Jewish help in administration and in the practice of learned professions. But be the reason what it may, the fact cannot be gainsaid, and a typical example is John of Damascus,[43] 'the last great doctor of the Greek Church and the man under whose hands its theology assumed final form'. His father Sergius was Treasurer under the Umayyads and after his death John himself became Vizier. In his writings and in those of his pupil Theodorus Abucara (d. 826 A.C.) there are polemic treatises on Islam cast in the form of discussions between Muslims and Christians, and evidently designed to help Christians to retain their faith in spite of the successes of Muslims as missionaries. They were characteristic of the people even more than of the times and now that neither Alexandria nor Antioch contributed all that passionate zest and fervour and heat to the theological controversies waged in Church Councils, those given to Greek dialectics like John of Damascus no doubt found some consolation in preparing such polemical treatises. Such writings were bound to react among the Musalmans also; but strangely enough Muslim politics assisted greatly in this reaction.

## THE SUNNI-SHIA SCHISM

As we shall see, Islam has one or two important schisms that have lived to our own day, but of heresy it has had, comparatively speaking, next to nothing, and these schisms came into existence over the question of succession to the Government of the new 'Church-State' of the Muslims. Ali was the son-in-law and cousin of the Prophet, and although he accepted the succession of Abu Bakr and then of Umar and finally of Usman, all by popular election or nomination by his predecessor or by his nominees and acclaimed by the people before he himself was similarly accepted as the Chief of the Faithful, it is a historical fact that when the Prophet passed away, he considered himself entitled to immediate succession, and although there is nothing to prove it beyond a doubt, it is probable that he based his title to succession on his relationship to the Prophet.

Abu Bakr had convinced the Muslims by citing the words of the Prophet himself that Prophets have no heirs, so that the Last of the Prophets

[42] David Samuel Margoliouth (1858–1940) was Laudian professor of Arabic at Oxford (1889–1937).

[43] St. John of Damascus (*c.* 675–*c.* 749), Greek theologian and 'Doctor of the Church'.

was held to have left no patrimony to be divided among his next of kin, let alone the question of a hereditary succession to his position as Chief of the Faithful. And in any case, Ali was not a son but only son-in-law, and the Prophet's uncle Abbas was still alive, so that when the Abbasids succeeded in uprooting the Umayyad power they did not swear allegiance to the successors of Ali, in whose interests they had so far appeared to be working, but set themselves up as *Khulafa*. If there was no equivalent of the Salic Law[44] to prevent succession through females, the Prophet's heir would have been the two sons of Ali by Fatima, the Prophet's youngest daughter, who alone left male issue and not Ali himself, so that it is very doubtful whether any title through heredity was ever formulated. But as so often happens, theory followed practice and the 'partisans' of Ali, who have survived to this day in the schism of the 'Shias' have since based the title of Ali and his descendants to the office of the Chief of the Faithful, the Successor of the Prophet, the Vicegerent of God in His Kingdom and the Head of the Islamic Republic on 'divine appointment' as well as heredity. After the first four *Khulafa*, the 'Truly Guided' who regulated the Islamic Commonwealth between them for 30 years, Muawiya,[45] the head of the family of Umayya, cousin of the family of Hashim, and from whom the Prophet descended, and their political rivals turned the Commonwealth or Republic into a dynastic monarchy preserving only the form of a popular election or rather acclamation. Before Islam the most powerful tribe of the Arabs was the Quraysh; it was the Warden of the Sanctuary at Mecca and managed the affairs of that locality. When the first revelation was received by the Prophet, this management was shared by a number of persons belonging to several of the principal families of the Quraysh, each of whom had charge of a particular function or department. The chief of these families were the families of Hashim and of Umayya and through the decline in prosperity of the former and the rise of the latter, it could safely have been predicted that before long the Umayyads would replace Hashimites who were still the premier political family in Mecca. But Islam cut across all these family divisions and replaced all this political patchwork by a 'Church-State' of which the Apostle of God was naturally and unquestionably the supreme head. The Umayyads opposed the spread of Islam as long as they could and their head Abu Sufyan[46] led the forces of Infidelity several times against the

[44] In normal usage, a rule of succession to the throne barring women, and men whose descent is only through females.

[45] Son of Abu Sufyan, he was the first Umayyad Khalifa.

[46] He belonged to the powerful Quraish (Kuraish) family of Abd Manaf. He was a rich

Prophet at Medina after having succeeded in driving him and his followers from their Meccan home. But Islam triumphed in the end, and on the conquest of Mecca by the Prophet in the eighth year of his exile, Abu Sufyan too acknowledged allegiance to the God of Islam and to His Prophet. Thenceforward he fought the battles of Islam and his fierce and revengeful wife Hind, who had offered a prize for the head of the Prophet's uncle Hamza, who had killed her father and brother in the first battle of Islam fought at Badr, and on his death at the battle of Uhud in the following year, had herself dismembered his body and even tried to eat his liver, had taken no mean part on one occasion in defending the tents of the women in the decisive battle of Yarmuk, when the superior forces of the Byzantine Empire repeatedly sought to overwhelm the Muslims and she had taunted her husband when pressed back by the enemy with being so valiant in the defence of Infidelity, and a coward in the defence of Islam! Whatever may have been the case with the convictions of Abu Sufyan, there is no doubt about those of Muawiya who was a sincere Muslim and had, on his conversion, been employed by the Prophet as one of the several amanuenses who used to take down the passages of the Quran soon after they were revealed to the Prophet. But that did not prevent his succumbing to the temptations that self-interest set before him in the disturbed condition of the 'Church-State' of Islam that followed the assassination of his kinsman Usman, the third of the 'truly guided' successors of the Prophet. And once the republic of Islam was replaced by the dynastic rule of the Umayyads, the dissolute lives of several of his successors and their policy in administration made it clear that they no longer looked upon it as the Kingdom of God but merely as their patrimony and an Arab hereditary monarchy. The Persians who had always despised their Arab neighbours in the pre-Islamic days—the 'Days of Ignorance', were an imperial race with an ancient history and quite distinct racial characteristics. On their defeat by the despised Arabs, they accepted the faith of their rulers with a rapidity that indicated neither genuine conviction nor political pressure so much as utter demoralisation. But they never forgave the Arabs their conquest of Persia and then Umayyad rule unlike that of the great Umar, during whose period of Khilafat Persia had been for the most part conquered, being more Arab than Muslims, had been little to allay this racial and political bitterness, so that when after Usman's murder Muawiya clamoured for vengeance on the murderers, many of whom were partisans

---

merchant and was initially hostile to the advent of Islam. Later, he accompanied the Prophet on his campaign against the Hawazin tribe. He died at the age of 88 in 651–2.

of Ali, and Ali preferred to vindicate the law of Islam after establishing himself a little more securely, and this led to the first outbreak of internecine war in Islam, the Persians as a nation espoused the cause of Ali and of his family and were ever a thorn in the side of the Umayyads. The greatest tragedy in Islamic history, the slaughter at Karbala[47] of the little band of 72 which formed the forces of Husain, the son of Ali, who had set out in 67 A.H. on the invitation of Kufa, his father's capital, to accept the allegiance as Khalifa as against Yazid, the son of Muawiya, nominated in the latter's lifetime without any precedent as his successor, is mourned to this day throughout the Islamic world by Sunni no less than Shia, the 'partisan' of Ali.

## PERSIAN NATIONALISM

But to the Nationalists of Persia it provided yet one more ground for their opposition to the rule of a primarily Arab dynasty inasmuch as Husain had married the daughter of the last of the Persian Kings when she had been brought a captive at the end of the Persian War and presented to him the most suitable husband for so noble a bride by the reigning Khalifa Usman. The Persians have ever since found an additional reason to be 'partisans', of Ali and of the descendants of Fatima because the line that runs from her second son Husain, the martyr of Karbala, is the line of the descendants of Shahr Banu, the Persian princess. How politics and racial differences have created the largest schism in Islam can be realised from the following quotation from so enlightened a Muslim as the Rt. Hon. Syed Ameer Ali, member of the Judicial Committee of the Privy Council and formerly a Puisne Judge of the Calcutta High Court.[48] He is so aggressively progressive that in his view the present sad plight of the Musalmans is entirely due to their ancestors' rejection, more than a thousand years ago, of the fantastic philosophising of Mutazila 'Hellenists', who caused the one and only Inquisition in Islamic history to be set up. He is not content with the obscurantist doctrine of the apostolic succession of infallible descendants of Ali, which could be equalled only by the doctrine of Papacy if Popes were not celibate but married and claimed the

[47] A place of pilgrimage west of the river Euphrates, about 60 miles from Baghdad. Husain, the only surviving grandson of the Prophet Mohammad, refused to pay allegiance to the ill-reputed Umayyad ruler, Yazid, son of Muawiya. He was slain along with his seventy-two comrades on the bank of the river Euphrates on the tenth of 61 A.H. (10 October 689).

[48] Syed Ameer Ali (1849–1928), leading scholar and author of many important books, including *The Spirit of Islam and History of the Saracens.*

dignity of St. Peter by right of hereditary succession, but must tack to it the right of succession to the Vicegerency of God in His Kingdom through the last Magian king of Persia. Writing with proper pathos of the sole survivor of the slaughter at Karbala, Ali, 'the sickly child whom Husain's sister Zainab (Zenobia) saved from the general massacre', who in after-life received the well-merited designation of 'Zain al-Abidin' (the Ornament of the Pious) he says, 'He was the son of Husain by the daughter of Yazdjard, the last Sassanid king of Persia and in him was perpetuated the house of the Prophet. *He represented also in his mother's right the claims of the Sassanians to the throne of Iran.*' Apart from the unutterably bizarre combination of the claims of the Sassanians and 'apostolic succession by divine appointment', one wonders whether it never struck a historian and a lawyer that at best the 'claims of the Sassanians to the throne of Iran' after the ignominious defeat, flight and death in exile of Yazdjard were no better than those of Yazid himself to the governance of Mecca after the ignominious submission of his grandfather Abu Sufyan when Mecca was conquered by the Prophet. We have seen how political, and in this case racial divisions as well, led to the largest schisms in the solid ranks of Islam, the schisms of Shias or 'partisans' of Ali and theory following on the heels of practice, an entirely distinct body of Theology, Tradition and Law and Ritual has since set up a terrific barrier between the two divisions. The main body of the Muslim world is designated *Ahl-i-Sunnat wal-Jamaat,* the adherents of the Prophet's Tradition and of the consensus or Agreement of the community and it is mainly of this, by far the largest of the two divisions, that I generally speak.

## THE KHARIJIS

A much smaller and yet for a time a very troublesome and even disastrous division was that which was caused by the 'Deserters' or Khawarij who left Ali's forces on the field of Siffiṇ when he very unwillingly accepted the demand of a considerable body of his supporters that he should consent to arbitration between himself and Muawiya whose General, no less than Amr ibn al-Aas, the conqueror of Egypt, fearing to be overcome in strategy, thought of snatching victory through a stratagem and ordered copies of the Quran to be suspended from the lances of his troops. On a too narrow and wooden-headed literalism, characteristic of fanatics, they turned round and blamed Ali for appointing *men* as arbitrators when God alone is declared in the Quran to be the Arbiter and Judge. In their desperate anger at the fratricidal war between Muslim and Muslim, some of them resolved, after their crushing defeat by Ali, at Nahrwan where they fought, as they did on subsequent occasions as well, with a grim determination and fearlessness worthy of a better cause, that peace could not be restored so long as the three principal protagonists, Ali, Muawiya and Amr ibn al-Aas lived and they should, therefore, be assassinated in order to save further Muslim bloodshed. Each of the three men, who agreed to do this, chose his man and on a fixed day all the three were to be killed. Ali's wound proved fatal. Muawiya's were less dangerous and he recovered, and as Amr happened to be ill, the *Qazi* who officiated for him at prayers fell a victim in his place. Naturally this added to the existing war between the Shias and the Umayyads, the further complication of war to the knife waged by both against the Khawarij or 'Deserters', whose remedy for the existing war only aggravated the disease. And as all these parties claimed to be fighting in the cause of Islam and that they were the only true Muslims and the others were all unbelievers or at least unpardonably gross sinners; so to the slaughter of the battlefield and occasional murderers such as we have just had occasion to take note of, were added imprecations against their enemies from the pulpits in every mosque. The Umayyads, however, happened to be the party in power, and although the Shias and the Khawarij both regarded them as 'Godless heathens who professed Islam but oppressed and slaughtered the true saints of God' there were many Musalmans who could not but see in them the upholders of some sort of law and order, and as such deserving their support or at least submission, without any condonation of their undoubted offence against good morals and the laws of Islam or a condemnation of all their opponents.

## THE AGE OF CONTROVERSIES

This political attitude, which was in fact fully justified and recommended by some of the Traditions of the Prophet, was sought to be based on a doctrine other than the obvious exigencies of the maintenance of order, and theory once more following practice, a dogma was discovered in a 'postponement of judgement' by the Muslims until it was pronounced by God Himself on the Day of Judgement. But these 'Postpones' or Murjites did not stop there. Once having opposed the political puritanism of the 'Deserters' or Kharijites, they proceeded, as the Shias had done, to elaborate a little theology of their own. The Kharijites had, in their puritanical zeal, declared that sinfulness meant infidelity and unless a sinner acknowledging his infidelity through sinning became Muslim again, he died an infidel, and even if he professed Islam with his lips, but had not repented before his death, he would eternally remain in Hell. To this the later Murjites opposed a doctrine of faith 'which is Pauline in its sweep'. Faith, they declared, and faith alone saved. On this arose the first great controversy in Islam, the controversy regarding *Iman* whether it meant conviction and profession, or mere conviction or confession of Islam in the heart even when outwardly professing some other belief, or needed, in addition to conviction of the heart and profession with the lips, a sinless life of good works. The next controversy arose with regard to the eternal question of Free Will, Predestination, and Foreknowledge. And in both cases, namely, in the case of the Murjites, for whom confession of Islam in the heart sufficed and in that of Qadrites, who attributed to man Qadr or Power over his actions, the close agreement of their ideas with those formulated and defended by John of Damascus and by the Greek Church generally, and the commencement of such theological speculation—at first in Syria and chiefly in Damascus unlike the more political controversies that swayed men and minds in Arabia, Mesopotamia and Persia irresistibly lead to the conclusion that it was the first fruits of Hellenism as it began to come into contact with the unsophisticated Muslim Arab of the desert. Although the latter controversy, namely, about Free Will and Necessity was sooner or later bound to arise in Islam as it has done in every faith, it seems that like the Murjite antinomianism it too had a semi-political origin. Two Qadrites are reported to have come to the celebrated ascetic Hasan of Basra (d. 110) through whom so many orders of Sufis trace their pedigree to Ali and thence to the Prophet himself, and to have told him that these kings who shed the blood of Muslims in their impious wars and did other grievous things disclaimed all responsibility for them and said that they had been decreed by God. To this Hasan al-Basri is said to have replied, 'The enemies of God lie'. These Murjites and Qadrites soon disappeared from the scene, but now 'we come from these drifting tendencies to a formal sect with a formal secession and a fixed name'. These are the Mutazila or Seceders who derive their name from an observation of the same Hasan al-Basri. A questioner had asked him whether the committer of a great sin could be a believer, as the Murjites said, or *ipso facto* ceased to be one, which was the opinion of the *Waidites*—those who laid stress on the threats (Waid) against sinners contained in the Quran,—and before he could answer, a pupil of his, Wasil ibn Ata (d. 131) broke in with an assertion of an intermediate position and leaving the circle which sat round the master went to another end of the mosque and began to develop his view to those who gathered round him. On this secession Hasan of Basra only said *Itazala 'anna*—he has seceded from us.

## THE 'GOLDEN AGE'

With the end of Umayyad rule and the victory of the Abbasids who used the grievances of the family and particularly of the descendants of the Prophet to undermine the government, came a complete change in the centre of gravity, typified by the transfer of the capital from Syria to Mesopotamia. The influence and power of the Persians increased, and to the Syrian source of Hellenism was now added the Persian source of Zoroastrianism and Manichæanism. 'At the court of the earliest of Abbasids it was fashionable to affect a little free thought. People were becoming enlightened and played with philosophy and science.' The Persianisation of the court at Baghdad led to a great deal more of Hellenisation than had been the case at Damascus, and though the new effervescence deservedly gave to this period the designation of the 'Golden Age', and men's minds were broadened, the contact of Islam and philosophy soon resulted in a conflict. Islam, as I have already indicated, survived that conflict, but as Melanchthon has said, there is never a discussion about religion by which religion is not a sufferer, and Islam as it came out of this conflict lost much of the old vitality of a faith of men who *lived* Islamic lives. As I shall presently show, it forced the defenders of this old faith to take up in the heat of controversy extreme positions that they would never have taken up if left to themselves, and subtle reasoning was soon pressed into service to support a needlessly literal interpretation of a teaching that had all the sensuousness and poetic beauty of the best and yet the simplest literature. What is worse, although this subtle reasoning served its purpose at the time, it was by no means sound, and during many uncreative centuries, bright Muslim lads have wasted the best years of youth and young men have grown into grey and weary and blear-eyed old men in the vain pursuit of unsound philosophy and unnatural science. With the sacred text alone, sooner or later, the true interpretation, based on the spirit as well as the letter, was bound to come. The emphasis on the letter of the sacred text, even when it went beyond the needs of the moment, would have disappeared with the moment of the need. But the elaborate reasoning which has survived those hot and dusty days of controversy has not only left the emphasis unaltered, but has misled generation after uncreative and uncritical generation into the belief that it too is as important for purposes of faith as the sacred text and is almost equally sacrosanct.

## MUCH DISCUSSION, LITTLE ACTION

Men like the two Imams who were pre-eminently Traditionalists, Malik ibn Anas and Ahmad ibn Hanbal, opposed discussion on all theological subjects and felt a shuddering repulsion because they could not have failed to realise in the first place that such discussions diverted the minds of Muslims from righteous *action,* which Islam demanded from the man of righteous *thought* before he could hope for salvation, and since they created an unwholesome distraction from which their ancestors had escaped, the appeal of the tradition of *salaf* was not the kind of patriotism by which their modern critics, like Syed Ameer Ali, try to mislead people. That is why Imam Ahmad ibn Hanbal would cast out those who supported his own opinions in a discussion as well as those who differed, for, in his view, the offence consisted not in holding a different opinion but in discussion and speculation. In the next place they could not have failed to realise the drift and tendency of those fantastic philosophies, bristling as they did with the most blasphemous possibilities. It is all very well to generalise about the 'rationalism' of Mutazila and to place the halo of philosophy round their heads. But even leaving out of consideration the loose conduct of at least some of them, if we scrutinise their precious philosophers in detail we cannot fail to discover the seamy side of their philosophising. Dragged by the tide of Hellenism they desired no less a freedom than to cut themselves off from their Islamic moorings and accepting Greek philosophy and science as they understood—and often misunderstood—then as the standard of truth they wished to measure Islam by their foot-rule. Some added to their nationalist antagonism to Islam as the product of an Arabian's brain, personal literary vanity and claimed to be able to compose a better work of art than the Quran, and most, if not all, of those who started the futile and foolish controversy on the question whether the Quran was eternal or had been created, hoped, apart from national antagonism or individual literary vanity, to 'reform' Islam not only out of recognition but out of existence, once they could establish it to be a creation of the Eternal Creator and, therefore, only of temporary binding force and utility. Two contemporary Indians have, in recent times, interpreted Islam under Western influences—Syed Ameer Ali and Sir Syed Ahmad Khan—and although Syed Ahmad Khan roused greater opposition among the orthodox in India than Syed

Ameer Ali, the difference between the view of the two on the subject of the sacred Text is characteristic. Syed Ameer Ali, the champion of the Mutazila, writes about it throughout as if it was the composition of the Unlettered Prophet of Arabia, no doubt a very praiseworthy and an astonishingly great production for such a man, such a place and such times, yet open to criticism and correction. Syed Ahmad Khan, the 'Naturee', who is out to reconcile everything in the Quran with the undisturbed laws of cause and effect in nature and to leave nothing to be swallowed as supernatural, is, however, so staunch in his conviction that the Quran is the uncreated and unchangeable Word of God that he would deny even the intermediation of the Archangel Gabriel. Bursting forth into poetry he says:

ز جبریل امین قران به پیغامے نمی خواہم
همه گفتار معشوقست قرآنے که من دارم

I desire not a Quran as a message from the Trusty Gabriel. The Quran that I possess is altogether the discourse of the Beloved.

To him, as he has explained fully, every word of the Quran is, both word and meaning, the Word of Allah existing from eternity containing the revelation of His eternal purpose made directly on the soul of His Messenger, Muhammad (on whom be peace and God's benedictions). He has interpreted it freely enough and incurred the anathema of his community, as Syed Ameer Ali has never done, and yet this other descendant of the Last of the Prophets who has proved one of the most effective of reformers in the history of his people, has never felt himself so hampered by the sacred Text as to wish to evade it on the ground of its being a temporary creation of God which served its purpose when it was first originated, and has at least in some respects, as Syed Ameer Ali clearly suggests, outlived its need and utility.

And yet, curiously enough, these 'rationalists', who doted on 'freedom' and demanded so much of it for some of their wildest fantasies, instigated that doctrinaire despot, Al-Mamun, who was thoroughly Persianised and under Persian tutelage, for a time wished a descendant of Ali and Fatima to succeed him, to set up the first and—God be thanked for it—the last Inquisition in the history of Islam. He died the very next year after it had been set up and his two immediate successors alone availed themselves of it, while the third, whatever may be said against his moral delinquencies, deserved every bit of the popularity he earned by abolishing it after it had been in existence for sixteen years.

## IMAM AHMAD'S SUCCESS AND THE RISE OF THE JURISTS

Imam Ahmad bin Hanbal's literalism and too exclusive a reliance on Tradition which he had so laboriously collected but did not himself authenticate, are the creed of a very small school today in the Muslim world, but the Muslim world can never outgrow his unflinching courage and determination to oppose the imposition of a belief in the uncreated character of the Quran on pain of death in this world which the Prophet and his truly-guided successors including Ali had never imposed on a Muslim even on pain of the tortures of the next world. The riotous crowds of Baghdad that supported him were not perhaps so much in love with his literalism and reliance on the Traditions of the Prophet and the usage of salaf or pious Muslim ancestors as with the resolute courage which made him suffer imprisonment and public scourging cheerfully and finally led to his death in prison. If 140,000 men and women of Baghdad followed his bier and he died 'in the odour of sanctity', as Syed Ameer Ali so chivalrously sneers, he died in an odour that he shared with the great martyr of Karbala who would not have his faith fettered by princelings on earthly thrones. His creed was his own, but the freedom for which he fought and which he won is our grand heritage to this day. We have already seen how the Prophet and his immediate successors and companions had discouraged theological discussions and it may be mentioned that so anxious was the Prophet that nothing should be confused with the pure Word of God that for a long time he would not allow his discourses to be taken down in writing, confining that to the Quranic revelations alone. When there was no longer any fear of such confusion he permitted his own sayings to be recorded by such of his companions as were anxious to do so, though no official amanuensis was employed for this purpose as had been done in the case of the Quran from the very outset. So long as he lived he declared the law of God when and as needed. But when he was no more, the need of a growing nation and state had to be satisfied and following his own authentic declaration, supported as it was by the principle enunciated by the Quran that he was to be taken as an exemplar by all Muslims whenever the Quran itself was silent, those who had to settle the affairs of the nation and the state after him eagerly sought guidance in his Traditions, i.e. words, deeds and consent implied by silence with regard to anything said or done within his knowledge.

This greatly stimulated the natural desire of the Muslims to collect his Traditions, and since, primarily and in the main, the necessity of the jurist provided the chief stimulus, the character of the corpus too that we have now is largely juristic. But when his own usage did not give a direct response when the jurists consulted it in any new case that arose, they had to arrive at a decision by the method of analogy or qiyas, for which too the Prophet's authentic Tradition had provided ample warrant. This was besides the Quran and the Hadith, the third source of Muslim law. There is a class of people who pose as rationalists and reformers but whose itch to create new doctrines is at bottom their disinclination to abide by the obligations of the old, or in fact of any doctrine including their own, whenever it became personally inconvenient to do so, and it has become a fashion with them to disparage the work done by the jurists of Islam, though even a glance at the work they have accomplished would suffice to convince an unprejudiced person to marvel at their enormous labour, their sound common sense which deserves the name of rationalism in the best sense of that expression and their eminent success in elaborating so soon a system of jurisprudence and a large body of laws covering all things spiritual. They allowed rationalism to have its full share in framing this system of laws and in fact could not have gone very far in their work without it as the fourth and last source of authority they were democratic enough to accept the consensus of the Muslim community, relying once more on an authentic tradition of the Prophet, that God would never let his followers agree on error. The result has been remarkably successful but this is not to say that there is no room for a revision if undertaken in the same reverent and responsible spirit after a like preparation for the task, and with equal devotion and diligence. The door of ijtihad or private judgement is still open though the janitor of the community's common sense must prevent anarchy from making a lodgement.

## THE FOUR SCHOOLS OF LAW

However, what we are concerned with here is the fact that the first discussions and disputations that pious Muslims permitted themselves after the demise of the Prophet were connected not with aqaid or theology, but with fiqh, or law which includes Civil Law as well as what is in the Christian Church known as Canon Law. Four schools of law have come down to us—but all are respected, and no such thing as orthodoxy or heresy can be predicated of any of these schools, and in fact a disciple of the founders of these schools could, without any inconsistency, subsequently attend the lectures of the founder of another. Law naturally needs conformity more than convictions and beliefs do, and Muslims as a rule definitely belong to one school or another, the oldest and most liberal being that of Imam Abu Hanifa,[49] a philosophical jurist whose system was perfected by his two disciples Qazi Abu Yusuf and Imam Muhammad. To this belong roughly the Muslims of Central Asia, Northern India and the Turks. Lower Egypt, Syria, Southern India and the Malay Archipelago, which Arab traders visited and where they settled as colonists, are adherents of the school of Imam Ash-Shafai[50] who took up an intermediate position between philosophical speculation in jurisprudence and a liberal adherence to Tradition. Upper Egypt and Northern Africa west of Egypt are attached to what may be called the historical school of Imam Malik bin Anas, the eminent Medina Traditionist, who is not quite so latitudinarian as Abu Hanifa, while practically only the Wahhabites in Central Arabia, the vigorous and even destructive puritans, follow the liberalist school of Ahmad bin Hanbal, though it may incidentally be mentioned that he was no lawyer but a simple Traditionist, who was a follower of Imam Shafai in law and never intended to establish a school of law. It was only his zealous followers who, after his tragic career of suffering and persecution, drew together and founded the fourth school of Muslim Law. There is a small class that are known as Ghayr-Muqqalidin or Non-Conformists, and sometimes as Ahl i-Hadith, the adherents of the Prophet's Traditions, in order to distinguish them from those who conform to opinions of a particular school and accept Qiyas or analogy as one of the sources on which Muslim Law may be based. But these generally claim Imam Ahmad bin Hanbal, as their Imam or leader. In other words, they have agreed among themselves to make the Imam's adherence to Tradition, against philosophical speculation in the field of Theology, the rule of their conduct in the field of jurisprudence as well. These alone characterise the liberalism of the other schools of law as against their literalism as biddat or innovation which is the nearest expression that Islam has to heresy, and it may be added that the destructive or irreverent lengths to which Muhammad bin Abdul Wahhab permitted his Puritanism to take him has led the Conformists to regard themselves as the orthodox party and these as heretics. There is, however, no such term as heresy applied to them and the only term of reproach employed is the designation of Wahhabi.

[49] (699–767); a leading jurist and founder of the Hanafite school which is named after him. People flocked to him in Kufa to hear him and to question him on the ritual and the law.

[50] (767–820); the founder of the Shafai (Shafíi) school of law. He belonged to the tribe of Quraish; he was a Hashimi and thus remotely connected with the Prophet. The main centres of his activities as a teacher were Baghdad and Cairo.

## THE AGE OF PERSECUTION

So far we have seen that the main division in the Muslim world has been more political than theological in its origin and schism rather than heresy is the proper term to employ in its case, and that the only other distinctions that followed were the minor divisions of the bulk of Muslims into four schools of law, to any of which the term heresy is even more inapplicable. But with the rise of the Mutazila as a distinct school of theology proper, we get the nearest approach to heresy in Islam. Professor D.H. Macdonald, of the Hartford Theological Seminary, cannot be accused of any partiality in favour of 'wooden-minded literalism' nor of any antipathy against the 'rationalism' of Mutazila whom he calls 'a group of daring and free-minded speculators'. In his remarkable lucid history of 'Muṣlim Theology' from which I have already quoted more than once, I should like to take a few more extracts. Writing of the latter, he says, 'They were applying to the ideas of the Quran the keen solvent of Greek dialectic and the results which they obtained were of the most fantastically original character. Thrown into the sea and utter freedom of Greek thought, their ideas had expanded to the bursting point and, more than even a German metaphysician, they had lost touch of the ground of ordinary life, with its reasonable probabilities, and were swinging loose on a wild hunt after ultimate truth, wielding as their weapons definitions of syllogisms. Their belief in the powers of the science of logic was unfailing, and, armed with Aristotle's "Analytics" they felt sure that certainty was within reach.' Referring to one of this group Abu Nazm,[51] 'who has the credit of having made use to a high degree of the doctrines of Greek philosophers', which led him to deny to God even the power to do anything that was not for the creatures' good and to make God's personality vanish behind an absolute law of right and utility, Professor Macdonald accurately sums up the whole movement when he says, 'He and all his followers were only playing with words like counters.' This 'keen solvent of Greek philosophy' was dissolving all Islamic activity and men, who valued Islamic ethics more than a heathen metaphysics which was destroying men's soul, refused to 'play with words like counters'. They would not discuss theology at all. They were too serious-minded to play with religion and too much in earnest to waste their energies in such metaphysical dalliance. Malik bin Anas used to cut off all discussion with *Bila Aaifa* (without asking how). He and others like him 'refused to go an inch beyond the statements in the

[51] A Mutazali theologian of the Basra School. A brilliant poet, a philologist of note, he occupies a most important place in the development of Muslim ideas.

Quran and the Traditions and to draw consequences however near the surface these consequences might seem to lie'. They were, as I have already indicated, even driven in their anxiety to avoid a theological speculation that was bristling with mischievous possibilities when not wholly sterile, to hold extreme positions which, if left to themselves, they would never have taken up. Al-Mamun, the 'doctrinaire despot,' that 'most dangerous of all beings', as Professor Macdonald rightly calls him, under the influence of these phantastic philosophers, imposed for the first time a test and instituted an inquisition, 'commanded that the death penalty for unbelief (*Kufr*) should be inflicted on those who refused to take the test', and subscribe to the Mutazila doctrines. And yet 'Orthodoxy'—as we are driven to call the vast bulk of the Muslim world that held views on which there was a general consensus or *ijma'* could not conscientiously deal a counter-stroke by laying down any articles of faith framed by itself and demand that the 'heretics' should subscribe to them. Imam Bukhari, the great compiler and verifier of Tradition, when himself subjected to inquisitory proceedings, remained at first obstinately silent and when at last persistent questioning drove him to an outburst, it did not go beyond a protest against the imposition of tests that the Prophet of God had never imposed. 'The Quran is the Word of God and is uncreated. The speech of man is created; and inquisition (*imtihan*) is an innovation (*biddat*).'

## IMAM AHMAD'S MARTYRDOM

The battle was already won by Imam Ahmad bin Hanbal's unflinching courage and steadfast perseverance in the line he had from the outset taken up. In his long examination before the officials of Al-Mamun and Al-Mutasim,[52] he contented himself with repeating either the words of the Quran which for him were proofs or Traditions as he accepted. Any approach to drawing a consequence he utterly rejected. When they argued before him, he remained silent. He was imprisoned and scourged and again cast into prison where he died. Some years after the scourging which he had so patiently borne, his son happened to notice that in the quiet of the night when he would offer extra prayers that were purely optional, he would remember one Abul Haitham in his devout supplications to God at the end of prayers and would continue to pray with a flood of tears entreating God's forgiveness and mercy for this Abul Haitham. His son had never heard of this man and thought that he must have been a saint of

[52] (b. 795), the son of Harun Rashid. After the death of Mamun Rashid, he ascended the throne in Baghdad in August 833.

some past generation of whom his father was perhaps a distant disciple.

His curiosity was sufficiently roused and one day he asked who this pious person might be that affected his father so greatly. And it was then that he learnt that Abul Haitham was none other than a notorious robber with a long career of crime. Asked why the Imam should pray so earnestly for such a vile person he was told that when Ahmad ibn Hanbal was being led through the streets of Baghdad weighted with heavy chains which he dragged along with difficulty and was to be publicly scourged if he still persisted in his contumacious opposition to the creed of the Khalifa, and in all that great city which at heart sympathised so fervently with him and shared his belief, none dared to show him the least sympathy outwardly; one man alone had the intrepid courage not only to express such sympathy but to rush to him, after dashing through the ranks of his large armed escort. That man was Abul Haitham. Before the astonished soldiers could arrest or drive him back he managed to tell Ahmad ibn Hanbal that he was a robber who persisted in his career of crime in spite of imprisonment on several occasions and scores of scourging. His back was one open sore and yet, he said, they had not been able to force him to give up his devilish deeds. The Imam was going to be subjected to his first scourging, and in Abul Haitham's opinion, his piety must be of the poorest kind if fear of that forced him to give up the Work of God. History bears ample witness to the fact that Ahmad ibn Hanbal did not; but he never forgot Abul Haitham for whom he prayed as for a saintly benefactor. Between the robber and the saint what a contrast and yet what a strange analogy! When I say orthodoxy had already won a victory when Imam Ahmad ibn Hanbal died in prison and 140,000 men and women of Baghdad followed his bier, I do not mean a victory for the contents of the Imam's creed. If it is at all represented by the school of law that bears his name, we have seen that a very small proportion of the Muslim world indeed shares it today. The victory rather was for the freedom of the individual believer's conscience from the imposition of a creed on which neither the Quran nor the Last of Allah's Messengers, through whom the Quran reached Mankind, insisted. This alone is orthodoxy and this is the negation of the very conception of orthodoxy as understood by non-Muslims.

## DISCUSSION CRAZE

But all were not proof against the temptation to argue with the fantastic philosophers of the Mutazila school. Even in the days of Al-Mamun some had displayed courage equal to that of Ahmad ibn Hanbal himself and a willingness to dispute the ground with the. Mutazila with arguments which

Ahmad heartily abhorred. One of these had travelled all the way from Mecca with his little son, and in a dramatic manner had thrown out a challenge to the Mutazila divines in no less a place than the largest mosque in Baghdad in the Rusafa quarter when it was overcrowded for the Friday service. Placing his boy against one of the pillars of the mosque in a very conspicuous spot he asked him whether the Quran was created or uncreated and the boy had boldly proclaimed that it was the uncreated Word of God, co-eternal with Him Whose Divine Purpose it revealed to His creatures. This was the biggest bomb-shell that could have been exploded in the capital city of the Abbasids and the stronghold of the Mutazila, and it exploded with a tremendous detonation. I will not explain here all that followed this explosion, contenting myself with indicating that finally the Meccan Shaykh succeeded in his effort to speak face to face with the Imperial innovator, and to argue with his Mutazila divines in his presence. Although Al-Mamun did not admit that the defeat of these divines with whom the Shaykh had by his invitation just successfully disputed, had convinced him that their creed—and his—was fallacious as the arguments with which they had sought to prove it, he confessed he saw there was much to be said on the other side as well, and he took the Shaykh's rebuke with regard to his dragooning the Muslims into a dogmatic conformity with his own views in good part. Afterwards others followed, but 'when the pious were eventually driven to dialectic weapons, their arguments show that these were snatched up to defend already occupied positions.'

## DEALERS IN DIALECTICS

Ahmad ibn Hanbal had relied solely upon *Naql* or Tradition and rejected *Aql* or reasoning altogether. This was an extreme position and however much one may approve the inexpediency of wasting one's energies in the trivial pursuits of the Mutazila 'rationalists', one cannot exclude reasoning in principle, especially when the Quran itself repeatedly appeals to the reason of mankind for confirmation of the truths it reveals. The mistakes of those who opposed the Mutazila with reasoning was that they snatched their own weapons. They too went to Greek Philosophy as to an armoury from which to equip themselves for the fray and Abul Hasan Ashari and Al-Baqillani and Maturidi who at last gave the Mutazila battle, their Plato, or rather their neo-Platonism and their Aristotle-cum-Plotinos, so effectively that they beat them on their own ground. Leaving those like Al-Farabi, Ibn Sina (Avicenna) and Ibn Rushd (Averroës) who studied philosophy for philosophy's sake, even though they had an interest in theology as well, and unlike Ibn Rushd who, like all his compatriots of Spain, had a horror of philosophy intruding in matters of faith, some of them did permit philosophy frequently to make excursions into the domain of theology, we find that far the larger number of those who took up the study of philosophy took it up mainly as theologians. The Mutazila, as I have said before, had set out to measure religion with the foot-rule of philosophy and these opponents of theirs neither did that nor did they attempt to measure philosophy with any measure furnished by their faith. But they were a kind of bi-metallists, who accepted both the standard of philosophy and of faith and set out to prove that the two were identical. Unlike the 'freethinkers', they had not set out on a quest for truth. The Quran and the Tradition for them was the Eternal Truth, but the glamour of great names dazzled them and they accepted this jumble of Plato,[53] Pythagoras, Aristotle[54] and Plotinus[55] for Truth as well and zealously commenced to reconcile this with the Quran and the Tradition. The unlearned had never been sceptical and the sporting instinct of mankind in mass which had led them to admire the heroic Ahmad ibn Hanbal must have dulled what little doubt they might have felt. But the schoolmen, many of whom must have been swinging on the fence, were made to fall safely on the side of the old faith by the new arguments advanced by these dealers in dialectics. Had this success served only its temporary purpose, nothing much may have been amiss. But, as I have indicated, alas! that success outlived its temporary purpose and the arguments with which the Ashari creed[56] was supported, having survived along with the creed, they have assumed a sacrosanct character that has long retarded progress in science and philosophy and, what is still worse, saddled the simple creed of Muslims with the weight of the old Greek incubus.

This much must, however, be said for the Ashari school of dialectics that the schoolmen shared to some extent the shuddering repulsion felt by men like the Imams Malik ibn Anas and Ahmad ibn Hanbal against all theological speculation. They believed in the truth of what they argued,

[53] (*c.* 427–347 B.C.), Athenian philosopher, a disciple of Socrates, who appears in most of his 35 dialogues.

[54] (384–322 B.C.), Greek philosopher, scientist and physician.

[55] (205–70 B.C.), Greek philosopher. He greatly influenced early Christian theology.

[56] Refers to the creed founded by the famous theologian of Basra (b. 873–4) Abul Hasan Ali. He was a Mutazalite, but disputed with his teacher on the fitness of God's predeterminations. He then wrote a large number of polemical works against the Mutazalites. He emerged as the founder of orthodox scholasticism (*Kalam*). The best known of the older Asharites were al-Bakkillani, and al-Ghazzali.

but they were anxious to confine it to the narrow circle of schoolmen. It must not be allowed to disturb the mental repose of the commonalty. This scholasticism or study of Kalam (Logic), as it was called, was hedged about with difficulties of restrictions. As Professor Macdonald says, 'Theologians recognised its trap-falls and doubts even for themselves, and lamented that they were compelled by their profession to study it. The public discussion of its questions was regarded as a breach of professional etiquette. Theologians and philosophers alike strove to keep these deeper mysteries hidden from the multitude.' He is of the opinion that the gap between the highly educated and the great mass is the fundamental and the greatest danger to Muslim society; but that is indeed true of all society, and the absence of an ordained clergy has made Muslim society far more immune from it than any other. However, one conclusion at which he arrives is indisputable: 'Muslim science has been always of the school; it has never learned the vitalising and disinfecting value of the fresh air of the market-place.' But this again may equally be said of all mediaeval science. Men like St. Bernard[57] would lament, at the least publicity in religious matters, that they had fallen on evil times and the Catholic faith had come to be discussed in the market-place.

## SUFISM

The Mutazila, after losing power at court and beaten in the schools, began to flounder more and more hopelessly in their philosophy and their conclusions became every day more and more unintelligible, until they finally disappeared from the scene. But thanks to the scholasticism which came into being through opposition to them, *Aql* as well as *Naql* came to be accepted as legitimate elements in Muslim Theology. To this a new element not unlike *gnosis* came to be added by the Sufis; these were the mystics who withdrew from the world like Christian anchorites to whose peaceful and quiet lives the Quran has approvingly alluded even when condemning their unnatural asceticism as a self-imposed obligation, not always fully consistently met. This was *Kashf*, the intuitive insight or minor revelation granted to the mystic in his ecstasy. Sufism originated very early in Islam and all orders of Sufis insist on connecting it with the Prophet through his cousin and son-in-law Ali or more rarely his friend and first successor Abu Bakr. But he who popularised it and at the same time gave to it a status that none but a learned divine, who had studied

[57] (1091-1153), the monk who was canonised in 1174 and created a 'Doctor of the Church' in 1830.

philosophy and theology and had been recognised as a master, could give, was Imam Ghazzali, whose confessions in his charming little volume, *Deliverer from Error*, gives the whole history of his life, thought and feeling. Says Professor Macdonald:

He led men back from scholastic labours upon theological dogmas to living contact with study and exegesis of the Word and the Traditions. What happened in Europe when the yoke of medieval scholasticism was broken, what is happening with us now, happened in Islam under his leadership. He could be a scholastic with scholastics, but to state and develop theological doctrine on a scriptural basis was emphatically his method. We should now call him a Biblical theologian.

At the same time, 'he brought philosophy and philosophical theology within the range of the ordinary mind'. Above all theology which an obsolete philosophy had made so artificial was at least humanised and the gap between the highly educated and the mass of Muslims was also greatly reduced. It warmed up the dry bones of theology, which the precision of logic had left cold with emotion, and it restored what George Elliot with naive candour calls 'the right of the individual to general haziness'.

But we must not press *Kashf* too far. As Ibn Rushd who, without doubting the *bona fides* of the mystics, was himself no mystic, truly says, anything so purely personal, anything which rested as it does so exclusively on the individual consciousness or rather sub-consciousness as the immediate knowledge of the Sufi, cannot be made the basis of any general system. Nevertheless, like vitamins in our food, the value of which science recognises today without being able to comprehend it like other elements of nutrition, it is of undoubted value, and ever since the era of Al-Ghazzali, *Naql, Aql* and *Kashf* have been accepted by the Muslim world as the three elements of its Theology.

## PERIOD OF DECAY AND THE VITALITY OF ISLAM

We have roughly traced the development of Muslim Theology but nowhere do we find any sign of a rigid orthodoxy dividing it from heresy, and if to any set of views the term orthodoxy is loosely applied for want of a better word, it must be understood to mean the views more or less generally shared by the vast bulk of the Muslim community at a particular time. It is true that, in the East, after the death of Imam Ghazzali, great names among Muslim thinkers come at greater intervals and that in the West too a century and a half later when the dynasty of the Muwahhids which the philosophical theologian and religious reformer, Ibn Tumart, a reputed favourite pupil of Ghazzali, had founded came to an end, Islamic thought seemed to get arrested in its further development. Naturally the views of the thinkers of the past which had already crystallised into schools now became so petrified that henceforward they approximated to a standard of orthodoxy, any serious departure from which would incur the opprobrious title of heresy. But there was no authority in the Quran or the Traditions that could justify such a rigid division and, whatever the practice, no theory of orthodoxy and heresy came into being even as a result of this stagnation. The stagnation itself was the result of perfectly natural causes, which a glance at Islamic history would disclose.

It was at the end of 488 A.H. that a new era commenced with the life of Ghazzali, at Baghdad, and abandoning his great position and brilliant prospects he wandered forth towards Syria, Palestine, and the Hejaz as a Sufi and that date marks a new era in the history of Islam as well. Within three years of the date, however, the Islamic world got involved in a life and death struggle with the crusading forces of the West which diverted all energy to the one subject of self-preservation. And hardly had the brilliant success of Nuruddin Zangi, the Atabek of Mosul, and of Saladin[58] rescued the Musalmans from the threat of Christian domination, while they were still far from immune from the Frankish onslaughts when came the Tartar wave which swept away all the civilisation and culture of the East. The eighth crusade led by Louis IX, of France, did not come to an end before 647 A.H. but the Tartar storm had already burst more than a generation previously in 615 A.H., when Chengiz,[59] issuing from the steppes with a savage following of a million Mongols, had moved upon Farghana and had swept away the forces of Khwarizm Shah like a mountain torrent swollen in the rains.[60] Khojand, Bokhara, Samarkand, Balkh, Herat, Rai, Dinawar, Hamadan, Nishapur—all were sacked and razed to the ground and reduced to ashes or otherwise destroyed, and the tale of victims of the Mongol sword in the Kingdom of Khiwa or Khwarizm alone exceeded several millions of peaceful citizens. 'In Transoxiana and Khorasan the civilisation of centuries was completely destroyed and the people were plunged into a depth of barbarism in which the remembrance of their former greatness and their whole future were alike engulfed. . . . The Mongolian eruption put an end to the intellectual life of Central Asia, for although Persia and the West generally recovered from the misfortunes,

[58] (1137–93), Sultan of Egypt and Syria. He defeated the Christians near Tiberias in 1187. A further crusade, headed by the kings of France and England, captured Acre in 1191, and he was defeated.

[59] Chenghis Khan (1162-1227), Mongol conqueror. By the time of his death the Mongol Empire stretched from the Black Sea to the Pacific.

[60] See *First Encyclopaedia of Islam, 1913–1936*, for Farghana, pp. 62–6.

Bokhara and Samarkand never regained their former mental activity, and their intellectual labours were henceforth entirely devoted to mysticism.' But what happened to Baghdad, the capital of the Abbasids and the centre of Islamic culture after the death of Chengiz or Jingiz when, at the invitation of the traitorous Alqami, the Shia vizier of the Khalifa, he sacked it in 651 A.H., made even the ravages of that 'scourge of God' seem by comparison insignificant. Men and women and children all were treated with like brutality and made the prey of blood lust. 'For three days the streets ran with blood and the water of the Tigris was dyed red for miles along its course. The horrors of rapine, slaughter and outraged humanity lasted for six weeks. The palaces, mosques and mausoleum were destroyed by fire and levelled to the earth for their golden domes. The patients in the hospitals and the students and professors in the colleges were put to the sword. In the mausoleum the mortal remains of Sheikhs and pious Imams and in the academies the immortal works of great and learned men were consumed to ashes; books were thrown into the fire or, where the Tigris was near, buried in its waters. The accumulated treasures of five centuries were thus for ever lost to humanity, and the flower of the nation was completely destroyed . . . Baghdad, the abode of learning, the seat of culture, the eye and the centre of the Saracenic world, was ruined for ever. The population before the sack was over two millions; according to Ibn Khaldun one million and six hundred thousand perished in the slaughter of six weeks. With the destruction of Baghdad the gloom of night settled on Western Asia.' Well may the historian exclaim: 'This is a period of famine for science and virtue', and it is nothing short of a miracle proving the imperishable vitality of Islam that it not only survived this cataclysm but that it tamed the descendants of Chengiz and Hulagu and converted them into champions of Islam and patrons of Muslim learning so soon after Sadi had sung the dirge of Baghdad and its Khilafat. A century later Tamerlane's whirlwind career of conquest completed the work of his ancestors and it is only during the last few generations that Islam has once more undergone a process of revivification and is anxious to remove from itself the reproach of stagnancy. Europe and Christendom have paid it back some of their old debt, and thus financed, they are once more undertaking fresh cultural enterprises.

## AN IMPORTANT WARNING

At this stage the greatest care has to be taken that Muslim thinkers do not fall into the old pitfalls of theologians or of philosophers. 'Free thought' had once more commenced its fantastic career with Western Education, but the temporal misfortunes of Islam have curbed its uncontrolled activity. The reaction too has to be carefully watched and kept under control. Naql or Tradition has to a great and growing extent regained its attractions and the respect due to it, but in Aql or the Reason, to which the earliest and the most authentic Tradition itself so frequently appealed, is always to be sought its truest confirmation. Poor Syed Ahmad Khan earned the appellation of Naturee, because he insisted on the consistency of the Word of God with what he called the Work of God, basing it, as I shall have occasion to show, on the clearest texts from the Quran. So far Ibn Rushd was right when he said that Philosophy agrees with Religion and Religion recommends Philosophy. Only we must be careful that this Philosophy is neither the narrow logic nor the obsolete and unnatural science of the old scholasticism and must exercise the caution of Ghazzali, that although nothing should be set down as unbelief that is not really so, and that the truths of science, whether mathematics, logic, physics, or any other that cannot intellectually be rejected should be fearlessly accepted, yet our intellectualism must not be permitted to lead us into an attitude and a belief that the scientists with their successes in their own departments are to be followed blindly in other departments also, and that all subjects are susceptible of the exactness and certainty of a syllogism in logic or are as demonstrable as the discoveries of natural science. Aql, moreover, is not reason, pure and simple, which is to exercise its sole sovereignty without the interference of a rival but must permit elbow room to intuition and other processes of the mind which have not hitherto been fully comprehended, classified and labelled by scientists. It is a good omen that great scientists themselves like Sir Oliver Lodge [author of Modern Scientific Ideas] are as convinced today as the merest obscurantist of an elder day that there are evidently things in heaven and earth which are still beyond the dreams of our philosophy. But a far more necessary warning than any of those already mentioned is necessary with regard to the schoolmen's superior attitude towards the commonalty. The desire to be exclusive in their possession of them is a natural failing of those that have been endowed with gifts in a more bounteous measure than their fellow beings and that is how autocracies and oligarchies, aristocracies and plutocracies have grown. Islam insists on a more equitable division of all things that it is within the power of man to divide, and just as it abhors the exclusive possession of power and pelf, so it abhors—and it abhors to a still greater degree—the exclusive possession of knowledge particularly of Religion, which creates a hierarchy. As I have already repeatedly stated it has no clergy, and yet if those intellectually more gifted than their fellow Muslims are not to exercise a check over the tendency to confine to themselves the knowledge that their superior cultural gifts enable them to possess, the ulama, that is the learned, are bound to approximate to an exclusive caste like the Brahmans or a hierarchy like the priests of Roman Church and for centuries they have shared some of the failings of the clergy of the Reformed Churches of Christianity. And the worst of these failings is that they lead the learned unconsciously to exaggerate the natural inequalities in the mental calibres of men. Take the spirit in which the Muwahhid dynasty of Spain which viewed philosophy with no disfavour and under which men like Ibn Tufayl and Ibn Rushd (Averroës) enriched the world with philosophic thought. They seem to have been troubled with the problem how much the people could be taught with safety and to have arrived at the solution that the bulk of the people should be taught nothing but the literal sense of the Quran, metaphors-quasi-anthropomorphism and that the educated lay public, which had already some inkling of the facts should be assured that there was really no difficulty between philosophy and theology. Ibn Tufayl's imaginary philosopher Hayy ibn Yaqzan,—'the living one son of the waking one' can best thrive on the deserted island and rising to the highest philosophic level reach the vision of the Divine and although the reformed and purified faith of a neighbouring island which is peopled is in truth the same as he has himself evolved unassisted on his desert island, it is good enough for the masses only, and he the theologian of nature must retire to his own island again and live the old solitary life. So sane a thinker as Ibn Rushd, who alone gave Aristotle to Europe, definitely lays down that there are two things in religion, literal meaning and interpretation, and that the literal meaning is the duty of the multitude and interpretation the duty of scholars, and though he rightly claims for the scholar freedom to interpret, without being tied down by any church dogmas as to what may not be interpreted, he is not only willing but anxious to tie down the scholar if necessary by the State to the extent that he must not communicate his interpretation to the multitude. Their faith must be carefully screened from all contact with the teachings of philosophers. But like so many schemes of mice and men that gang aft agley, such systems of obscurantism fall to pieces and do not work for long. The people refuse to be blindfolded. It must be said to the credit of Syed Ahmad Khan that he has proved a true rationalist in his democratic ideal and has mercilessly exposed the futility and the mistake of Ibn Rushd's unnatural and irrational division of mankind into philosophers and fools. God the Creator of all mankind, of fools as well as philosophers, did not send His final message through the Last of the Messengers for philosophers only nor did He send two messages, one for philosophers and another for fools. True, there are things enough and to spare that all cannot equally well comprehend. No one in his senses would suggest that the scholar and the scavenger are equally highly endowed with intellect. But if they are equally subject to a moral law, and equally responsible for their actions in this world, it would argue injustice in the Creator if He had not endowed both of them with sufficient intelligence to comprehend that moral law and to understand His Divine Purpose. And after all that Purpose is no riddle that philosophy alone can solve. It is plain and within the compass of the meanest intelligence. It is writ large all over Nature, and he who runs may read. The bishop and his butler may not be equally good theologians as Popes and prelates define a theologian; but they can be equally good servants of God, and it is this what religion is for, if it has indeed any purpose to serve, besides that of eternal disputations and creed-making. Muslims, alas! have so often misunderstood the challenge that Allah throws down in the Quran more than once, asking the unbelievers to produce ten chapters or even one chapter like it. Allah is no stylist to whom a well-turned verse could be matter for boasting. He does not compete with Imra-ul-Qais or Labeed for the honour of Ukaz or Al-Majannah. And curiously enough the critics of the Quran fall into the same mistake when they suggest comparison of the Quran with human literary products. They forget that there is not one of those works of art that they would compare with the Quran and adjudge to possess greater literary excellence but makes its appeal to a more or less limited circle.

## THE QURAN: EVERY MAN'S BOOK

Where the Quran excels in style apart from its contents is in the universality of its appeal and its intelligibility to fools as well as philosophers, dull, prosaic men no less than poets revelling in their fine frenzy. All may not derive the same kind of enjoyment from it, but to all it conveys clearly enough the concluding message God sent to mankind. There are no such things as literal meaning and interpretation. If speech is not the art of concealing thought but of expressing it, the Quran, like any other literary product must have some thoughts to express, some meaning to convey, and it is immaterial how we arrive at a comprehension of these thoughts and an understanding of that meaning so long as we do arrive there. If literal meaning would take us to our destination, by all means let us all take that road, philosophers as well as fools. If, on the contrary, interpretation alone can lead to it, let us all follow that path, fools as well as philosophers. But if either literary meaning or interpretation fails to lead us to our destined goal, of what earthly use is it? No road in the world runs absolutely straight and always on the same level. For miles and miles it may go on straight and smooth, and yet some natural obstacle like a lake or a hill intervenes and may have to be skirted and traversed in a zigzag way or like a spiral. Are we to refuse to take the road that safely brings us at last to our destination simply because we cannot walk on as the crow flies? The object is to get there the best way we can for that is why we take the road. Not that for every wayfarer the road possesses the same interest or charm. They all agree with regard to the object of their journey, which is to reach their destination, but to some the beauty of the wayside itself will make an appeal which it may not to others that have no eyes for such beauty. Yet even here, the Quran's great miracle is that all without exception find some beauty or other in the road, and to none is the way dull and wearisome.

The Quran is God's word truly enough; but it is and must be in man's ill coin. Just as the Quran repeatedly assures those unbelievers who clamoured for a miracle, such as an angel bringing God's message to mankind, that an angel and not a man like Muhammad would certainly have been chosen for the task if angels and not men tread this territorial globe and lived and worked and died here, so it tells the Arabs who were to be the first faggots to light the fire that God's message to mankind to be delivered by them is worded in their own Arabic tongue. And it repeatedly asserts its clarity. The Quran must, therefore, be simple enough, if it was meant by Allah whose message it contains, to be intelligible to the dwellers of the desert. For an Ummi or an unlettered nation even the Apostle chosen was an Ummi. How then could the Quran be a mystery to all mankind except the philosopher who could solve it by the 'Open Sesame' of his interpretation? The only way to make it a riddle is to look in it for riddles. And if we understand anything of the psychology of such simple folk as the dwellers of the desert, who had to preach the new Evangel, Allah must have talked in the Quran in pictures and parables. Not philosophical concepts and abstractions but images sufficiently concrete for the untutored mind must have been employed. And that is precisely what we find. But if we must not look for riddles in the Quran and thereby make it a philosopher's riddle, we must not be so wooden-minded as to have no use for a metaphor. If there is one thing worse than turning rhetoric into a syllogism it is petrifying a parable. Metaphysics and anthropromorphisms are alike foreign to the whole spirit of the Quran, and if we just let it soak into our consciousness as it must have soaked into the consciousness of the Arabs more than 1300 years ago, we shall get all the philosophy we need to last us through life and carry us into the Great Beyond. This is the possible canon of interpretation to be applied to a book like the Quran, and howsoever one may differ from Syed Ahmad Khan in the results at which he has arrived, this much must be said for him that he has convincingly enunciated this canon in his exegesis of the Quran. He does not presume to question the visions of a Sufi in his ecstasy but since they are not objective and cannot convince those who have not shared such an experience, he lays them on one side. The philosopher too who would cogitate endlessly about Essence and Attributes, Freewill and Necessity he leaves to his own devices. But the plain average man is his concern and him he is out to convince that the King of the whole of this Creation is one that is Good, that He and He alone must be served and Muhammad (on whom be Allah's benedictions and peace) has brought for them a clear enough message, the last and the only certain Word of God, which tells them how God can be served, what obligation there is on them to serve Him and how easy it is after all to do so. It was not until very recently that I read his Tafseer, which he could not unfortunately complete through pressure of educational work in later life, and apart from certain matters of detail and one or two matters of more essential importance on which I have thankfully received enlightenment from it, I had arrived at my main conclusions quite independently of it. This cannot be a matter for boasting for, as I view it, every man of average intelligence would reach the same destination if he would only not hamper his progress with the impedimenta of theologians, literalists or philosophical speculators. Remember, the message was first addressed to the untutored Arabs and even if we are as bad as the Bedouins and no worse by following the same road, we can, with God's help, find our destined goal. I have no more prejudice against philosophy than had Syed Ahmad Khan, and there is still ample room in the Church of Islam for all philosophers. Only they must not make Muslim Theology their battle-ground and divert the energies of Muslims from righteous action, of which the Muslim world stands sorely in need, into vain disputations. There is ample room for the mystic also, but let him develop his kashf or gnosis to the fullest extent that his deep religious emotions are capable of, without letting Sufism degenerate into a wild fantastic ritual, or worse still, leading him to consider his kind above and beyond the claims of Islam's Shariat, which prescribes the simplest of duties for all alike.

## LAST WORDS

I have now said all that I need say about my religious antecedents and my present attitude towards Islam and its theology and I fear I have said it at much greater length than I wished, and would have done if I had been able to devote more time that expression and concentration require. But an inherent and almost ineradicable tendency towards diffusion and a fatal attraction for tangents found a good ally in the condition of my prison life when work at a stretch, which I have always preferred, was impossible and only snippets of time were available for dashing off a few scores of lines at a time. Doubtful as I feel about completing my task I feel almost certain that even if I am enabled to do so within a reasonable time I would not have the leisure for any but the rapidest revision before I hand over the manuscript to the printers. But in the circumstances of which now the reader shares the knowledge with the writer, he thinks he can rely on a generous measure of the reader's indulgence. I do not pose as an authority on Islam; but I do hope I am a Muslim, and as such it is my first duty to share such truth as I have with my fellow beings. I would close this part of the book with the citation of a short chapter from the Quran in which the Prophet's life has been briefly reviewed and the duty he owes to Allah for His mercies has been simply stated:

سُوْرَةُ وَالضُّحَىٰ مَكِّيَّةٌ وَّهِيَ اِحْدَىٰ عَشْرَةَ اٰيَةً

بِسْمِ اللّٰهِ الرَّحْمٰنِ الرَّحِيْمِ

وَالضُّحَىٰ ۙ وَالَّيْلِ اِذَا سَجَىٰ ۙ مَا وَدَّعَكَ

رَبُّكَ وَمَا قَلَىٰ ۗ وَلَلْاٰخِرَةُ خَيْرٌ لَّكَ مِنَ

الْاُوْلَىٰ ۗ وَلَسَوْفَ يُعْطِيْكَ رَبُّكَ فَتَرْضَىٰ ۗ

اَلَمْ يَجِدْكَ يَتِيْمًا فَاٰوٰى ۙ وَوَجَدَكَ

ضَآلًّا فَهَدٰى ۝ وَوَجَدَكَ عَآئِلًا فَاَغْنٰى ۝

فَاَمَّا الْيَتِيْمَ فَلَا تَقْهَرْ ۝ وَاَمَّا السَّآئِلَ فَلَا

تَنْهَرْ ۝ وَاَمَّا بِنِعْمَةِ رَبِّكَ فَحَدِّثْ ۝ ع

Me also my Allah found an orphan and rescued; me also He found wandering in search of truth, and I believe guided, and me also He found in the sorest of a mortal's needs, the needs of the Spirit even more than those of the body and satisfied them in ample measure. The least that I must do for such divine mercies is to deal with orphans with loving kindness, to assist to the best of my ability such as have a question unanswered about my faith and to proclaim the bounty of Him that created me and sustains me.

# Appendix

## THE MISUNDERSTANDING AND ITS CAUSES

AFTER A VERY LENGTHY recital of my individual experiences and a statement of my position and attitude, I should, in all conscience, now plunge into the heart of my subject. But I fear I shall not succeed in the purpose I have in view in offering this exposition of Islam if I did not give as brief and yet as adequate a history as I can of the misunderstanding that exists between Islam and the West. The estrangement itself none will deny; but the average reader, for whom I write, is not likely to know how it came about, and it is only when he has got a fair idea of its genesis and growth that with his present expanded outlook and his desire to avoid the pitfalls of prejudice, he would do that justice to Islam for which it has waited in vain for thirteen centuries. In order not to be considered guilty of unfairness, a suspicion that will nullify the whole of my appeal for fairness from others, I shall, as far as possible, cite Europeans and Christians and base this part of the book on their writings, often transcribing their very words.

One of the most sympathetic writers on Islam among Englishmen after Gibbon and Carlyle, though nonetheless a frank believer in its inferiority to Christianity, was Bosworth Smith, who gave a series of lectures at Harrow, where he was a Master, before the select circle of friends and subsequently published them in one volume *Mohammad and Mohammadanism*. In one of these lectures he said:

> During the first four centuries of Mohammadanism, Christendom could not afford to criticise or explain; it could only tremble and obey. But when the Saracens had received their first check in the heart of France, the nations which had been flying before them faced round, as a herd of cows will sometimes do when the single dog that has put them to flight is called off; and though they did not yet venture to fight, they could at least calumniate their retreating foe. Drances-like [sic], they could manufacture calumnies and victories at pleasure: —
>
> Quoe tuto tibi magna volant; dum distinet hostem,
> Agger murorum, neo inundant sanguine fossoe.

The disastrous retreat of Charles the Great, through Roncesvalles, and the slaughter of his rear-guard by the Gascons, is turned by Romance-mongers and Troubadors into a signal victory of his over the Saracens; Charles, who never went beyond Pannonia, is credited, in the following century, with a successful Crusade to the Holy Sepulchre, and even with the sack of Babylon.

It will be my duty to mention some of these calumnies and to repudiate them, but before I do that, it is necessary for Muslims and Christians alike to enquire, in some detail, into the causes and conditions that gave rise to them.

I, for one, honestly believe that even if the Muslims had never contributed that brilliant and inspiring chapter to the history of the world which they did by their conquests in Spain, France, Southern Italy and Sicily and by their rule over large areas in Europe, which in Spain itself lasted for eight long centuries, they would have carried out their mission in the world far more truly if they had succeeded in having in Europe today just as many fellow-Muslims as they have in China, which they never conquered nor ruled. Believing this as I do, I cannot be accused of insincerity in wishing what the follower of so militant a faith as Islam is reputed to be, is not expected to wish; that there had not been all this warfare between Muslim and Christian, and consequently no need on the part of Christian chroniclers to manufacture calumnies against Islam along with the manufacture of victories over Muslims. From the point of view of religion the 'flaming onset' of victorious Islam cannot be contemplated in the light of all the subsequent history of Islamic mission, without a good deal of regret.

But perhaps our regrets are in vain and it would be better to take it more philosophically and say that ours is all that time has passed over and nothing is in a safer place than what has been. For it seems that the Dark Ages of Christendom that witnessed the dawn of Islam were in any case too unenlightened and too contentious to appreciate the truth of Islam. The men in whose public life their polemics was the most engrossing and perhaps also the most debasing element could not be expected to have summoned patience enough to understand what looked like an alien creed. According to the Muslim view, which such study of Hebrew and Christian religion as I have recently been able to make, fully confirms, is that Jesus (on whom be peace) was, like John the Baptist, a Prophet of Israel who had resumed the interrupted tradition of Israelite prophesy, and that quite in a different sense from that of St. Paul, he had come not to destroy the Law as enunciated by Moses but to fulfil it. He was, like all prophets, a reformer of the faith of his spiritual ancestors that had got corrupted and submerged in the course of time. And although I hold, as a Muslim, that all religion is intended by the Divine Being, Who sends His Apostles and Messengers to various groups and divisions of mankind, geographically and historically separated from each other, to be universal and not tribal or local, and therefore Jesus could not have meant what was understood by some at least of his early and most intimate followers from the words 'Salvation is of the Jews', and could not have intended that the Gentile should remain beyond the pale of his immediate mission-field which lay in Judea.[1] From God at least, Who had created him for His own purpose, the fact could not have remained hidden that his ministry was to be exceedingly brief, and for such a brief life of public activity the work that was entrusted to Jesus could not have been unlike that of the older Prophets of Israel, Elijah (Elisha), Amos[2] and Hosea,[3] Isaiah[4] and Jeremiah,[5] Ezekiel[6] and the Second Isaiah. They all had a definite place in the history of Israel and emphasised particular aspects of Divine Truth which had been neglected more than others. They all fulfilled the Law in the truest sense of the word and did not come to destroy it. Juda had had her troubles as well as the Northern Kingdom of Israel that had parted company with the Southern after Solomon's reign,[7] and even though she was inclined to regard herself as the favourite of Yahovah, who had sent back from her gates the Assyrian that destroyed the sister state, she got as severe a lesson as history has ever taught an unrighteous people, in the havoc wrought by Nebuchadnazzar, a century and a quarter later and in the wrong captivity in Babylonia.[8] And this experience, while it chastened the Jews, also estranged them a little from Yahovah, who was regarded not only with wholesome awe but with a fear untempered with love. He was not perhaps a tyrant, but he was certainly a hard taskmaster who was not a little vindictive in vindicating his neglected righteousness. The henotheism[9]

[1] Roman-Greek name for South Palestine.

[2] The prophet Amos, who was supposedly active in parts of Israel in the mid-eighth century B.C.

[3] Also a prophet, who was active during a period of Assyrian military invasions.

[4] The first in order of the major Old Testament prophets, son of Amoz.

[5] A prophet who was active in Judah *c.* 627–587 B.C.. A major prophetic work of the Hebrew Bible/Old Testament is attributed to him.

[6] A sixth century B.C. priest amongst the Jews exiled in Babylonian territories. A major prophetic work in the Hebrew Bible/Old Testament is also attributed to him.

[7] Famous king of Israel, the second son of David and Bathsheba.

[8] (*c.* 630–562 B.C.); founder of the New Babylonian Empire. In the West he is remembered chiefly for his deportation of the Jews to Babylon in 586 B.C.

[9] A term first employed by Max Mueller in 1860 for a primitive form of faith which, as

that had overlaid Mosaic monotheism had certainly gone, and but for the Hellenism of the Dispersal, which interposed mediators between a transcendental God and man, stimulated the creation of divine hypostases[10] and culminated in the Logos of Philo, the senior contemporary of Jesus. Judaism was as monotheistic as Islam itself. But the sole sovereign of all creation needed atonement and propitiatory sacrifices and a rigid adherence to the priestly ritual elaborated largely in the Babylonian captivity. The Sadducees[11] who governed the Church-State, such as it was after the Restoration under Gentile paramountcy, had the 'liberalism' of indifference to the faith of their ancestors; but it was the Pharisees and Scribes[12] that were the most vigorous element in Judaism at the time and they in their legalism and formalism had erected rigid barriers between the Creator and those whom He had created and loved and wished to lead. It was these barriers that Jesus came to destroy and not the Law of God enunciated by Moses. The Law he fulfilled by transforming the legalism of the Pharisee with the aid of God's transcending Love. It was the crying need of Israel then, and the heroic effort of Jesus to infuse love into the legalism of the Pharisee, which culminated in the soul-stirring scene enacted at Calvary[13] which was worthy of one whom the Quran describes as 'illustrious in this world and in the hereafter' and 'one of those near (to God)'. When in the fullness of time he passed away, he left behind him an exquisitely loveable personality and an example of firmness undivorced from gentleness that must have given fresh courage and resolve to millions of drooping spirits in their encounter with the devil within and without. But he was no theologian who cared to leave to his followers the legacy of involved labyrinthine dogma as rigid as the formalism of the Pharisees themselves, or an elaborate scheme of Church Government and a hierarchy that could shame the empire-builders of Rome with its regular gradation or a cycle of fasts and feasts and rites and ceremonies and fashion plates of vestments surpassing in variety and imposing effect the best efforts of heathen priestcraft. Yet all this has been done in his name and with the

---

distinct from monotheism, recognises the existence of several gods. It stands mid-way between polytheism and monotheism.

[10] This probably refers to the Greek word Hypostasis which, in popular language, was used for 'objective reality' as opposed to illusion.

[11] A major party within Judaism (*c.* second century B.C.–A.D. 70). They were mainly aristocrats, associated with the Jerusalem priesthood.

[12] A class of experts on the Jewish law. Most were Pharisees.

[13] The place of Christ's crucifixion, just outside Jerusalem. According to tradition it was the burial place of Adam.

sanction of his precept or example, while the loving kindness that was his chief message to mankind, the peace on earth, goodwill to men, that he wished to be his memorial, did not, alas! survive him long. Muslims will not wonder at the reception they met with at the hands of Christians if they know that fellow-Christians that dared to differ from them in the smallest particular met with nothing better. And Christians today, who think intolerance is the badge of every faith but their own, will be able to unravel the mystery of their own intolerance towards Islam that does exist, and in such ample measure too, even though they are not conscious of its existence, and will, it is my earnest wish and hope, discard it once for all like so many ancient and medieval superstitions that they have discarded in recent days.

I have already explained at some length how far-reaching was the effect of the first controversy among the followers of Jesus, when Paul evolved a Christology of his own from his inner consciousness and gnosis. It began with the extension of the field of missionary effort to the lands of the Gentiles and to this Peter and the Galilean disciples did not take long in agreeing. Then came the application of the Law to them, and it appears that here too the concession came from these disciples and not from their erstwhile persecutor, the stern Pharisee of Tarsus. They were willing to patch up a truce by freeing the Gentiles from the 'Yoke of Law', but matters did not rest there. The next question that demanded an immediate answer was: 'What about the Jews among the Gentiles?' Peter and his party would not concede liberty from the Law to the Jews; but to this Paul would never agree. To the Galilean disciples Jesus was the Jewish Messiah; to Paul he was the Saviour of the whole human race. In his conception of Christ, the Cross acquired not only a new proportion and value but also a new significance. It became the central fact of his life and the mainspring of his teaching and marked the entire abolition of the economy of Law.

The Law was a sign of Servitude due to the sin of Adam. Grace was the sign of Sonship due to the redemption wrought by Christ on the Cross. Consequently, it became, along with the Spirit, a token from God that the dispensation of Law and Servitude ended and a dispensation of Grace and Sonship began. Just as Saul the Pharisee persecutor of the Christians must have maintained that to seek 'justification' by Grace was 'of none effect', so Paul the suddenly and miraculously converted Christian and divinely created 'Apostle of the Gentiles', maintained that to seek 'justification' through the works of Law' made the Grace of Jesus Christ 'of none effect'. This was a startling innovation and to the Galilean apostles, who had been the companions and disciples of Jesus during his ministry, it was altogether a different Gospel from that which they had received from the Master himself, and, as I have said before, not only did they not agree to it but it was never accepted south of the Taurus Range. In depending upon his superior Gnosis and dispensing with the sayings and the story of Jesus alike, Paul set an example that other Hellenists were not slow to follow. The claims of St. Paul are, after all, nothing peculiar to him, and even in recent days we have had examples of Editor-Proprietors of groups of newspapers who have habitually seen to it that their views are systematically and artistically worked into the news which their 'Own Correspondents' send to their groups of newspapers. If challenged by some stickler for facts, they have boldly justified this practice by declaring that they were purveyors of truth and not facts. When, however, once we leave the moorings of historical and objective fact and, cutting the painter, sail out in search of some haven of purely psychological and subjective Truth, it is not so easy as it looks to avoid the fate of a derelict. Paul's Hellenistic ideas of freedom from the 'Yoke of Law', heirship of Christ, vicarious atonement, individual redemption through faith alone, apart from works of Law, and mystic union with God in Christ who had pre-existed from all eternity as the Son and Heir, and after Resurrection ascended to heaven and 'sat to the right hand of the Father' led by a very intelligible process and by every gradation to a form of Gnosticism[14] which was even more Hellenistic than Paul's own Gnosis. They were distinctly the disciples of Paul, however far they may have carried his anti-Jewish and Hellenistic tendencies. 'Paul', says Wilhelm Bousset,[15] Professor of New Testament Exegesis, in the University of Göttingen, 'was the apostle whom they reverenced and his spiritual influence on them is quite unmistakable. The Gnostic Marcion[16] docetic[17] has rightly been characterised as a direct disciple of Paul. Paul's battle against the Law and the narrow national conception of Christianity found a willing following in a movement the syncretic origin of which directed it towards universal religion.' St. Paul's ideas were here developed to their extreme consequences though Bousset adds that this was done 'in

[14] Gnosticism was considered a heresy by the early Church Fathers, particularly for its appeal to secret traditions, its deprecatory view of the Creator God, and its docetic view of Christ.

[15] (1865–1920), New Testament scholar. He made extensive investigations into the connections of later Judaism and early Christianity with the contemporary Hellenistic religion.

[16] (d. 160). Known to be a heretic. By the end of the third century most of the Marcionite communities had been absorbed in Manichaeism. His Christology was Docetic, a point Mohamed Ali seemed familiar with.

[17] Docetism was a tendency in early Church which considered the humanity and suffering of the earthly Christ as apparent rather than real.

an entirely one-sided fashion such as was far from being in his intention'.

Curiously enough this other conflict of Hellenism with Hebraism had also a Jew, and no Gentile, for a leading figure, Cernithus of Ephesus, being one of the principal exponents of this Gnosticism. The Gnostic 'heresy' grew apace and one of its earliest forms was called Doketism, 'from its exaggeration of Paulinism into a complete repudiation of the historic Jesus whose earthly career was stigmatised as a mere "phantom" (Dokesis)'. It altogether denied Resurrection and Judgement, and maintained the Adoptionists' doctrine that Jesus became Son of God only at his baptism, a mere temporary 'receptacle' of the Spirit, until the Ascension, which took place, according to this view, before the death on the Cross. These 'progressives' repudiated the Jesus of 'the flesh' in favour of one who comes by water only (that is, the outpouring of the Spirit in baptism) and not by the blood of the Cross. The Pauline doctrine of the Cross was a stumbling-block to them and they rejected the sacrament of the blood and wine. According to one of their books 'The Acts of John', which did not, of course, find a place within the Canon of Orthodoxy, the blinded multitude below the Mount of Olives[18] had tortured not the 'Lord', whom the posse had arrested, but a mere bodily shape which they took to be Christ, while the real Christ 'stood by and laughed'. In another of their compilations, 'The Gospel of Peter', which met with no better fate, Jesus hung upon the Cross 'as one feels no pain' and was 'taken up' before the end. The 'illuminati' also denied the actual sending of 'God's only begotten Son' into the world, and the 'propitiation' for the sins of mankind. If Paul's Gnosis led him to one set of views, theirs led them to another and there was no standard of fact by which to measure such Gnostic Truth.

The result was what could easily have been foreseen. The most violent and substantial controversy and conflict was the first-born of the contact of Hebraism and Hellenism in the History of the Christian Church, and the freedom from the 'Yoke of the Law' did not stop there but soon had a most disastrous development in moral laxity in the next stage of Doketism—a laxity of which evidences are easily discernible in one of the Epistles of Paul, in which he condemns the toleration of fornication and even incest. Among certain branches of the Gnostics, such as Nicolaitians,[19] Philionites, Borborites,[20] etc., unbridled prostitution seemed

[18] A site of sanctuaries during the reigns of David and Solomon, and a traditional burial ground. It is also near the site of the Garden of Gethsemane where Jesus was arrested, and the supposed location of the ascension of the risen Jesus.

[19] Sectaries mentioned in the New Testament where they appear as the advocates of a return to pagan worship.

[20] A sect of libertine Gnostics which flourished from the second to the fifth centuries.

to have been a distinct and essential part of the cult. To be fair to the Gnostics it must be remembered that of their actual writings, which were extraordinarily numerous, very little has survived. They were sacrificed to the destructive zeal of their ecclesiastical opponents, so that we have to depend either upon fragments and extracts from Gnostic writings to be found in the works of the Fathers who attacked Gnosticism, or worse still, on the opinions of these furious opponents of theirs as to their views and vices. In some cases the sources quoted by the Fathers have lately met with very unfavourable criticism and the opinion has been advanced that some of them had fallen victims of the mystification of a forger! With this word of caution, I may safely cite the following judgement of Professor Bacon, of the University of Yale. 'The Doketists', he says, 'with their exaggerated Hellenistic mysticism . . . showed an almost contemptuous disregard for historic Jesus, a one-sided aim at personal redemption by mystic union of the individual with the Christ-Spirit, to the disregard of "the law of Christ", even in some cases of common morality.'

Against the rapid growth of this 'heresy' men like the author of the Pastoral Epistles—1st and 2nd, Timothy and Titus, 100-110 A.C.—and Ignatius and Polycarp,[21] resorted in a state of panic, to the authority of the past and relied on 'ecclesiastical discipline, concrete and massive miracle in the story of Jesus, particularly on the point of the bodily—or as they would have said, the "fleshly"—resurrection'. To them the record of his 'words' became thenceforward a fixed and superhuman standard or rule in the 'new laws', and they gladly turned to the tradition handed down in the Mathaean sayings in the Gospels according to Matthew and Luke and of the Petrine story in the Gospel 'according to Mark'. They, however, did not contain 'reflections on the sense of Sonship', nor the Pauline view of 'the pre-existent divine wisdom tabernacling in man, producing a second Adam as elder brother of a new race, the children and heirs of God'. In fact the Gospel according to St. Mark, the earliest to be compiled, was, on account of its hazy outline of Jesus, the favourite of the Gnostics themselves even though, like the other Synoptics,[22] it does not make Jesus out to be God, which Jesus was to them, pure and simple. So a new Gospel was needed which would 'spiritualise' the 'Apostolic' teaching of the

[21] See entry Testament of our Lord in Galilee, in *The Oxford Dictionary of the Christian Church*, p. 1353.

[22] Refers to the three 'Synoptic Gospels', i.e. Synoptic problem, which arises from the occurrence of a large amount of common subject-matter and often similar phrasing in more than one Gospel.

Synoptic Gospels and yet strongly react against Doketic and Antinomian 'heresy'. And the 'theologian of Ephesus' who has come to bear the name of 'John' and taken for the disciple that died long before it was compiled, produced the Fourth Gospel. He reverses the natural order that 'sound doctrine' must be based on Divine Scripture, inasmuch as he sits down to write Divine Scripture which he based on the conception of 'sound doctrine' entertained by a partisan in heated and turbulent polemics. It is not a Gospel in the general sense of the word, but 'a theological treatise, an interpretation of the doctrine of the person of Christ, written that the readers "may believe that Jesus is the Christ, the Son of God and that believing, they may have life in his name" (20:31)'. Real history, as the author already cited himself admits, was no longer attainable and in any case the author of the Fourth Gospel 'does not aim to be a historian but an interpreter of doctrine' and 'aims to give not fact but truth'. Even 'the material borrowed is handled with sovereign superiority', with the result that his transmutation of such original sources as he relied upon 'makes hardly the pretence of being history' and is 'frankly theology or rather apologetics!'

The dialogue ... does not aim to repeat remembered sayings but follows the literary form which prevailed since Plato had been the classic model for presenting the themes of philosophy. . . . Instead of parables we have allegories. There are important omissions dictated by the requirements of 'sound doctrine'. 'Again and again synoptic scenes are retouched and new scenes are added in a way to present a consistent picture of the "tabernacling" of the pre-existent Son of God in human flesh. . . . In a word evangelic tradition as it had hitherto found currency still lacked the fundamental thing in the Christology of Paul—the Incarnation Doctrine. Paul conceived the story of Jesus as a supernatural drama, beginning and ending in heaven at God's right hand. Even Mathew and Luke, carrying back the adoption to Sonship from the baptism to the birth, had not essentially changed the pre-Pauline point of view. . . . Jesus was still, even in Mark, just the prophet, mighty in deed and word, raised by God, from among his brethren and for his obedience exalted to the Messiahic throne of Glory. How could this satisfy churches trained in the doctrine of Paul? The fourth evangelist depicts the person of Jesus, consistently and throughout, despite his meagre and refractory material, along his line of Christology. . . . Tacitly but uncompromisingly Petrine tradition is set aside. . . . The Fourth Gospel, as its Prologue forewarns, is an application of the story of Jesus as tradition reported it, of the Pauline incarnation doctrine formulated under the Stoic Logos theory. It represents a study in the psychology of religion applied to the person of Christ. Poor as Paul himself in the knowledge of the outward Jesus, unfamiliar with really historical words and deeds, its doctrine about Jesus became, nevertheless, like that of the Great Apostle of the Gentiles, the truest exposition of "the heart of Christ".'

Here is a frank historian but equally fervent partisan of Paul and of the fourth evangelist. His facts cannot be denied, but naturally there was, at the time when this 'the truest exposition of "the heart of Christ"' came to be prepared, a bitter and violent controversy. I have already told the story of the Church of Jerusalem, the nearest approach to a real Khilafat of Jesus in the Christian Church, and how the poor Nazarites[23] and Ebionites[24] were hounded out, and finally driven back either into the Jewish Synagogue from which these despised 'Judaizers who wished to fulfil the Law and not to destroy it, had come or absorbed into the Gentile and now Catholic and Orthodox Church'. That was the ultimate result of one controversy, the conflict between Hellenism and Hebraism, in which Hebraism was worsted, and the Apostle of the Gentiles who applied to the disciples of Jesus and their supporters such epithets as 'super-extra apostles', 'ministers of Satan', and 'dogs of the Concision', came victoriously out of the fray.

The second conflict lasted much longer. Here, indeed, Greek meets Greek! Gnosticism, as we have already noted, was the offspring of Hellenism itself, and it had opposed the Judaizers even more bitterly than Paul and 'John'. In fact it had the most violent dislike of the Mosaic dispensation and identified Yahovah with the Prince of Darkness. It is supposed to have been promulgated towards the end of the first century, almost simultaneously with the capture and destruction of Jerusalem by Hadrian, and the expulsion of Jews and Christians from Jerusalem, which abounded in so many traditions relating to Jesus as a man and the intermixture of his followers with non-Judaic people through this dispersal following on Paul's Gentile ministry had the greatest possible influence on the rapid growth of Gnostic 'truth' to replace Galilean 'fact'. When it threatened to engulf what little was left of the Christianity of Jesus, it compelled Christians of less extreme views to combine into a Catholic Church which, equally relentlessly, pursued it and all the sub-sects into which this 'heresy' had branched out. These included the Marcionites, the Carpocratines,[25] the Basilidians,[26] the Velentinians, the Egyptian

[23] A body of Israelites especially consecrated to the service of God who were under vows to abstain from eating or drinking the produce of the vine, to let their hair grow, and to avoid defilement by contact with a dead body.

[24] A sect of Jewish Christians which flourished in the early centuries of the Christian era.

[25] Followers of Carporates, probably a native of Alexandria. The Carpocratians, who survived till the fourth century, preached a licentious ethic, the transmigration of souls, and the doctrine that Jesus was born by natural generation.

[26] The followers of Basilides, a theologian of Gnostic tendencies who taught at Alexandria in the second quarter of the second century.

Gnostics known as Ophites who shared with other Egyptian Gnostics their notions concerning the eternity of matter, the æons, the creation of the world in opposition to the will of God, the tyranny of the Demikeye who had created the inferior world and 'the divine Christ united to the man Jesus in order to destroy the Empire of the Usurper'. 'This freely growing Gnostic religiosity', says Bousset, 'aroused in the Church an increasingly strong movement towards unity and a firm and inelastic organisation towards authority and tradition. An organised hierarchy, a definitive canon of the Holy Scriptures, a confession of faith and unbending doctrinal discipline, these were the means employed.' While these heretics, who combined with Hellenism a Persian dualism and some elements of Babylonian planetary worship, delighted in giving a free rein to the wildest imagination and peopling the world of religion with Platonic phantoms, they ran a neck-to-neck race with their opponents who had a passion for definition found in the extreme indefiniteness of the theology of Jesus, just the material to put into their rigid moulds and in Greek theology just that language which with its extreme flexibility lends itself so readily to an involved and labyrinthine theology. Of this we shall see a good deal when we reach the Nicolean[27] and post-Nicolean controversies; but in the meantime it will suffice to mention how the Gnostic minority was stigmatised by the majority which now becomes the Catholic Church and Orthodoxy. In Timothy 4:1 these speculations of the Gnostics are denounced as 'seducing spirits and doctrines of devils' and among the titles they received in the sub-apostolic age are 'servants of Satan, beasts in human shape, dealers in deadly poison, robbers and pirates'. The very worst motives 'pride, disappointed ambition, sensual lust and avarice' are recklessly imputed to the heretics and no possibility of morally innocent doubt, difficulty or difference in thought is admitted.

Among Gnostic heresies has to be included Manichæism, the latest development of Gnosticism, though in its original home in the East it was not so much a development of Gnosticism as a distinct religion professedly blending the teachings of Jesus with the old Persian Magism. 'Towards the close of the 3rd century,' write the authors—the great theologians Adolf Harnack[28] and Mr. Connyblare—of the article on Manichæism in the Encyclopædia Britannica,

> two great religions stood opposed to one another in Western Europe, one wholly

[27] Sectaries mentioned in the New Testament where they appear as the advocates of a return to pagan worship.

[28] (1851–1930), German Church historian and theologian. He made himself complete master of the early Christian literature.

Iranian, namely, Mithraism, the other of Jewish origin but not without Iranian elements, part and parcel probably of Judaism which gave it birth, namely, Christianity. Mithraism was peculiarly the religion of the Roman garrisons and was carried by the legionaries wherever they went, and soldiers may have espoused it rather than the rival faith, because in primitive age Christian discipline denied them the sacraments on the ground that they were professional shedders of blood. Although in its austerity and inculcation of self-restraint, courage and honesty, Mithraism suited the Roman soldiers, its cumbrous mythology and cosmogony at last weakened its hold on men's mind and it disappeared in the 4th century before a victorious Catholicism. Yet it did not do so until another faith equally Iranian in mythology and cosmological belief had taken its place.

This was the faith of Mani, which spread with an astonishing rapidity on account of its combination of a thorough-going materialistic dualism with an exceedingly simple spiritual worship and a strict morality; its adaptability from the first to individual requirements of the ignorant as well as the wise, and of the man of the world as well as of the religious enthusiast and ascetic, and the simple and convenient solution that it offered to a problem that had become peculiarly oppressive to the human race in the second and third centuries, the problem of Good and Evil. The Manichæan system was one of consistent uncompromising dualism and in its fantastic philosophy of nature, the physical and the ethical were not distinguished, so that it was thoroughly materialistic. The dual principle of light and darkness which was such a prominent element in Magism was still more emphasised. The Avesta[29] not only formed the background of Mani's faith as the Old Testament formed that of Christianity, but Mani seems to have quarrelled with later Magism because it was not dualistic enough. Mani co-ordinates good with light and evil with darkness. This to him is no figure of speech but light is actually good and darkness evil. Religious knowledge involves the knowledge of nature and her elements, and redemption consists in a physical process of freeing the elements of light from the darkness. God is the head of the kingdom of light. The other kingdom is that of darkness but has no 'God' at its head. Satan and his demons were born of the kingdom of darkness. These two kingdoms stood opposed to each other from all eternity, touching each other on one side but remained unmingled. Then Satan began to rage and made an incursion into the kingdom of light, into the earth of light. God now begot the primal man and equipped him with five pure elements to fight against Satan, but the latter proved himself the stronger and the primal man was,

[29] The sacred books of the Zorastrians or Parsis, which set forth the theology and religious system of the ancient Persians.

for the moment, vanquished. And although the God of light now Himself took the field, totally defeated Satan and set the primal man free, the latter had already been robbed of part of his light by the darkness and the five dark elements had already got mingled themselves with the generation of light. These mixed elements are the elements of the present visible world with its self-contradictory character and the forming of the world is in itself the beginning of the deliverance of the imprisoned elements of light. While the formation of the world is considered to be the work of good spirits, the creation of man is referred to the prince of darkness. Adam was engendered by Satan in conjunction with 'sin', 'cupidity', and 'desire' but the spirit of darkness drove into him all the portions of light he had stolen in order to be able to dominate them the more securely. Hence Adam is a discordant being, created in the image of Satan, but carrying within him the stronger spark of light. Eve, who is seductive in sensuousness, but with a small spark of light also in her, is given to him by Satan as his companion. Thus these first human beings stood entirely under the domination of the devil but the glorious spirits took them under their care from the very outset sending æons to them (including Jesus) which instructed them regarding their nature and in particular warned Adam against sensuality. But the first man fell under the temptation of sexual desire. In the course of history the demons have sought to bind men to themselves by means of sensuality, error and false religion, and among them is to be reckoned, above all, the religion of Moses and the prophets. The good spirits, on the other hand, have carried on their process of distillation with a view to gaining the pure light that exists in the world and with the mechanism of the twelve constellations of the Zodiac, a great wheel with buckets, the portions of light set free from the world are poured into those reservoirs of light, the sun and the moon, where they are purified anew and attain finally to the kingdom of pure light and to God Himself. These portions of light scattered in the world awaiting their deliverance, the Western Manichæans called the Jesus patibilis. Jesus impatibilis, however, was probably one of the prophets who like Noah and Abraham (perhaps Zoroaster and Buddha) had descended from the world of light. But that was not the historical Jesus, the devilish Messiah of the Jews. He was a contemporaneous phantom of Jesus who neither suffered nor died. The religion that had proceeded from the historical Jesus he repudiated altogether with its founder and Catholicism as well as Judaism he looked upon as a religion of the devil. But he looked upon Christianity as it had been developed among the Gnostic sects of Basilidians and Marcionites, Christianity proper as he considered, to be a comparatively valuable and sound religion. And of course he held the apostle Paul, from whom Gnosticism had received its cue, in high estimation, explicitly rejecting the Book of Acts.[30] He himself, on his own claim, is to be reckoned the last and the greatest of prophets, who took up the work of Jesus impatibilis and of Paul. He is the 'leader', the 'ambassador of the light', the 'Paraclete'. The good spirits had been attempting to save men by imparting to them the true Gnosis concerning nature and her forces but he is the first who brought full knowledge. The ethics that he taught was that of rigid asceticism, forbidding the eating of all unclean food which included bodies of animals and wine, every gratification of sexual desire and all traffic with things generally, in so far as they carry in them elements of darkness. These together with an exceedingly rigorous system of fasts, aggregating to nearly a quarter of the year and hours of the four prayers determined with equal exactness, each prayer being preceded by ablutions, made his system too hard for the ordinary man, so that he conceded the principle of a twofold morality like that of the Catholic Church, that of the religious orders and that of secular Christians. The elect were to be rigid ascetics while the hearers were ordinary men of the world. At the head of all these stood teachers (Mani himself and his successors); then followed the administrators and then the elders. According to St. Augustine, who was himself for nine years a hearer, there were twelve teachers and seventy-two administrators. This system first penetrated the Greek-Roman Empire about the year 280 A.C., and gaining a firm footing by the beginning of the fourth century, it spread very rapidly after the Council of Nice. Its adherents were recruited on the one hand from the old Gnostic sects and on the other from the large number of the cultured who were striving after a rational yet in some manner Christian religion. It gave itself out as Christianity without the Old Testament, which had proved a stumbling block to so many Christians. It rejected the doctrine of Incarnation and severely criticised the Catholic Church. The Christian Byzantine and Roman Emperors from Valens[31] onwards enacted strict laws against Manichæans. It nevertheless flourished and in Rome itself between 370 and 440 A.C. gained a large amount of support, specially among the scholars and public teachers. Leo the Great was the first who took energetic measures along with the State authorities against this system. Valentinian III decreed banishment against its

[30] The fifth book of the New Testament, written by St. Luke, the author of the Third Gospel. It traces the progress of the Christian Church from the Ascension of Christ to St. Paul's first visit to Rome.

[31] See *The Oxford Dictionary of the Christian Church*, p. 1423.

adherents and Justinian punished them with death. In North Africa it was extinguished by the persecution of the Vandals.[32] But it continued to exist elsewhere both in the Byzantine Empire and the West and in the early part of the Middle Ages it gave an impulse to the formation of new sects, which remained related to it. Perhaps the Priscillianists[33] of Spain too were influenced by it; but at any rate the Paulicians[34] and Bogomoiles[35] as well as the Catharists[36] and the Albigenses[37] are to be traced back to Manichæism. Thus it accompanied the Catholic Church until the 13th century even though not in its original form which Mani gave to it but as modified by Christian influences. Yet, as in the case of other forms of Gnosticism, we would know little of it today but for Muslim historians. Many of their books were 'destroyed by the Christian bishops acting in conjunction with the authorities', and what little is known through Christian sources is to be found, characteristically enough, in a book in Latin known as *Acta Archelai*, purporting to be an account of a disputation between Mani and the bishop Archelaus of Cascar, in Mesopotamia, translated from the original in Syriac into Greek and soon afterwards into Latin. The writers of the *Encyclopædia Britannica* article pay a well-deserved compliment to Muslim chronicles when they say 'of these (sources) the Mahommedan, though of comparatively late date, are distinguished by the excellent manner in which they have been transmitted to us, as well as by their impartiality. They must be named first because ancient Manichæan writings have been used in their construction.' And yet Musalmans had as much cause to abhor Manichæism as Christians. Nevertheless the seat of the Manichæan pope continued to be in Muslim territory and the writers already cited say that 'even after the conquests of Islam the Manichæan Church continued to maintain itself; indeed, it seems to have become still more widely diffused by the victorious campaigns of

[32] A Germanic people, originally from the Baltic area, who settled in the Danube valley in the fourth century.

[33] The followers of Priscillian, a layman who took up a kind of Gnosticism introduced into Spain by an Egyptian named Marcus.

[34] The members of a sect of the Byzantine Empire. Their name may be derived from St. Paul, who they held in special veneration, or, more probably, from Paul of Samosata, with whom they had affinities.

[35] A medieval Balkan sect of Manichaean origin.

[36] Cathari, a name applied to several sects or a group of Manichaeans. But it is mostly used for a medieval sect, which first came to be known in Germany in the second half of the twelfth century.

[37] A medieval term for the inhabitants of parts of south France, and hence applied to the heretics who were strong there in the late twelfth and early thirteenth centuries.

the Mohammedans, and it frequently gained secret adherents among the latter themselves'.

Besides Gnosticism in its variegated forms, which were so violently denounced and relentlessly crushed, there were other 'heresies' such as that of the Phrygian Montanists, who persisted in their wild enthusiasm of prophecy 'imbibed from their male and female apostles, the special organs of the Paraclete',[38] when the newly formed 'Church' found that unregulated prophecy as a free gift of the Holy Spirit to all Christians was a prolific source of inconvenience, and arbitrarily decreed that the fountain of prophecy had now dried up. In the condition in which the Gospels have come down to us, it is highly unsafe to dogmatise and say what precisely was the teaching of Jesus himself on the one subject on which he talked so incessantly to his disciples, namely, the kingdom of God. I may, however, remark, parenthetically, that as a Muslim it is my belief that his teaching was the same as that of the Quran, or of all the prophets that had preceded him; and if we had a better record of the views of the Galilean disciples than we have in the Synoptic Gospels and the Acts, it would have confirmed the teaching subsequently embodied in the Quran, unless of course they had reasons of their own, as some Muslims like Syed Ahmad Khan and the adherents of the Ahmadiya movement have plausibly suggested, for disguising their real views in order to cover up the traces of Jesus after the reputed 'resurrection from the dead' on the third day. But from the records of early Christian teaching and of subsequent Church history, as they are, one thing is clear. From the crucification and all that followed it right down to the middle of the 2nd century there was the most lively expectation of the second advent of Christ, and nothing could be more natural after the way in which early Christianity had inherited Jewish theology, bodily taking over the Old Testament and accepting a good deal more of Judaistic speculation as a mere intellectual presupposition. This included, of course, the most absorbing topic of the Jewish world for some centuries before the birth of Jesus as well as during his ministry, namely, the Apocalypse.[39] The watchword certainly rings throughout the New Testament—'the Lord is at hand'. As we have seen, St. Paul, 'the Apostle of the Gentiles' as he styles himself, and the second founder of Christianity as he has been since

[38] Johannine epithet of the Holy Ghost. It is traditionally translated 'Comforter'.

[39] 'Revelation of the future'. A literary genre which can be traced to post-Biblical Jewish and early Christian eras; it especially comprises works in highly symbolic language which claim to express divine disclosures about the heavenly spheres, the course of history, or the end of the world.

styled, effected the transformation from a Hebraistic to a Hellenistic Christianity. Greece was the sovereign power in all the world of ancient culture and so Christianity, as preached by this propagandist to the cultured world of Europe, was Hellenised and philosophised. 'Philosophy offered a vehicle which could be applied to the contents of Christianity. The Platonic theism which had adopted the conception of the Logos made a place for Christian terms of philosophy within the Godhead.' And so St. Paul and the author of the Fourth Gospel between them had taken more than half the journey from primary religion, which was, apparently, all the concern of the Galilean disciples, to theology and the rest was being taken at break-neck speed by their extravagant disciples, the Gnostics. But while this journey was being undertaken, Christianity was manifesting itself as 'enthusiastic'. The end of the world was held to be close at hand. Neither the story nor the sayings of Jesus were recorded by those who could have perpetuated a full and authentic account of his ministry because of their vivid expectation of the immediate end of the world and of his second advent. Curiously enough the one Hebraistic Apocalypse that somehow managed to scrape through into the canon of the New Testament, the Book of Revelation, was ascribed to the same apostolic author as the Hellenistic Fourth Gospel. Although the anticipations of the future prevalent among the early Christians had some fluctuating elements that remained in a state of solution and 'were modified from day to day partly because of the changing circumstances of the present by which the forecasts of the future were regulated, partly by indications—real or supposed—of the ancient prophets always admitted of new combinations and constructions' (A. Harnack).

It would suffice here to indicate, for those who are not familiar with Christian scriptures, the shape of the Messianic Kingdom from one canonical New Testament Apocalypse of Christianity. After Christ has appeared from heaven in the guise of a warrior and vanquished the anti-Christian world-power, the wisdom of the world and the devil, indulging in terribly sickening slaughter as unlike the teaching of the Sermon on the Mount,[40] as it is possible to conceive, those who have remained steadfast in the time of the last catastrophe, and have given up their lives for the faith, shall be raised up and shall reign with Christ on this earth as a royal priesthood for one thousand years. At the end of this time Satan is to be let loose again for a short season; he will prepare a new onslaught but God will miraculously destroy him and his hosts. Then will follow the

[40] The discourse of Jesus setting forth the principles of the Christian ethic.

general resurrection of the dead, the last Judgement and the creation of a new heaven and a new earth. Such enthusiastic expectations were inseparably bound up with the Christian faith down to the middle of the 2nd century and although they were then gradually thrust into the background they would never have died out had not the circumstances altered. As year followed year and decade followed decade and yet the Lord that was at hand did not arrive to usher in the Millennium and the Messianic Kingdom that was to come did not come and seemed to tarry, the early enthusiasm could not be indefinitely maintained. People began to resume the thread of their interrupted worldly life instead of remaining for ever 'other-worldly'.

While this enthusiasm was cooling down Greek thought was interpreting the contents of Christianity and the Gnostics who abhorred everything Judaic, including the Apocalypse, found supporters even in a Church party in Asia Minor—the so-called Alogi—who rejected the whole body of Apocalyptic writings and denounced the Book of Revelation as a book of fables.[41] Controversy had raged for a long time when Dionysius, Bishop of Alexandria,[42] who was convinced that the victory of mystical theology over 'Jewish' Chiliasm or Millenarianism would never be secure so long as the Book of Revelation passed for the writing of St. John and kept its own place in the canon, raised the question of its apostolic origin. He carried his point and in the 4th century it was removed from the Greek canon. For many centuries it was thus kept out by the Greek Church and in the meantime court theologians, like that prince of trimmers, Eusabius,[43] [sic] entertained the imperial table with discussions as to whether the dining hall of the Emperor—the second David and Solomon, the beloved of God—might not be the New Jerusalem of John's Apocalypse! Thus 'mysticism and political servility between them gave the death-blow to Chiliasm in the Greek Church. It never again obtained a footing there; for, although, late in the Middle Ages, the Book of Revelation—by what means we cannot tell—did recover its authority, the Church was, by that time, so hopelessly trammelled by a magical mysticism as to be incapable of fresh developments' (A. Harnack). In the Semitic Churches of the East, and in that of Armenia, the apocalyptic literature was preserved much longer than in the Greek Church. The Western Church which was more conservative than the Greek, and whose theologians had little turn for

[41] The Alogi—a group of heretics in Asia Minoı (*c.* A.D. 170).

[42] 'The Great' Bishop of Dionysius (d. *c.* 264).

[43] It should read as Eusebius.

mystical theology and had, on the other hand, a tendency to reduce the Gospel to a system of morals and Church government, utilised Chiliasm for their own purpose. The opposition of Marcion and the Gnostics made them all the more firm in their support of the canonicity of the Book of Revelation and in the West Millenarianism was still a point of 'orthodoxy' in the 4th century. But after the end of that century it gradually disappeared partly through the influence of Greek theology but chiefly through the new idea of the Church wrought out by Augustine on the basis of the altered political situation of the Church. He was the first to teach that the Catholic Church itself was the Kingdom of Christ which had commenced with the appearing of Christ and was, therefore, an accomplished fact.

But while 'acute Hellenisation' was digging the grave of Chiliasm, there was another side to it, the equally acute 'secularisation' of the Church against which the most ardent Christians could not but protest. In spite of the tremendous influence St. Augustine has exercised over Christendom and the Church dogma, even he could not completely extirpate the old Millenarianism. All that he could accomplish was to banish it from official theology.

It still lived on, however, in the lower strata of Christian society, and in certain under-currents of tradition it was transmitted from century to century. At various periods in the history of the Middle Ages we encounter sudden outbreaks of Millenarianism, sometimes as the tenet of a small sect, sometimes as a far-reaching movement. And, since it had been suppressed, not as in the East, by mystic speculation, its mightiest antagonist, but by the political Church of the hierarchy, we find that wherever there is Chiliasm, in the Middle Ages, it makes common cause with all enemies of the secularised church. It strengthened the hands of the Church democracy; it formed an alliance with the pure souls who held up to the Church the ideal of apostolic poverty . . . and in the revolutionary movements of the 15th and 16th centuries . . . it appears with all its old uncompromising energy. If the Church and not the State was regarded as Babylon and the Pope declared to be the Anti-Christ, these were legitimate inferences from the ancient traditions and the actual position of the Church. (A. Harnack)

I thought it necessary to give such a lengthy outline of the history of Millenarianism and such a long-drawn exposition of its spirit because unless we grasp its real significance we shall be misled into condemning with Christian orthodoxy the undoubted extravagances of Montanism without appreciating its historical necessity and the energy of its protests against the growing worldliness of the Church of Christ. In one aspect Montanism was the central reaction of the primitive Christian 'enthusiasm' against the forces which were transforming its character. The man whose name the movement bears, Montanus, appeared in Mysia, near the border of Phrygia, about the year 156 A.C., bringing revelations of the 'Spirit' to Christendom. About that very time a change had begun to take place in the outward circumstances of Christianity. The Christian faith had hitherto been maintained in a few small congregations scattered over the Roman Empire; and these congregations were provided with only the most indispensable constitutional forms. This state of things passed away. While, on the one hand, the Churches now found numbers within their pale who stood, no doubt, in need of instruction, and, as the ordained clergy always think, also in need of clerical supervision and regular control, the enthusiasm for a life of holiness and separation from the world of the earlier days did not, on the other hand, sway many minds any longer. Many were not new converts and those who were merely born and had not become Christians did not feel the same fervour. Besides, Christianity was no longer confined to the poor and the lowly. Christians were now already found in all ranks and occupations, in the imperial palace, among the officials and in the halls of learning as well as in the abodes of labour and among the slaves. Secular tendencies, as I have already stated, were now plainly visible and warning voices were naturally raised against this. The Church did not heed these and, as Harnack says, 'marched through the open door into the Roman State' and settled down there to Christianise the State by imparting to it the word of the Gospel, but at the same time leaving it everything except its gods. On the other hand, she furnished herself with everything of value that could be taken over from the world without overstraining the elastic structure of the organisation which she now adopted. With the aid of its philosophy she created her new Christian theology; its polity furnished her with the most exact constitutional forms; its jurisprudence, its trade and commerce, its art and industry, were all taken into her service; and she contrived to borrow some hints even from its religious worship. With this equipment she undertook, and carried through, a world-mission on a grand scale. But believers of the old school who protested in the name of the Gospel against this secular Church, they joined an enthusiastic movement which had originated in a remote province, and had at first merely a local importance. There, in Phrygia, the cry for a strict Christian life was reinforced by the belief in a new and final outpouring of the spirit—a coincidence which has been observed elsewhere in Church history—as for instance among the early Quakers[44]

[44] A Christian sect founded in the mid-seventeenth century England, and formally organised in 1667.

and in the Irvingite Movement. These zealots hailed the appearance of the Paraclete[45] in Phrygia, and surrendered themselves to his guidance. But the Church that had already waged a bitter and violent controversy with Gnosticism was not going to tolerate such energetic protests. As in the case of the Gnostics, but certainly with far less justice, the Church poured down its condemnation on these disturbers of the order it was bent on setting up. 'Their enthusiasm and their prophesying were denounced as demoniacal; their expectation of a glorious earthly kingdom of Christ was stigmatised as Jewish; their passion for martyrdom as vainglorious; and their whole conduct as hypocritical. Nor did they escape the more serious imputation of heresy on important articles of faith; indeed, there was a disposition to put them on the same level with the Gnostics'. The burden of the new prophecy seems to have been a new standard of moral obligations with regard to marriage, fasting and martyrdom. But Montanus had larger schemes in view. He wished to organise a special community of true Christians to wait for the coming of the Lord. The small Phrygian towns of Pepuza and Timion were selected as the headquarters of his Church. Funds were raised for the new organisation, and from these the leaders and missionaries, who were to have nothing to do with worldly life, drew their pay. Two women, Prisca and Maximilla, were also moved by the Spirit, whose commands they uttered in a state of frenzy like Montanus, urging men to a strict and holy life. For twenty years this agitation seems to have been confined to Phrygia and the neighbouring provinces; but when after 177 A.C., a persecution of Christians broke out simultaneously in many provinces of the Empire and like every persecution it was regarded as the beginning of the end, the desire for a sharper exercise of discipline and a more decided renunciation of the world, combined with a craving for some plain indication of the Divine Will in these last critical times, had prepared many minds for an eager acceptance of the tidings from Phrygia. And thus within the large congregations, 'where there was so much that was open to censure in doctrine and constitution and morals', conventicles were formed in order that Christians might prepare themselves by strict discipline for the day of the Lord. But during a whole generation preceding this crisis the authority of the Episcopate had been immensely strengthened, and the bishop who considered that this new enthusiasm 'disturbed the peace and order of the congregations and threatened their safety', became all the more resolute enemies of Montanism. Some of

[45] Johannine epithet of the Holy Ghost.

these bishops arranged a disputation with Maximilla and her following; but it turned out disastrously for its promoters, a certain Themiso in particular having reduced the bishops to silence. Another bishop attempted to refute Prisca, but with no better success. These proceedings were never forgotten in Asia Minor, and the report of them spread far and wide. 'In after times the only way in which the discomfiture of the bishops could be explained was by asserting that they had been silenced by fraud or violence.' It is to this spirit of the Church in the controversy that we may well attribute the slander against Prisca and Maximilla that they were more remarkable for their wealth than for their virtue. This was the commencement of the excommunication or secession of the Montanists in Asia Minor. An extreme section arose there rejecting all prophecy and the Apocalypse of 'John' along with it. The majority of the Churches and bishops appear to have broken off all fellowship with the new prophets, while books were written to show that the very form of the Montanist prophecy was sufficient proof of its spuriousness. In Gaul and Rome the prophets of Montanism seemed for a while more favourable, the confessors of the Gallican Church at Lyons being of the opinion that communion ought to be maintained with these zealots. There was a momentary vacillation at Rome when the bishop received a letter to this effect from the Church of Gaul. But in A.C. 202, Rome took the decisive step to refuse to communicate with Asiatic Montanists, Praxeas of Asia Minor, the relentless foe of Montanism and himself one of the leaders of Monarchian Moralist heresy, having succeeded in persuading the Roman bishop to withhold his letters of conciliation. Every bond of intercourse was broken and in the Catholic Churches the worst calumnies were retailed about the deceased prophets and the leaders of the societies they had founded. But in many Churches outside Asia Minor a different state of affairs prevailed, those who had accepted the messages of the new prophecy not at once leaving the Catholic Church in a body, but simply forming small conventicles within the Church. But even here an open rupture could not be indefinitely postponed. The bishops and their flocks gave offence to the spiritualists on so many points that at last it could no longer be endured. There was no rivalry in the West between the old organisations and the new as in Asia and Phrygia, for the Western Montanists recognised in its main features the Catholic organisation as it had been developed in the contest with Gnosticism. But they desired that God Himself should be left the sole Judge in the congregation which the bishops wanted more and more to be under their own control, and the demand that the 'organs of the spirit' should direct the whole discipline of the congregation contained an implicit protest against the actual constitution of the Church. And, characteristically enough, the Latin Church would surrender nothing on the point of Church government. Even before this latent antagonism was made plain there were many minor matters which were sufficient, considering the transfer of the partisans, to precipitate a rupture in particular congregations. In Carthage, for example, it would appear that the breach between the Catholic Church and the Montanist Conventicle was caused by a disagreement on the question whether or not virgins ought to be veiled. For nearly five years (202–7) the Carthaginian Montanists strove to remain within the Church; but at length they quitted it and formed a congregation of their own.

It was at this juncture that Tertullian,[46] the most famous theologian of the West, left the Church whose cause he had so passionately espoused against pagans and heretics. In fact, he was the creator of Christian literature in Latin. Cyprian who contested with the bishops of Rome the hegemony of Christendom was ever aware of his dependence upon Tertullian, whom he called his Master, and Augustine whose dominating influence Christianity has not yet been able to shake off, 'stood on the shoulders of Tertullian and Cyprian and these three North Africans are the fathers of the Western Church'. But like Origen[47] in the East who was really the first great theologian of Christianity after Paul and the Fourth Evangelist and was nevertheless dubbed a heretic centuries after he had passed away, the Church did not spare Tertullian and he stood condemned as a heretic. If Montanus himself disdained all knowledge and learning, that could not be said at least of Tertullian. Well able to speak and write in Greek and familiar alike with its prose and poetry, on the theological side, he had not only carefully read the works of his predecessors in the Church like Justin, Tatian, Irænus, Clementi and others and even many Gnostic treatises, in particular the writings of Marcion but he was equally familiar with the old historians of Greece and Rome and 'the accuracy of his historical knowledge is astounding'. He had also studied with earnest zeal the Greek philosophers and particularly Plato and the writings of the Stoics.[48] From the philosophers he had been led to the medical writers and having been intended by his father for law, he had not only studied it

[46] Quintus Septimus Florens Tertullian (*c.* 160–*c.* 225), African Church Father. He was brought up in Carthage as a pagan. He enjoys the title of Father of Latin theology.

[47] (*c.* 185–*c.* 254), Alexandrian Biblical critic, exegete, theologian and spiritual writer.

[48] A Greeco-Roman school of philosophy founded at Athens. The system is described as a form of materialistic pantheism or monoism in contrast to Platonic idealism on the one hand and Epicurean hedonism on the other.

but enjoyed the reputation of being one of the most eminent jurists. This last, however, was at once his strength and his weakness. He was a passionate controversialist whose entire life was lived in the atmosphere of conflict, and this would have well served the cause he now espoused for even 'heat without light' with which his style is sometimes charged, was something in the vein of the frenzy of prophets and prophetesses. But although convinced that the Church had forsaken the old paths and entered on a way that must lead to destruction, he was, perhaps, too much of a lawyer to break away completely from the faith established by a constitutional Church. Harnack says of him, truly enough, that

he well understood the meaning of Christ's saying that he came not into the world to bring peace but a sword: in a period when a lax spirit of conformity to the world had seized the churches he maintained the vigour evangellicus not merely against the Gnostics but against opportunists and a worldly-wise clergy. Among all the fathers of the first three centuries Tertullian has given the most powerful expression to the terrible earnestness of the Gospel.

But the same Harnack says elsewhere of him that he lacked along with the other later followers of Montanus 'the over-mastering power of religious enthusiasm', and that 'in place of an intense moral earnestness we find in Tertullian a legal casuistry, a finical morality from which no good could ever come'. It was in all probability his legal training that was 'responsible for his litigiousness, his often doubtful shifts and artifices, his sophisms and *argumentationes ad hominen*, his fallacies and surprise'.

Western Montanism, at the beginning of the 3rd century, admitted the legitimacy of almost every point of the Catholic system. It allowed that the bishops were the successors of the apostles, that the Catholic rule of faith was a complete and authoritative exposition of Christianity and that the New Testament was the supreme rule of the Christian life. Montanus himself and his first disciples had been in quite a different position. In his time there was no fixed divinely instituted congregational organisation, no canon of the New Testament Scripture, no anti-Gnostic theology and no Catholic Church. When Montanus proposed to summon all true Christians to Pepuza, in order to live a holy life and prepare for the day of the Lord, there was nothing whatever to prevent the execution of his plan except the inertia and lukewarmness of Christendom. But this, says Harnack, was not the case in the West at the beginning of the third century.

At Rome and Carthage, and in all other places where sincere Montanists were found, they were confronted by the imposing edifice of the Catholic Church, and they had neither the courage nor the inclination to undermine her sacred foundations. This explains how the later Montanism never attained a position of influence. In accepting, with slight reservations, the results of the development which the Church had undergone during the fifty years from 160 to 210, it reduced itself to the level of a sect. Tertullian exhausted all the resources of dialectic in the endeavour to define and vindicate the relation of the spiritualists to the 'psychic' Christians; but no one will say he has succeeded in clearing the Montanistic position of its fundamental inconsistency.

After their separation from the Church, the later Montanists had become narrower and pettier in their conception of Christianity. Their asceticism had degenerated into legalism, their claim to a monopoly of pure Christianity had made them arrogant. In the third century their influence began to decline from day to day. Prophecy could not be resuscitated. Only at rare intervals 'a vision might perhaps be vouchsafed to some Montanistic old woman or a brother might now and then have a dream that seemed to be of a supernatural origin. . . . It was only in the land of its nativity that Montanism held its ground till the 4th century'. In Carthage, there existed, down to the year 400, a sect called Tertullianists, providing in this survival a striking testimony to the influence of that teacher. But as we have already indicated, he too had failed to keep alive the old fervour because 'he was under the dominion of more than one ruling principle and he felt himself bound by several mutually opposing authorities'. 'It was,' says Harnack,

> his desire to unite the enthusiasm of primitive Christianity with intelligent thought, the original demands of the Gospel with every letter of the Scripture and with the practice of the Roman Church, the sayings of the Paraclete with the authority of the bishops, the law of the Churches with the freedom of the inspired, the rigid discipline of the Montanists with all the utterances of the New Testament and with the arrangements of a Church seeking to set itself up within the world. . . . The growing violence of his latest works is to be accounted for, not only by his burning indignation against the ever-advancing secularisation of the Catholic Church but also between the incompatibility between the authorities which he recognised and yet was not able to reconcile. After having done battle with the heathens, Jews and the Marcionites, Gnostics, Monarchians and the Catholics, he died an old man, carrying with him to the grave the last remains of primitive Christianity in the West.

What the bitter controversy with the Gnostics had commenced, the equally bitter and perhaps more violent controversy with the Montanists completed and the Catholicism was now rigid and inflexible in its beliefs and organisation, as willing as it was potent to crush minorities without any discrimination and with every weapon on which it could lay its hand. Already, we learn, the controversy with Montanism had turned Northern Asia into a slaughterhouse and, in its insensate fury, had inflicted terrible sufferings on the human race.

There was, besides, the 'heresy' of the Novatians, who rejected the temporal efficacy of repentance and who afterwards attached themselves to the Montanists; and there were the Monarchian 'heresies' of Praxeas[49] and Sabellius[50] who, insisting on the Monarchy of the Father would confound the Father and the Son. Praxeas maintained that the Father was so intimately united with the man Jesus Christ, His Son, that He suffered with Him the anguish of an afflicted life and the torments of an ignominious death! This was the other extreme to which Pauline Christianity was driven by the extravagances of the Gnostics. Then there were schisms such as those associated with Paul of Samosata and Donatus. These heresies and schisms, along with the main controversies already mentioned had helped to keep up a continuous and bitter conflict with the Church of Christ from the times of the Apostles themselves and, as we have seen, the temper and tone of the combatants displayed little of Christian charity. Indeed the time was ripe for Nicæa and its aftermath when controversy was destined to descend from mere bitterness to bloodshed.

And yet it is admitted that there was no longer such serious peril to the life and thought of the Christian Church as had existed earlier when the introduction of Jewish or pagan elements into the faith of the Church was threatened and had to be vigorously resisted 'if the Church was to retain its distinctive character'. 'No vital interest of the Christian faith', writes Rev. A.E. Garsia, D.D., Principal of the New College, Hampstead, 'justified the extravagant denunciations in which theological partisanship so recklessly and ruthlessly indulged' in the post-Nicene period. So far the Church had managed to survive both neglect and persecution and had grown into an *imperium in imperio* which attracted Constantine. He sought to strengthen his empire and stabilise his power with the help of Christianity in which he hoped to secure a fairly numerous and well-knit body of his subjects. This *imperium in imperio* had existed for three centuries within the dominions of Roman Emperors as a disciplined society with jurisdiction of its own religious magistracy strictly exercised over the minds of the faithful. What Constantine, however, failed to see was

[49] He is said to have arrived in Rome towards the end of the second century from Asia, where he had suffered imprisonment for his faith, and to have succeeded in turning the Pope against the Montanists.

[50] Very little is known about him. He was probably an early third century theologian of Roman origin. Sabellianism is an alternative title for the Modalist form of Monarchianism.

the almost inevitable effect of the interaction of State and Church, which, in spite of the theocracy of the Old Testament and the insistence of Jesus himself on the Kingdom of Heaven, came to be conceived by his followers, as he became a more and more remote figure with the passage of time, as separate entities with undefined jurisdictions and unlimited ambitions. The Church *imperium* was, as we have seen, already engaged in the process of formulating, however imperceptibly, creeds and confessions that should confine the wandering imaginations of its members within limits of orthodoxy. Episcopal censures were not free even before from temporal discomforts. The Christian Emperor on the throne was not so desirous perhaps as the Church of the success of sound doctrine, but all the same he was anxious in his own interests for uniformity, and willing to lend to the Church the support of the civil arm. In the altered circumstances Episcopal censures were unlikely to leave anything to distinguish them from the sentences pronounced by magistrates, except perhaps their more apparent rigour and their less apparent justice. In the ante-Nicene period only ecclesiastical penalties, such as reproof, deposition or ex-communication, could be imposed. In the post-Nicene the union of the Church and State transformed theological error into legal offence. As Gibbon pithily sums up, the prerogatives of the King of Heaven were settled or changed in the cabinet of an earthly monarch and the sword of the tyrant was often unsheathed to enforce the reasons of the theologian.

Now exile and extermination were to add their temporal terror to those of deposition and excommunication, and the sword was to be the arbiter between the contending creeds associated with the name of the Prince of Peace. From a poor persecuted people, hiding in the catacombs outside Rome, who could be thrown to the lions and 'butchered to make a Roman holiday', Christians had become, after Constantine's politic conversion, a power behind the imperial throne, and would, within another two or three centuries of that remarkable transformation, presume to dictate to the successors of the first Christian Emperor, and even refuse to them a solitary church in all their kingdom in which to celebrate the Easter if they did not subscribe to the creed of Nice.

Constantine, although still unbaptised, was an interested spectator of the first battle royal fought out under the new conditions, and it was this battle that gave at the first General Council of Nicæa, the Trinity of Three Persons of one and the same substance to the Godhead of Christianity. There were the Tritheists who believed that these three Persons, God the Father, God the Son and God the Holy Ghost, were three distinct and infinite substances, co-equal and co-eternal, composing the Divine

Essence. There were the Sabellians who believed that these were Three Beings, possessing all the divine attributes in perfection, eternal and infinite, and yet so intimately present to each other and to the whole universe as to present themselves as One Being manifesting Himself under different forms and capable of being considered under different aspects. They regarded Jesus as only a man and believed that a certain energy proceeding from the Supreme Father had united itself with the man Jesus, thus constituting him the son of God. This peculiar doctrine, which Gibbon regards as an approach to Unitarianism, was the cause of serious disorders in the Christian Church and had led to the promulgation, by origin of the doctrine of three distinct personalities in the Godhead, a modification, in reality, of the ancient paganism suited to the character of the people who had adopted the creed of Jesus.

Between these two views, the quasi-Unitarianism of the Sabellians and this Tritheism, lay the view of the Lucian of Antioch, as interpreted by his disciple Arius, the excommunicated Presbyter of Alexandria, who was opposed by the successful competitor, in the election to the Episcopal throne, Alexander, and with the latter was his astoundingly energetic and persistent deacon and future successor, Athanasius. Arius believed that the three Persons were real Persons and not merely three attributes to which Sabellianism seemed to reduce them; but of these the Second Person had been created from nothing by the Will of the Father. He, in his turn, created all things and shone with reflected light and governed the Universe in obedience to the will of his Father and Monarch. The real contest was, as is too well known, between Arius and the party that had already succeeded in Alexandria. When Arius began to expound his doctrine at Nicæa with the gentleness and modesty, perhaps dictated by policy as well as temperament, such was the fury of the more numerous party of the Alexandrian bishop that it stuffed its fingers into its ears at the Arian 'blasphemy'. And this has ever since been the characteristic feature of the General Councils of the Christian Church. We, who hold a different faith and plead in the interests of peace and reconciliation, have got to persuade Christendom to give up that ancient habit of stuffing its fingers into its ears.

The decision and victory turned eventually on the ingenuous admission contained in a letter of the patron of the Arians that *Homoousion*[51] or Consubstantial[52] was incompatible with the principle of their theological

[51] The term used in the Nicene Creed to express the relations of the Father and the Son within the Godhead and originally designed to exclude Arianism.

[52] Of one and the same substance or being. The word is used especially of the eternal relationship which subsists between the three Persons of the Holy Trinity.

system. All the other parties pooled their strength against this admission and Consubstantiality of the Father and Son was in this manner established for all times as the creed of the Christians, though wide differences existed among the victors, as I have already explained, as to the interpretation of Homoousion.

But it is not that with which we are here concerned. Our concern is rather with the bitterness which the contest generated. Gibbon is not guilty of any exaggeration when he says that 'the heretics who degraded, were treated with more severity than those who annihilated the person of the Son'. With people in such a frame of mind no victory, however conclusive from the point of view of the Church, could be conclusive from the point of view of the peace of Christendom. That word Homoousion which had proved so convenient at a critical moment in the battle, so bristled with difficulties that peace was not possible. The pure and distinct equality of substance was sought to be tempered, on the one hand, by the pre-eminence of the Father, which was acknowledged as far as it was deemed compatible with the independence of the Son, and on the other, by the internal connection and spiritual penetration which indissolubly unites the divine persons. This latter was the doctrine of circumincessio, which Gibbon characterises as 'perhaps the deepest and darkest corner of the whole theological abyss'. St. Hilary,[53] the zealous bishop of Poitiers, 'from the peculiar hardships of his situation, was inclined to extenuate rather than to aggravate the errors of the Oriental Clergy. . . . The oppression which he had felt, the disorders of which he was the spectator and the victim, appeased, during a short interval, the angry passions of his soul'. And it was then that, according to Gibbon, 'unwarily deviating into the style of a Christian philosopher,' he wrote:

It is a thing equally deplorable and dangerous that there are as many creeds as opinions among men, as many doctrines as inclinations, and as many sources of blasphemy as there are faults among us; because we make creeds arbitrarily and explain them as arbitrarily. The Homoousion is rejected, and received, and explained away by successive synods. The partial or total resemblance of the Father and of the Son is a subject of dispute for these unhappy times. Every year, nay every moon, we make new creeds to describe invisible mysteries. We repent of what we have done, we defend those who repent, we anathematise those whom we defended. We condemn either the doctrine of others in ourselves or our own in that of others; and reciprocally tearing one another to pieces, we have been the cause of each other's ruin.

[53] St. Hilary of Poitiers (*c.* 315–67), the 'Athanasms of the West'. His defence of orthodoxy led to his condemnation at the Synod of Biterre (356) and to a four-year exile to Phrygia by the Emperor Constantins.

This is a most significant judgement, coming as it does from one who was known as the 'Mallens Arianorum' and the 'Athanasius of the West', who was a most zealous opponent of Arianism[54] at a time when it was threatening to overrun the Western Church and undertook the task of repelling the irruption. Little knowing at the time that he himself would soon be the victim of an imperial rescript of banishment to remote Phrygia, one of the first steps he took in this direction was, in fact, to secure the excommunication by the Gallican hierarchy of the Arian bishop of Arles and of two of his prominent supporters. When we remember that he shared to the full fury of the theology with the other controversialists of the time, that he even impeached an orthodox bishop of Milan and had the mortification of hearing the supposed heretic, when summoned before the Emperor, give satisfactory answers to all the questions proposed that he, characteristically enough, called the lately deceased Constantius son of Constantine, Antichrist, a rebel against God and a 'tyrant whose sole object had been to make a gift to the devil of that world for which Christ had suffered'. We can, I think, appreciate the significance that Gibbon rightly attaches to this unconscious deviation 'into the style of a Christian philosopher'.

For the War of Substances[55] soon gave place to a War of Similarity. The questions mooted with the same fierce ardour, if not more, were now whether there was a likeness between the Father and the Son, or a similarity of Substance instead of Consubstantiality. There were the Anomaeans[56] who resolutely denied the likeness and held that an infinite difference existed between the Creator and the most excellent of His creatures. This obvious consequence of the Arian view was maintained by Aetius on whom the zeal of his adversaries bestowed the surname of the Atheist! Armed with texts of Scripture and Aristotelian logic he soon acquired the fame of an invincible disputant and the friendship of the Arian bishops,—'till they were forced to renounce and even to persecute a dangerous ally, who by the accuracy of his reasoning had prejudiced their cause in the popular opinion and offended the piety of their most devoted followers'. On the other side were the Homæans who held that the Son was different from other creatures and similar only to the Father. These two were, of course, Arians, since they regarded the Son as a creature and denied

[54] The principal heresy which denied the true divinity of Jesus.

[55] In the Christian doctrine of the Godhead, the word is used to express the underlying Being, by which all Three persons are One.

[56] The fourth century exponents of a doctrine closely akin to Arianism. They distinguished God's creative will (his fatherhood) from his absolute and undivided essence.

Consubstantiality. But the most numerous sect that had now arisen was that of those semi-Arians who, while still denying Consubstantiality or Homoousion, asserted the doctrine of a similar substance and at the Council of Selencia their opinion would have prevailed by a majority of 105 to 43 bishops. 'The Greek word,' says Gibbon, 'which was chosen to express this mysterious resemblance bears so close an affinity to the orthodox symbol that the profane of every age have derided the furious contests which the difference of a single diphthong excited between the *Homoousions* and the *Homoiusions*.' Like the 'profane of every age' we may not deride, but we must certainly deplore the serious consequences to the peace of a large part of the world resulting from such doctrinal differences. At first it was Arius and his adherents that had to bear the brunt for their 'unorthodox' beliefs, and then by a sudden reversal of fortune, it was the turn of Athanasius and other victors of Nicæa to suffer no less cruelly at the instigation of their defeated and persecuted rivals. The banishment of Arius, the condemnation of his writings to flames, and the denunciation of nothing less than capital punishment against those in whose possession they should be found, were the immediate sequel of Nicæa. But only three years later, the turn of the tide brought Arius and his supporter and fellow-student Eusebius, bishop of Nicomedia,[57] back and subsequently Athanasius and two other leaders of orthodoxy, the bishops of Antioch and Constantinople, were deposed and afterwards banished by the same Constantine. It was a curious commentary on the momentous decision taken in his presence at the first General Council of the Catholic Church that when at last he was baptised a little before his death it was at the hand of Eusebius, of Nicomedia, who had been exiled to Gaul for refusing to accept its anethemas, though, unlike Arius, he had accepted the creed of Nicæa. In the reign of his son, Constantius, the heretics had their fill of vengeance, though they too did not escape scot-free. If Constantine saw in the one Catholic Church the best means of counteracting the movement in his vast empire towards disintegration, and realising how dangerous dogmatic squabbles might prove to its unity, sought uniformity, his son Constantius was even more desirous of uniformity, but only to satisfy the craving of despotism. So capricious was he in his tastes and so easily offended by the slightest deviation from his imaginary standard of Christianity that he persecuted with equal zeal those who defended Consubstantiality, those who asserted Similar

[57] Leader of the Arian party in the first half of the fourth century. At the Council of Nicaea (325), he signed the Creed. His followers were commonly known by his name.

Substance and those who denied the likeness of Father and Son. In the West, Arianism had little success, except among the Germanic tribes whose story I shall presently tell. But, thanks to Constantius and Valens, in the East, Arianism could not be snuffed out so easily as the victors of Nicæa had imagined. For 40 years, from 340 to 380 A.C., Constantinople was their principal seat and fortress. As a consequence of this, their opponents were deprived of the public exercise of their religion in the very capital of the empire. However, as, unlike the Arians in the West, they were not so few in numbers in the East, nor so feeble in power, the result was a constant controversy leading to the use of invectives and not unoften followed by blows. Tertullian had boasted that a Christian mechanic could readily answer such questions as had perplexed the wisest of the Greek sages, and apparently the Greek sages were amply revenged where Gregory, of Nyassa, describing Constantinople said:

This city is full of mechanics and slaves who are all of them profound theologians and preach in shops and streets. If you desire a man to change a piece of silver he informs you wherein the Son differs from the Father; if you ask the price of a loaf, you are told by way of reply that the Son is inferior to the Father; and if you enquire whether the bath is ready, the answer is that the Son was made out of nothing.

The capricious Constantius, alternately embraced and condemned the sentiments, and successively banished and recalled the leaders of the factions, and the five successive expulsions of Athanasius from his Episcopal throne in Alexandria, epitomise the varying fortunes as well as the perpetual conflict of the parties. While this lasted, it was not unusual in Alexandria, which detested Arianism and loved its bishop, for devotions in churches to be interrupted by the soldiery, the doors of sacred edifices to be battered, congregations to be attacked with every horrid circumstance of tumult and bloodshed, consecrated virgins to be stripped naked, scourged, and violated and the houses of the wealthy to be plundered 'with impunity and even with applause'. And what occurred at Alexandria was repeated in ninety other Episcopal cities of Egypt. In Rome popular fury took the form of murder of the adherents of an unwanted extra bishop in the streets, in the baths, and even in the churches, which recalled the massacres of Marius and the proscriptions of Sylla. In Constantinople, Paul, its bishop, was also driven from his throne no less than five times in the space of fourteen years, and the populace vented its wrath against the special officers entrusted with carrying out such unpopular orders. Describing the incident connected with the transportation of the remains of the first Christian Emperor from a chapel in a ruinous condition into the Church of St. Acacius, which the people were led to regard as a wicked profanation, 'one of the ecclesiastical historians has observed, as a real fact, not as a figure of rhetoric, that the well before the Church overflowed with a stream of blood which filled the porticoes and the adjacent courts'. In Thrace[58] and in Asia Minor the sacraments of the Church were administered to the reluctant victims by priests whose principles they abhorred. 'The rites of baptism were conferred on women and children who, for that purpose, had been torn from the arms of their friends and parents; the mouths of the communicants were held open by a wooden engine while the consecrated bread was forced down their throat; the breasts of tender virgins were either burnt with red-hot egg-shells or inhumanely compressed between sharp and heavy boards.'

In trying to suppress the Novatians in Paphlagonia, the soldiers, although they succeeded in slaying many, were themselves vanquished by an irregular multitude armed only with scythes and axes, and almost all the four thousand soldiers were left dead on the field of battle. The successor of Constantius has himself left on record that 'whole troops of those who were styled heretics were massacred . . . and towns and villages were laid waste and utterly destroyed'. The most curious fanatics, however, were the Donatist Circumcellians.[59] Under their leaders styled 'Captains of the Saints', principally armed with a huge and hefty club which they termed an 'Israelite', and using the well-known sound 'Praise be to God' as their war-cry, they 'diffused consternation over the unarmed provinces of Africa . . . burnt villages, which they had pillaged, and reigned the licentious tyrants of the open country'. They even engaged and sometimes defeated the troops of the province. Their horror of life and desire of martyrdom let them to resort to 'religious suicides'. For this they would often stop travellers on the public highways and give them the alternative of a reward if they would consent to kill and of instant death if they would refuse. As Gregory Nazianzen pathetically lamented 'the kingdom of heaven was converted by discord into the image of chaos, of a nocturnal tempest and hell itself'.

Lest it may be considered that these were temporary outbursts of royal or popular passion when bad sovereigns ruled, let us see what happens when a man like Theodosius is called by Gratian to share with him the burden of Empire and succeeds Valens in the East. We find in him the

[58] North-east region of Greece, bounded north by Bulgaria, east by Turkey, and south by the Aegean Sea; in classical times, part of the area associated with the worship of Dionysius.

[59] They were a body in the African Church who became divided from the Catholics.

same keen anxiety for uniformity, but unlike Constantius and Valens he was not favourable to Arianism. The steps he hastened to take to enforce his will soon made the creed of Nicæa 'Catholic'. For he totally extirpated paganism and crushed the 'heresy' of Arius. On receiving the sacrament of baptism, 'as the Emperor ascended from the holy font still glowing with the warm feelings of regeneration', he dictated (28 February 380 A.C.) a solemn edict which proclaimed his own faith and prescribed the religion of his subjects. 'It is our pleasure' (such, says Gibbon, is the Imperial style) 'that all the nations which are governed by our clemency and moderation should steadfastly adhere to the religion which was taught by St. Peter to the Romans; which faithful tradition has preserved; and which is now professed by the pontiff of Damascus and by Peter, bishop of Alexandria, a man of apostolic holiness'; and after stating the Nicene creed and authorising those who adhered to it 'to assume the title of Catholic Christians', the edict proclaims that 'as we judge that all others are extravagant mad men, we brand them with the infamous naive of Heretics; and declare that their conventicles shall no longer usurp the respectable appellation of Churches'. And then comes the conclusion to be expected from such piety. The edict goes on to say, 'Beside the condemnation of divine justice, they must expect to suffer the severe penalties which our authority, guided by heavenly wisdom, shall think proper to inflict on them.' And the feeble remnant of the Catholic party in Constantinople, which was animated with joyful confidence, did not have to wait long for the fulfilment of the promise of persecution of the Arians so clearly and emphatically held out in the Imperial edict. The very next day after his entry into the Capital after a victorious campaign, Theodosius summoned to his presence the Arian Patriarch and offered to him the alternative of subscribing the Nicene creed or of instantly resigning to the orthodox believers the use and possession of his Episcopal palace, the Cathedral of St. Sophia,[60] and all the churches of Constantinople. Demophilus accepted poverty and exile and his removal was immediately followed by the transfer to an inconsiderable congregation of Homoousians of the hundred churches which they were insufficient to fill, whilst the far greater part of the people was excluded from every place of religious worship. Gregory Nazianzen, who had hitherto preached in the room of private house, and was even then not secure from the tumultuous interruptions of the Arians who issued from the Cathedral of

[60] The famous church at Constantinople and one of the most perfect examples of Byzantine architecture. In 1453 the church was converted into a mosque.

St. Sophia, 'a motley crowd of common beggars, who had forfeited their claim to pity, of monks who had the appearance of goats or satyrs and of women more terrible than so many Jazebels', who broke open the door of the house and did much mischief with sticks, stones and firebrands, was now conducted by the Emperor (26 November 380 A.C.) through the streets in solemn triumph. Theodosius then placed him with his own hands on the archiepiscopal throne of Constantinople in St. Sophia, which was now occupied by a large body of the Imperial Guards. But St. Gregory himself confesses that on the memorable day of his installation the Capital of the East wore the appearance of a city taken by storm and in the hands of a barbarian conqueror. Soon afterwards the Emperor declared his resolution (10 January 381 A.C.) of expelling the bishops and their clergy who should refuse to believe, or at least, to profess the doctrine of the Council of Nicæa and his lieutenant, Sapor, armed with the ample powers of a general law, a special commission and a military force, conducted the ecclesiastical revolution and established the Emperor's religion in all the provinces of the East. 'The writings of the Arians', says Gibbon, 'would perhaps contain the lamentable story of the persecution which afflicted the Church under the reign of the impious Theodosius; and the sufferings of their holy confessors might claim the pity of the disinterested reader' In a footnote he adds that he does not reckon Philostorgius 'the Eunomian historian has been carefully strained through an orthodox sieve'.

A General Council of the Church was held at Constantinople (May-July 381 A.C.) which reasserted the creed and the theological system of its predecessor of Nicæa, and unanimously ratified the equal Deity of the Holy Ghost. In the space of 15 years (380-394 A.C.) Theodosius promulgated at least 15 severe edicts against the heretics and more especially against those who rejected the Nicene doctrine of Trinity. Heretical Bishops and Presbyters were exposed to the penalties of exile and confiscation if they preached the doctrine or practised the rites of their sect. Their religious meetings, whether public or secret, by day or by night, were proscribed and the building or ground used for the purpose was forfeited to the Imperial domain. They were gradually disqualified for employment and the Eunomians, who distinguished the nature of the Son from that of the Father, were declared to be incapable of making their wills or receiving any advantage from testamentary donations. The guilt of the Manichæan heresy was deemed of such magnitude that it could be expiated only by the death of the offender, and those who scoff today at the ritualism of other religious communities and at the importance attached to it by the 'adulterous generation' of Pharisees ought to know that the edicts of the Wise and Good Theodosius inflicted nothing less than capital punishment on the Andians or Quartodecimans whose only offence was that they always kept the Easter, like the Jewish Passover, on the 14th day of the first moon after the vernal equinox, instead of having fixed Easter to a Sunday, like the Roman Church and the Nicene Synod. Every subject of the Emperor might exercise the right of public accusation, but the office of the Inquisitors of the Faith was first instituted under the reign of Theodosius. While this was the rigidity of the Christian theology, what was the condition of Christian religious life? These same ecclesiastics 'had scandalously degenerated from the model of apostolic purity' and 'the most worthless and corrupt were always the most eager to frequent and disturb the episcopal assemblies. . . . Their ruling passion was love of gold and love of dispute. Many of the prelates who now applauded the orthodox piety of Theodosius had repeatedly changed, with prudent flexibility, their creeds and opinions; and in the various revolutions of the Church and State, the religion of the Sovereign was the rule of their obsequious faith.'

It may be said, however, that the bark of Theodosius was worse than his bite and that the execution of his penal edicts was seldom enforced. But when the Church had thus secured the State for the enforcement of its wishes and edicts had been issued, prescribing secular penalties for things within the domain of individual conscience, episcopal censures could no longer be called merely censures and the enforcement of the penal edicts was only a matter of time. In fact the theory established by Theodosius was practised, in the fullest extent, by his rival and colleague, Maximinius, 'the first among the Christian princes, who shed the blood of his Christian subjects on account of their religious opinions'. Priscillian, the Bishop of Avila, in Spain, and six of his associates, including a noble matron of Bordeaux, the widow of a renowned orator, who were all burned alive at Treves, were 'the first human sacrifices formally offered up under the improved conditions to the greater glory of reinforced Christianity. Thereafter the blood of the heretics was the cement of Christian amity' (H.G. Wells). Priscillian was a Spanish theologian and the founder of a party, 'which in spite of severe persecution for heresy', continued to subsist in Spain and Gaul until after the middle of the 6th century. He was a wealthy layman who had devoted his life to a study of the occult sciences and the deeper problems of philosophy. He was largely a mystic and regarded the Christian life as continual intercourse with God. His favourite idea is that which St. Paul has expressed in the words 'know ye not that ye are the temple of God', and he argued that to make himself a fit habitation for the divine a man must, besides holding the Catholic faith and doing works of love, renounce marriage and earthly honour and practise a hard asceticism. It was on the question of continence in, if not renunciation of marriage, that he came into conflict with the authorities. Priscillian and his sympathisers who were organised into bands of spiritales and abstinentes, like the Cathari of a later day, indignantly refused the compromise which by this time the Church had established in the matter. This explains the charge of Manichæanism levelled against Priscillian.' His study of occult sciences could equally easily explain the accusation of magic in those days; but nothing except the most perverse partisanship and falsehood and injustice can explain the added accusation of 'licentious orgies' against people who wanted 'continence in, if not renunciation of marriage'. To complete the irony of the whole situation, the man who had solicited their death and had beheld their tortures was Ithacus and 'the vices of that profligate bishop were admitted as a proof that his zeal was instigated by the sordid motives of interest' (Gibbon).

Although Priscillian had in the meantime been made a bishop and had several bishops among the leading Priscillianists, some of them were deposed for their zeal as ascetics and he and six others, as we have just seen, were burned alive. In fact no matter what the antecedents and the merits of a man may have been, if he dared to differ from the Church in the least, he could not escape the dangerous imputation of heresy. We have already noted the cases of Origen and Tertullian. Here is another, no less than Jerome himself who, 'for his talk of the *Sordes nuptiarum*, had been similarly accused (of Manichæanism) and to escape popular indignation had retired to Bethlehem'. 'The official Church', says F.C. Conybeare, 'had to respect the ascetic spirit to the extent of enjoining celibacy upon its priests, and of recognising, or rather immuring, such of the laity as desired to live out the old ascetic ideal. But the official teaching of Rome would not allow it to be the ideal and duty of every Christian. Priscillian perished for insisting that it was such; and seven centuries later the Church began to burn the Cathari by thousands because they took a similar view of the Christian life.' For long the prevalent estimation of Priscillian as a heretic and Manichæan rested chiefly upon such eminent authorities of the Church as Augustine and Leo the Great, although at the Council of Toledo, in 400, fifteen years after Priscillian's death, when his case was reviewed,

> the most serious change that could be brought was the error of language in rendering α'γε'νητος as *innascibilis*. It was long thought that the writings of the 'heretic' himself had perished, but in 1885, G. Schepss discovered, at Würzburg, eleven

genuine tracts, since published in the Vienna *Corpus*. 'They contain nothing that is not orthodox and commonplace, nothing that Jerome might not have written,' and go far to justify the description of Priscillian as 'the first martyr burned by a Spanish Inquisition'.

There was, remarks Gibbon, 'scandalous irregularity' in the proceedings in this case, and adds that

> since the death of Priscillian, the rude attempts of persecution have been refined and methodized in the Holy Office (of the Inquisition) which assigns their distinct parts to the ecclesiastical and secular powers. The devoted victim is regularly delivered by the jurist to the magistrate and by the magistrate to the executioner; and the inexorable sentence of the Church, which declares the guilt of the offender, is expressed in the mild language of pity and intercession.

The first instance of the application of the Theodosian law against heretics had the approval of the Synod which met at Treves, in the same year, but Ambrose of Milan and Martin of Tours 'can claim the glory of having, in some measure, stayed the hand of persecution' (Rev. A.J. Grieve, *Encyclopædia Britannica*).

Even though these two ardent ecclesiastics condemned it

> many bishops approved the act. While Chrysostom disapproved of the execution of heretics, he approved 'the prohibition of their assemblies and the confiscation of their Churches'. Jerome, by an appeal to Deuteronomy (XIII:6-10), appears to defend even the execution of heretics. Augustine found a justification for these penal measures in the 'compel them to come in', of Luke (XIV:23), although his personal bearings were towards clemency. Only the persecuted themselves insisted on toleration as a Christian duty. (Rev. A.E. Garvie, *Encyc. Brit.*)

As for Ambrose and Martin, their condemnation of the execution at Treves was, as Gibbon observes, only due to a 'humane inconsistency'. 'The cause of humanity and that of persecution have been asserted by the same Ambrose with equal energy and equal success', and the influence which Ambrose and his clerical brethren had acquired over the Youth of Gratian and the piety of Theodosius was 'employed to infuse the maximum of persecution into the breasts of their Imperial proselytes'. They had established it as a principle of religious jurisprudence that the prince is, in some measure, guilty of the crimes of heresy and paganism if he neglects to prohibit or punish them.

Pagan temples were now not only shut but, in spite of the great beauty of many of them, and the utility of all as buildings that could at least be converted to secular uses, were for the most part destroyed. The bishops often assisted in this work of destruction, with an army of zealous monks without authority and without discipline. The most noteworthy of the temples that were thus razed to the ground was the temple of Serapis in Alexandria, which rivalled the pride and magnificence of the Capitol.

The libraries of Alexandria were the most important as well as the most celebrated of the ancient world. Under the enlightened rule of the Ptolemies a society of scholars and men of science was attracted to their capital. Ptolemy Sofer had already begun to collect books; but it was in the reign of Ptolemy Philadelphus, that the libraries were properly organised and established in separate buildings. He sent men into every part of Greece and Asia to secure the most valuable works and no exertion or expense was spared in enriching the collections. Ptolemy Eugestes, his successor, is said to have caused all books brought into Egypt by foreigners to be seized for the benefit of the library, while the owners had to be content with receiving copies of them in exchange.[61] There were two libraries at Alexandria, the larger in the Brucheum Quarter was in connection with the Museum, a sort of academy, while the smaller was placed in the Serapeum. When Caesar set fire to the fleet in the harbour of Alexandria, the flames accidentally extended to the larger library of Brucheum, and it was destroyed. Mark Antony endeavoured to repair the loss by presenting to Cleopatra the library from Perganum.[62] The Kings of Perganum had vied with the Ptolemies in their encouragement of learning and despite the obstacles presented by the embargo placed by the latter upon the export of papyrus, so successful was the rivalry of the Attali that their library numbered 200,000 volumes when Mark Antony[63] removed it to Alexandria, to replace Cleopatra's burnt library. This was, very probably, placed in the Brucheum, as this continued to be the library quarter of Alexandria until the time of Aurelian. It is very probable that one of the libraries perished when the Brucheum Quarter was destroyed by Aurelian, in 273 A.C. Thenceforward the Seraphim became the principal library. In 389 or 391 A.C., an edict of Theodosius ordered the destruction of the Seraphim[64] and this library was 'pillaged and destroyed' by zealous

[61] For details, see *The Cambridge Encyclopedia*, p. 985.

[62] The town was situated *c.* 50 miles north of Smyrna and *c.* 15 miles from the sea, on a hill 1,000 feet above the surrounding plain. In the second century B.C. it became one of the greatest centres of art and culture in the ancient world.

[63] (*c.* 83–30 B.C.); Roman statesman and soldier. He was related to Julius Caesar and was commander in the war against Pompey. He met and was captivated by Queen Cleopatra, whom he followed to Egypt.

[64] Heavenly beings mentioned in Jewish scriptures. They are described as having six wings and being stationed above the throne of God.

Christians under the rule of their Bishop Theophilus.[65] 'Nearly twenty years afterwards,' says Gibbon, 'the appearance of the empty shelves excited the regret and indignation of every spectator whose mind was not totally darkened by religious prejudice.' That this destruction of pagan lore was quite characteristic of the zealots who executed the decree of Theodosius is amply evidenced by their destruction of Christian lore itself that was tainted by 'heresy'. Every modern scholar of Christian theology warns us to handle with caution the sources of information that are now available for a study of various 'heresies' because they are almost always the polemical writings of their successful adversaries who not only crushed the minorities called 'heresies' but also destroyed their religious literature.

Yet such is prejudice that when long after the Dark Ages, that had dawned soon after the establishment of Christian rule had passed away, thanks to the enlightenment due in the main to the sons of the Arabian desert, and Christians had learnt to take interest in Greek philosophy revived by Muslims and even to use in reconstructing their theology and building up their scholasticism, these very Muslims, to whom Christendom owed its revival of learning, were accused of such savage hatred of learning that they were alleged to have destroyed this library of Alexandria. The only source for this horrible calumny is the historian Abul-Faraj or Abulpharagius, who, for all the unconscious disguise of a Saracenic name, was no other than Mac-Gregor M'clitrin or Bar-Hebræus, not only a good Christian but from 1264 to 1286 the *Maphrian*, a dignitary second in rank to the Patriarch, of the Monophysite Jacobite Church that owed and still owes its existence to the tolerance of Islamic rule when Catholicism and Orthodoxy have, between them, snuffed out all other 'heresies'. He wrote in Syriac a chronicle of universal history, political and ecclesiastical, in three parts and also issued a rescension of his political history in Arabic, under the title of a 'Compendious History of the Dynasties,' which was edited and translated by that staunch enemy of Islam, Pocock [sic], in 1663.[66] In this, more than six hundred years after the conquest of Egypt by the Arabs, we find this little gem which has furnished innumerable Christian writers with excellent material with which to point a moral against Islam and adorn a tale for the edification of Christendom. He says:

[65] (d. 412). Patriarch of Alexandria. In the first years as patriarch he took an active part in suppressing the remnants of paganism in his city.

[66] Edward Pococke (1604–91); Orientalist and Fellow at Corpus Christi, Oxford (1628). In 1663 he issued the Arabic text (with a Latin translation) of the book referred to by Mohamed Ali.

John the Grammarian, a famous peripatetic philosopher, being in Alexandria at the time of its capture, and in high favour with 'Amr (the Muslim conqueror of Egypt), begged that he would give him the royal library. 'Amr told him that it was not in his power to grant such a request, but promised to write to the Khalifa for his consent. 'Umar, on learning the request of his General, is said to have replied that if those books contained the same doctrine with the Qur'an, they could be of no use, since the Qur'an contained all the necessary truths; but if they contained anything contrary to that book they ought to be destroyed; and therefore, whatever their contents were, he ordered them to be burnt. Pursuant to this order, they were distributed among the public baths, of which there was a large number in the city where, for six months, they served to supply the fires.

'Since the Dynasties of Abulpharagius,' says Gibbon, 'have been given to the world in a Latin version, the tale has been repeatedly transcribed; and every scholar with pious indignation has deplored the irreparable shipwreck of the learning, the arts and the genius of antiquity.' 'For my part,' he continues,

> I am strongly tempted to deny both the fact and the consequences. The fact is indeed marvellous; 'Read and wonder', says the historian himself; and the solitary report of a stranger who wrote at the end of six hundred years on the confines of Media is overbalanced by the silence of two annalists of a more early date, both natives of Egypt, and the most ancient of whom, the patriarch Eutychius, has amply described the conquest of Alexandria. The rigid sentence of Umar is repugnant to the sound and orthodox precept of the Mohammedan canonists: they expressly declare that the religious books of the Jews and Christians, which are acquired by the right of war, should never be committed to flames, and the works of profane science, historians or poets, physicians or philosophers, may be lawfully applied to the use of the faithful.

Mr. D.G. Hogarth, Keeper of the Ashmolean Museum at Oxford, who is no friend of Islam, in his article on Alexandria, in the *Encyclopædia Britannica*, while discarding the story of Bar-Hebræus, refers to the 'disgraceful pillage of the library in A.D. 389', so that Gibbon can be excused, if, with lesser religious prejudice, he refers to 'the mischievous bigotry of the Christians who studied to destroy the monuments of idolatry'. In fact, the Catholic contemporaries of the Khalifa Umar and of Amr bin al-As would have approved of Gibbon's sarcasm, when, in concluding this episode, he writes: 'If the ponderous mass of Arian and Monophysite controversy were indeed consumed in the public baths, a philosopher may allow, with a smile, that it was ultimately devoted to the benefit of mankind.' The latest editor of Gibbon, Professor Bury, who does not seem to agree with him in his conclusions, and thinks that 'the silence of the chronicles of Theophanes and Nicephorus does not count for much, as they are capricious and unaccountable in their selection of facts,' and that 'the silence of Tabari,[67] and Ibn Abdul Hakam is more important, but not decisive', nevertheless adds that 'of far greater weight is the silence of the contemporary John of Nikin, who gives a very full account of the conquest of Egypt', and 'in fact is the sole contemporary source for the Saracen conquest.'[68] He says Weil agrees with Gibbon and finally quotes the verdict of Susemihl: *Umar Sand 642 schwerlich noch Bücher in Alexandria zu verbrennen.* And yet so hard-lived is religious bigotry that even after the convincing proofs of the apocryphal character of the story related by Abulpharagius, Renan, who had come to discard Christianity itself in the popular acceptation of that word, still held fast to his anti-Islamic prejudices. In a lecture on 'Islamism and Science,' the author of *Averroës and Averroism*, acknowledged that Umar did not burn, as we are often told, the library of Alexandria; that library had, by this time, nearly disappeared. But adds, characteristically enough, 'the principle which he caused to triumph in the world was in a very real sense destructive of learned research and of the varied work of the mind.' In other words, the small incident that could indicate the love of ignorance and stupidity on the part of the early Muslims is acknowledged to have been a fabrication; but what it was designed to indicate is vehemently asserted by the judge himself to have been more than proved.

In the face of such calumnies the matter deserves closer examination. It is indeed unthinkable that people so deeply attached to the *Sunna* or usage of their Prophet, who wanted them to regard wisdom whenever they found it as their own lost property to which they had a better title than he with whom he found it, and who asked them to seek knowledge even if it be in China, would sacrifice hundreds of thousands of books to such childish logic as that attributed to Umar. Such of the polytheists of Mecca, who had been captured in Islam's first battle at Badr, as were literate, were offered their release by the Prophet himself if they would only teach a Muslim lad to read and write. Zaid ibn Thabit,[69] the chief

[67] (839–923), renowned Arab historian. He travelled widely from his hometown in Persia and wrote a major commentary on the Quran, and a history of the world from creation until the early tenth century.

[68] A word used by medieval writers of the Arabs generally and later applied to the Muslims against whom the crusaders fought. The term was not used by the Muslims themselves.

[69] It is said that as a boy Zaid already knew a number of *Suras* when Mohammad settled in Medina. He recorded his revelations and settled the correspondence with the Jews, whose language or script he is said to have learned in 17 days or less. He was entrusted with the government of Medina by Umar and Usman, when they went to perform the *Haj*.

amanuensis of the Prophet, who used to take down the revelations as he received them, and was entrusted, on that account, by the Prophet's first Khalifa or successor, Abu Bakr, to transcribe all these fragments into one volume, was subsequently placed by 'Usman, the third Khalifa, at the head of the Commission appointed to make several copies from this volume and send out to newly conquered territories of Islam, when all private and unauthorised copies were withdrawn and destroyed, was himself ordered by the Prophet to learn Hebrew from a Medina Jew in order to be able to study the religious literature of Judaism. With such an example before him, how could 'Umar destroy the religious literature of the Christians? Not much better is the foundation for the report which Professor Bury cites in this connection with regard to some books of the Fire-worshippers ordered to be destroyed by 'Umar in the course of the Persian conquest, and we can leave him to get such consolation as he can find in the conclusion at which he finally arrives—that 'it is quite credible that books of the Fire-worshippers were destroyed by 'Umar's orders; and this incident might have originated legends of the destruction of books elsewhere'. There is a well-authenticated injunction of the Prophet asking Muslims to hold fast to the usage of his 'truly guided successors' as well as his own, and if Umar had ordered the destruction of any such books, it is hardly possible that any Zoroastrian, Christian or Jewish literature in the conquered territories could have survived and still less likely that the Muslims should have been the possessors of such vast libraries as history has shown them to be. Yet some of the oldest copies of the Bible and other sacred and theological manuscripts have been discovered in these regions rather than in the territories that remained to Christendom after the first flaming onset of the Muslims and the writers of the article on 'Libraries', in the *Encyclopædia Britannica*, record it as their deliberate judgement that 'it is certain that the libraries of the Arabians and the Moors of Spain offer a very remarkable contrast to those of the Christian nations during the same period'. But so grudging is a Christian praise of Muslims that even that obvious judgement is qualified with a footnote to the effect that 'among the Arabs, as among the Christians, theological bigotry did not always approve of non-theological literature and the great library of Cordoba was sacrificed by Almanzor to his reputation for orthodoxy', in 978 A.C. This is such a surprising generalisation, and the manner in which the incident of Almanzor's destructive trickery is alluded to is so misleading that I must give a few details that would go to show that 'theological bigotry' did not disapprove of 'non-theological literature among the Arabs as among the Christians', and that only some of the books out of the famous library of Cordoba were destroyed by an astute but unscrupulous statesman who had usurped authority in his master's kingdom and that although he could not avoid the guilt of this more or less open treachery he wished at least to disprove the suspicion of the Spanish Muslims and Berbers that he had added to this secular offence the further offence of being irreligious. Had theological bigotry among the Arabs been indeed as great as it is suggested, we would not have succeeded to the heritage of so many works of a purely non-theological character as we have done in spite of the destruction caused by the Crusaders and the Tartars. It is not strange at all that in the first century of Islam literary activity should have been less prominent than it became later, if we remember that when the Prophet received his call even the cultured Quraysh[70] in Mecca, the most populous city of Arabia, could boast of no more than 17 literate persons. By the time the Prophet departed from this world, literacy had become fairly common among the Muslims and Medina had become a literary centre which began to attract foreigners and non-Muslims as well. Like the Prophet and the early *Khulafa*, the descendants of the Prophet, whose learning was as great as their piety, 'received with distinction the learned men whom the fanatical persecutions of Justinian's successors drove for refuge into foreign lands'. In the time of Justinian himself a historic school at Athens had been closed. Modern Europe dates its birth from, and in fact calls it, the Renaissance when admittedly Christendom recovered through the revival of pagan letters its sense of the dignity of human nature and, emancipating itself from the chains of Christian theology, learnt to live and to enjoy human life as something divine and not bearing the ineffaceable mark of the devil. It cannot, therefore, be said that Gibbon was prejudiced against the Church of his faith when he wrote:

> The Gothic arms were less fatal to the schools of Athens than the establishment of the new religion, whose ministers superseded the exercise of reason, resolved every question by an article of faith, and condemned the infidel or sceptic to eternal flames. In many a volume of laborious controversy, they exposed the weakness of the understanding and the corruption of the heart, insulted human nature in the sages of antiquity, and proscribed the spirit of philosophical inquiry, so repugnant to the doctrine, or at least to the temper, of an humble believer. The surviving sect of the Platonists, whom Plato would have blushed to acknowledge, extravagantly mingled a sublime theory with the practice of superstition and magic, and as they remained alone in the midst of a Christian world they indulged in a

[70] With the preaching of Mohammad the story of the Qurayash becomes practically that of Islam. Two illustrious Qurayash (Kuraish) were Abu Bakr and Umar.

secret rancour against the government of the Church and State whose severity was still suspended over their heads.

Still, about a century after the reign of Julian,[71] 'the Apostate', from whose reign the pagans, to whom he was of course a hero, reckoned their calamities, the industrious and able, though superstitious, Proclus[72] was permitted to teach in the philosophic chair of the Academy and when he died, his life, completed by two of his disciples, exhibited the deplorable picture of what Gibbon calls 'the second childhood of human reason.' 'Yet,' he adds, 'the golden chain, as it was fondly styled of the Platonic succession, continued forty-four years from the death of Proclus to the edict of Justinian, which imposed a perpetual silence on Athens and excited the grief and indignation of the few remaining votaries of Grecian science and superstitions.' The edicts against paganism, strictly interpreted, involved the cessation of neo-Platonic propagandism. Justinian ensured the suppression of the schools not only by withdrawing the revenue but, as Gazler says, he 'confiscated the property of the Platonic Academy[73] and forbade, at the University of Athens, teaching in philosophy and law'.[74] Seven philosophical friends who dissented from the religion of their sovereign sought, in a foreign country, the freedom which was now denied them in their native land and, credulously believing that the Republic of Plato was realised in the despotic Government of Persia, experienced so great a disillusionment on their arrival there that they precipitately returned. But, as Gibbon remarks, from this journey they derived a unique benefit which one would not have expected from the opinion formed by the Athenian philosophers, in their exaggerated disappointment, of the Persian 'Barbarians' and their ruler, Chosroes, 'required that the seven sages, who had visited the court of Persia, should be exempted from the penal laws which Justinian enacted against his pagan subjects; and this privilege, expressly stipulated in a treaty of peace, was guarded by the vigilance of a powerful mediator.' When in the time of Justinian's successors the academies of philosophy and medicine founded by the Nestorians at Edessa[75] and Nisibis had been broken up, their professors and students

[71] (332–63), Roman Emperor. With regard to the Church, his policy was to degrade Christianity and promote paganism.

[72] St. Proculus (d. 446), a well-applauded preacher.

[73] After the death of Plato, his nephew Speusippus, succeeded him as head of the Academy of Athens which with varying fortunes persisted until its closure by Justinian in A.D. 529.

[74] In 529 Justinian closed its schools as exponents of surviving paganism, and shortly afterwards the Parthenon and other temples were converted into churches.

[75] Home of the Nestorian 'Persian school'. In 641 it fell into the hands of the Arabs, but continued to be an important Christian centre for several centuries.

took refuge in Persia and Arabia. Many betook themselves to Medina where the descendant of the Prophet, the Imam Jafar as-Sadiq,[76] had gathered round him a galaxy of talented scholars.

The Umayyads at Damascus were not such patrons of learning as their successors the Abbasids at Baghdad had the opportunity of becoming; but this was not because the spirit of Islam was opposed to learning and inquiry. In fact, with a few exceptions, particularly that of Umar II, their religion sat very lightly on them. They were much more like the old pre-Islamic Arabs of the desert, for whom the luxurious life of the court had provided great opportunities for self-indulgence than their Meccan trading and warring ancestors had enjoyed, than like the simple God-fearing Muslims of the days of the Prophet and his Companions, who combined a wise rulership of newly conquered territories with the hardy life of the soldier and a self-restraint that would be the despair of many a professed anchorite. Often, Muslims only in their outward religious observances, they were at heart pagans whom the pious Muslims, who devoted their lives to earning, deeply abhorred; and the one branch of literature which they did encourage was, characteristically enough, poetry, which in its pre-Islamic sensuality, pride and passions and love of tribal warfare, had been given a very wide berth by the Muslims ever since the days of the Prophet. With wine and women went also the song in the old Arab way at the Umayyad court. Islam too had its poets from the earliest times, but like Labid and Hassán ibn Thábit and the converted Kab ibn Zubayr and Aisha, they had turned the talents towards religious poetry and panegyrics of the Prophet and such poetry as the Umayyad *Khulafa* came subsequently to encourage with all its accompaniments of violent passions, vice and self-indulgence, knew what to expect from true Muslims from the fate of Abu Mihjan,[77] who had made his peace with Islam towards the end of the Prophet's life, but was several times flogged and finally exiled for his love of wine which he celebrated in his verse, and perhaps for his amorous intrigues. Another such case was that of Jarwal ibn Aus, known as Al-Hutaia, a wandering poet whose keen satires led to his imprisonment by Umar.[78] In that first century after the Prophet's death the work of conquest and consolidation did not leave much time for any other pursuits; but the

[76] The fourth Shia Imam, Ali, Hasan and Husain being the first three, who was present at the Battle of Karbala but could not participate owing to his illness.

[77] An Arab poet. As a pagan he fought against the Prophet and was one of the defenders of Taif. He was banished by Umar, the second Khalifa, in 637. His vocation is founded on his wine songs.

[78] 'The dwarf', the well-known poet who was imprisoned by the second Khalifa.

love of learning was the first fruit of Islam and, characteristically enough, the pious Muslims, when they turned towards learning, commenced to gather together the scattered Traditions of the Prophet and to base Muslim Jurisprudence on a thorough understanding (*tafaqquh*) of the Quran and on the precept and example of the Prophet.